DATA ENTRY
ACTIVITIES FOR MICROCOMPUTERS

3D EDITION

WILLIAM E. BUX, M. ED.

KENNETH L. GORMAN, DEAN
COLLEGE OF BUSINESS
WINONA STATE UNIVERSITY
WINONA, MINNESOTA

SOUTH-WESTERN EDUCATIONAL PUBLISHING

Editor-In-Chief: *Robert E. First*
Developmental Editor: *Diana Trabel*
Senior Production Editor: *Mary Todd*
Instructional Designer/Software Editor: *Donna Craighead*
Consulting Editor: *Nikki N. Wise*
Production Services: *Navta Associates, Inc.*
Internal Design: *The Quarasan Group, Inc.*
Cover Design: *Lamson Design*

I(T)P
International Thomson Publishing

Preface

*T*he development of *Data Entry Activities for Microcomputers, 3rd Edition* was guided primarily by the feedback received from classroom teachers who used the second edition. Many of the 13 activities in the third edition are new and completely different from the previous edition. Activity 13 is a culminating activity that brings together skills students learn in earlier activities, while providing only a minimal amount of instruction. This activity can be weighted and used as a final exam. Each activity has its own dexterity drills for students to use as practice.

Data entry has been streamlined to accommodate interruptions and class periods of different lengths. The activities are timed, and data correction is allowed at four different levels. Going back through each field for data correction is easy and fast. If a student is interrupted during an activity, the data may be stored on a student data diskette. When students return, they may begin their work where they left off.

Several print options have been included in this software. All data that a student enters may be printed or displayed at the end of each activity. The error analysis may be printed or displayed at the end of each activity. The error analysis shows the number of errors made, student's accuracy, rate measured in words per minute, strokes per hour, and letter grade.

The software is completely menu driven and easy to use, either with or without a mouse. The computer screens are very user-friendly.

MICROCOMPUTER SYSTEMS

*D*ata Entry Activities for Microcomputers is designed to run on the IBM PC, PS/2, IBM compatibles, Macintosh SE, SE30, Classic, LC, IIs, or higher, and the Tandy 1000.

FEATURES OF ACTIVITIES.

*T*he text-workbook is organized as a series of activities. Each activity includes the following features:

Data Entry Application and Job Description
Some activities introduce the students to the principles involved in at least one business system, such as payroll or accounts payable. Other activities give the students experience and general knowledge in such topics as a census survey, automobile registration, insurance application, student class registration, and radio listener survey.

Input Fields
An input field is a specific area of a record set aside for recording a particular type or category of data. Some examples of input fields are name field, street field, state field, and ZIP code field. Whenever data is key-entered into any of those fields, it is assumed that the data belongs to that particular category of data. For instance, an operator in the payroll department would not place the gross amount of pay in an employee's street address field.

Dexterity Drills
Each activity contains instructions for students to complete two dexterity drills. There are alpha-numeric and numeric-only (keypad) drills. Dexterity drills are designed to build a high degree of keyboarding speed and accuracy. The computer calculates the student's speed and accuracy for each drill.

Step-By-Step Instructions
Each activity contains instructions for entering data into the microcomputer from realistic source documents. The instructions are designed to help the student key-enter the data quickly and effectively. A student progress report on each activity can be printed.

Vocabulary
Included in each activity are special words or phrases that are introduced and tested in each activity. Students can enhance their business acumen by understanding the definitions of these words and phrases.

Study Guide
Each activity includes a study guide that covers the business principles and the data entry procedures discussed in the activity.

OUTLINE OF ACTIVITIES

*G*enerally students will begin work with Activity 1 and continue through to Activity 13. However, the teacher may choose to omit or repeat some activities. This judgment should be made on the basis of the needs and objectives of each student as well as on the amount of time and number of microcomputers available. The features of each activity are summarized below.

Activity 1   In this activity students are introduced to microcomputers and how they may be used in data entry. After becoming familiar with the computer, students prepare source documents and key-enter data for a corporate softball league.

Activity 2   In this activity students learn about computerized inventory. After preparing the source documents for a perpetual inventory system, students key-enter the data for the inventory setup, point-of-sale transaction, and inventory update. Stock items are identified by the Universal Product Code (UPC) number.

Activity 3   In this activity students develop knowledge of point-of-sale invoices used in an office supply store. Students key-enter the quantity, stock number, and description for sales transactions.

Activity 4   In this activity students learn about accounts receivable transactions for a home cuisine delivery service. The extension amounts are calculated automatically by the computer after the quantity and unit price have been key-entered by the students.

Activity 5   In this activity students become familiar with accounts payable procedures. Sales ticket information is entered into the computer.

Activity 6   In this activity students are introduced to different types of payroll calculations. Students must set up and update a payroll master file for a company. The type of pay calculations are hourly rate, salary, and salary plus commission.

Activity 7   In this activity students become familiar with the type of information required on a census survey and the purpose of a census.

Activity 8	In this activity students learn what information is required on an automobile insurance application.
Activity 9	In this activity students are introduced to a driver's license application.
Activity 10	In this activity students learn about information on an automobile registration application and the reasons to register your vehicle.
Activity 11	In this activity students are introduced to student class registration. Different class scheduling methods are discussed, and registration forms for college courses are entered into the computer.
Activity 12	In this activity students become familiar with a listener survey for a radio station. A listener survey is usually taken to find out what type of music the audience wishes to hear.
Activity 13	In this activity students bring together several activities at the same time. Payroll, accounts payable, and inventory will be used and updated in this activity. The final project is similar to a key-entry practice set.

PURPOSE OF THE BOOK

*T*he primary purpose of this text-workbook is to develop the speed and accuracy of students' data entry skills. Upon completion of the thirteen activities in this text-workbook, the students will have a good foundation of data entry procedures. All of the activities simulate actual business experiences. Thus, in addition to learning data-entry skills, students also gain valuable knowledge of the business world.

Table of Contents

Activity 1

Introduction To Data Entry

LEARNING OBJECTIVES

Upon completion of this activity, you will be able to:

→ **1** Define data, data entry, information, source document, and hard copy.

2 Define electronic spreadsheet software and electronic database software.

3 Identify the components of a computer system and describe their functions.

4 Define disk, disk drive, and concentric circles.

5 Care for a disk.

6 Understand the basic keyboard differences between IBM, Tandy 1000, and Macintosh microcomputers.

7 Key-enter the data for two intramural softball teams.

8 Use the special keys and key combinations that perform editing functions.

WHAT IS DATA ENTRY?

*D***ata entry** is the process whereby data is key-entered into the computer by an operator. (In this text-workbook, **key-enter** refers to the process of keying data at the keyboard and pressing the ENTER or RETURN key.) **Data** refers to the raw facts (alphabetic characters, numeric characters, and special symbols) that are processed by the microcomputer. **Information** is data that has been processed to produce usable, meaningful report formats such as sports statistical reports, merchandise inventories, payroll records, and registration forms.

Data entry operators frequently use two types of application software packages—spreadsheet and database—to key-enter data. An **electronic spreadsheet** displays data in a series of rows and columns that form a grid. The operator key-enters data and keys formulas that can calculate the data. Calculations (such as adding, multiplying, and dividing) can be performed across columns and down rows. An **electronic database** is used to create electronic files, similar to a card-catalog. The operator can key-enter, retrieve, and update data in a manner that permits easy access and retrieval. The data can be sorted using different criteria, and reports may be generated that show specific information.

The forms on which the data is originally recorded are known as **source documents.** Data is key-entered into the microcomputer from these documents. Source documents are usually kept as backup material just in case something goes wrong and the original data must be re-entered into the computer.

WHO KEY-ENTERS DATA?

*E*ither data entry operators or individuals working with the data usually key-enter data. For example, persons working in the payroll department might key-enter the data pertaining to payroll, and persons in the accounts receivable department might key-enter the data pertaining to accounts receivable.

Data is usually key-entered in the same sequence as it appears on the source document. Generally, a left-to-right, top-to-bottom flow from the source document is used.

Key-entering data immediately at the time of a transaction allows for faster service and quicker updates of results (output). For example, bank tellers enter deposits and withdrawals for customers while they wait. Regardless of whether a person is key-entering a batch of data from many source documents at one time or is key-entering data immediately at the time a transaction is made, that person must be very careful that the data entered is completely accurate to ensure correct results.

EQUIPMENT TO BE USED

In this course you will be using either an IBM, IBM compatible, Tandy 1000, or Macintosh microcomputer system. Each of these computer systems consists of the following distinctive components.

The **central processing unit** (CPU) is commonly referred to as the brains of the microcomputer. The CPU is composed of a control unit, an arithmetic/logic unit, and an internal primary storage (memory) unit. The **control unit** contains electronic circuits that direct the microcomputer to process data. The arithmetic/logic unit performs arithmetic operations including adding, subtracting, multiplying, and dividing. The main memory (also known as internal memory or primary storage) stores the software program instructions and the data during processing. A software program instructs the CPU and directs other hardware components, such as a printer.

The **keyboard** is the most common input device for microcomputers. The keyboard is made up of alphabetic (a, b, c ...), numeric (1, 2, 3 ...), symbol (#, @, $ ...), function (F1, F2, F3 ...), and special purpose keys (such as Ctrl, Shift, and Tab). The data is displayed on the screen and is stored in memory as the data is keyed. The **monitor** or **CRT** (cathode ray tube) is simply a television-like screen upon which the microcomputer can display data as it is key-entered into the microcomputer. The monitor can also display the results of processing if the software contains a print or display option. The software that accompanies this text-workbook contains a print or display option. Therefore, the user can either print the results on an attached printer or display them on the monitor.

Secondary (auxiliary) storage units allow data and instructions to be kept outside the main microcomputer memory. Two common types of secondary storage are disks and hard disks. A **disk** (sometimes called a **diskette**) is an auxiliary storage device on which data and information can be stored or retrieved. The **disk drive** has a small slot into which a disk is inserted and the disk drive will read or write data from or to the disk. A disk is a thin, flexible plastic surface covered with a thin coat of metal oxide. The disks normally used in microcomputers are either 5¼ or 3½ inches in diameter. Some microcomputers also have hard disks. A **hard disk**, which consists of one or more disk platters, is sealed inside the CPU.

Data is arranged on a disk in concentric circles. **Concentric circles**, called **tracks,** are circles within circles. Each one of the circles gets smaller, and none of them are connected to each other. Small magnetic spots of data are recorded on (written) or retrieved from (read) the disk by the read/write head. The **read/write head** never touches the disk. Instead, it floats extremely close to the disk and records or retrieves data electronically. During the reading process, data is copied from the disk into the microcomputer's main memory. Thus, after data is read from the disk, it is contained in both microcomputer memory and on the disk.

A **printer** is a device used to print information on paper when instructed to do so by the computer. A printed report or form is sometimes called **hard copy**. Usually the operator can instruct the computer to save data or results on a disk. The operator can then obtain hard copy at a later date.

CARE OF DISKS

Disks are fragile. Following these instructions is essential for obtaining good results from the 5¼ and 3½ inch disks.

- Do not bend the disk.
- Use only a soft felt-tip pen when writing on the disk label.
- Keep the disk away from any magnetic fields, such as the computer monitor.

- Do not touch the exposed area of the disk.
- Do not expose the disk to extremely hot or cold temperatures.
- Carefully insert the disk into the disk drive.
- Replace the disk in its envelope immediately after use.
- Store disks in an upright position in a storage container.
- Do not place anything on top of a disk.
- Do not insert or remove a disk from the disk drive when the "in-use" light is on or when the disk drive motor is running.

KEYBOARD DIFFERENCES AND SPECIAL KEYS

The computer, monitor, disk drive, and printer components are similar for the IBM, IBM compatibles, Tandy 1000, and Macintosh computers. However, there are some significant differences between the keyboards that should be noted. In addition, five special keys and key combinations are used as editing commands with the *Data Entry Activities for Microcomputers* software. Some of the keyboard differences and special keys are described below and on the following page.

RETURN or ENTER. This is keyed after a response is made at the computer keyboard. Pressing this key indicates to the computer that the response that has been entered is complete. This key is called the RETURN key on Apple computers and the ENTER key on Tandy 1000 and IBM computers. The ENTER key is designated with this symbol (↵) on the IBM. The term **key-enter** means to key the data for a field and press the RETURN or ENTER key.

Numeric Keypad. On the IBM and Tandy 1000 computers the numeric keypad is used to key-enter numeric data. On each of these computers, the numeric keypad is located on the right side of the keyboard and may be used in place of the number keys on the top row of the main keyboard. On the IBM computer the 2, 4, 6, and 8 keys on the numeric keypad also have four directional arrows for moving the cursor within and between data fields. When the computer is turned on, the directional arrow keys on the keypad are active and the numbers on the keypad are inactive. To activate the numbers on the numeric keypad, simply press the

NUM LOCK key one time. Each time the NUM LOCK key is pressed, the status of the numeric keypad numbers and directional arrows will toggle back and forth. When the number keys on the numeric keypad are active, the plus (+) key is active and may be used as the RETURN or ENTER key.

The Macintosh extended keyboard also provides a numeric keypad, as well as a num lock key.

Directional Arrows (←) (→). When the left or right arrow key is pressed, the cursor is moved in the direction of the arrow through the data field. As the cursor moves through the text in the field, no data is changed. The operator must stop the cursor at a given point and re-key the correct data.

TAB. When the TAB key is pressed, the cursor is moved to the next field on a data entry screen.

F8. When the F8 key is pressed, the cursor will move to the previous record during data entry. Once data entry is completed, pressing the F8 key will allow you to edit your data.

F9. When the F9 key is pressed, the cursor will move to the next record during data entry. Once data entry is completed, pressing the F9 key will allow you to analyze the results of your data entry session.

F10. When the F8 key is pressed, the timer will stop and your data entry session will end.

HOME. When the HOME key is pressed, the cursor will move to the top of the screen.

END. When the END key is pressed, the cursor will move to the bottom of the screen.

Appendix D lists the keystrokes used to navigate on the screens in this software program

⌘-J. When the ⌘ key is pressed and held down while the J key is pressed, the cursor will move to the previous record during data entry.
⌘-K. When the ⌘ key is pressed and held down while the K key is pressed, the cursor will move to the next record during data entry.

INPUT FIELDS

You have volunteered to be the data entry operator for Wellingham, Inc., Corporate Softball League. You will enter the data for the game between the Titans and the Hawks on April 12. The data is recorded on a form for keeping the softball statistics. This form is illustrated in Figure 1.1.

WELLINGHAM, INC. **Corporate Softball League**

Titans vs. Hawks   April 12

Employee Number	Last Name	Init.	Team	Dept.	At Bats	Hits	Runs	Errors

FIGURE 1.1 Wellingham, Inc., Corporate Softball League Form

You will key-enter the game statistics for both teams for the April 12 game between the Titans and the Hawks. In this activity you will enter all of the data listed on the source document (softball statistics sheet) for 24 softball players.

As discussed previously, data is key-entered into the computer from source documents. The data written for the Wellingham, Inc., Corporate Softball League statistics sheet will be key-entered into fields on the data entry screen. A **field** is a group of one or more consecutive spaces reserved for only one type of data. For example, the player's employee number, last name, team, and errors are separate fields on the softball statistics form. A **record** is a collection or group of fields relating to the same subject. The data in fields can be numeric, alphabetic (alpha) or alpha and numeric (alphanumeric). Fields that are programmed or identified to accept numeric data will only accept digits. Fields that are programmed to accept alphabetic data will only accept letters and symbols. Fields that are programmed to accept alphanumeric data will accept digits, letters, and symbols.

Data is often classified and coded on **source documents** to identify similar groups of people or items. Classifying and coding data speeds up the processing of data and may make it easier to summarize data when preparing reports. Code numbers or letters are used to identify the groups or items. For example, instead of key-entering lists of occupation titles, a 2-digit code might be used to identify each occupational title (09 may represent teacher, 35 may represent dentist, and 76 may represent lawyer).

If 3-digit numbers were used to identify items, 001 to 999 could be used as identifiers. In key-entering data, "leading zeros" are often used in spreadsheets and in data bases to have consistency in field size. For example, if you were keying the item number 3, it would be keyed 003, 47 would be keyed 047, and 334 would be keyed 334. When using dates (month, day, and year), a leading zero is also used (10/03/--). When you see leading zeros on source documents, key them.

The input fields for this activity are:

Employee Number. This field is nine characters in length. This number is assigned to each employee working at Wellingham, Inc.

Last Name. This field is a maximum of twelve characters in length and represents the last name of each team member.

Init. This field is a maximum of two characters in length and represents the initials of the first and middle names of the players.

Team. This field is a maximum of six characters in length and contains the names of the teams playing softball.

Dept. This field is a maximum of eight characters in length and is large enough to contain the names listed for those departments participating in the softball league. This field tells in which department each player works.

At Bats. This field is one digit in length and tells how many times each player was at bat.

Hits. This field is one digit in length and tells how many hits each player made.

Runs. This field is one digit in length and tells how many runs each player scored.

Errors. This field is one digit in length and tells how many errors each player made.

Step-by-Step Instructions

GET READY

Follow the start-up procedures for your computer that are found in Appendix A.

COMPLETE ALPHA-NUMERIC DEXTERITY DRILL

```
8125 4200229 TITANS 9500276 676CR 053665
1135520 06692 00815953 214663 HITS 52107
262119 008571 37182 RUNS 690016 6579 201
ERRORS 579442 311076 ME 631091 74259 567
36790 079524977 20010136 TEAM 638 575942
```

STEP 1   From the *Activities* menu, select *Activity 1 Spreadsheet Statistics.*

STEP 2   Select *Alpha-Numeric Dexterity Drill* by either double-clicking on it or highlighting it and selecting *OK.*

The display on your screen will be similar to that shown in Figure 1.2.

FIGURE 1.2

> ✍ **Note: If you do not want to continue with the drill at this time, either:**
>> **A. Select *Cancel*. This pass will not be recorded**
>>> **OR**
>> **B. Select *OK*. This pass will be labeled incomplete.**

> ✍ **Note: One data pass is defined as one attempt to complete an activity.**

STEP 3   Enter the data for each line. Space between the groups of data where spaces appear on the screen. Press *enter* or *return* at the end of each line. This drill will be timed automatically, beginning when you strike the first character or number.

STEP 4   Select *OK* when you have finished key-entering. When you select OK, the timer stops automatically. Your accuracy score for each line will appear, along with the words per minute and strokes per hour.

STEP 5   Select *Review* to review any errors that were made. After you have reviewed your performance, select *OK*. You may generate a report of your performance by using the report software feature. To do this, from the *File* menu, select *Open Report*, and highlight *Activity 1 Spreadsheet Statistics*. Select *Alpha-Numeric Dexterity Drill* and select *Get Report*. When the report appears on your screen, from the *File* menu, select *Print*.

STEP 6   Repeat the Alpha-Numeric Dexterity Drill as many times as instructed by your teacher. To repeat the drill:

     A. Repeat Steps 1 and 2.
     B. If you completed the previous drill, select *New*. If you left a drill unfinished, select *Open* and then complete the drill.
     C. Repeat Steps 3 through 5 above.

> ✍ **Note: The instructions for completing the remaining Alpha-Numeric Dexterity Drills in this book will be less detailed. If necessary, you may refer to the step-by-step instructions listed here.**

COMPLETE KEYPAD DEXTERITY DRILL

```
47474  58585  69696  96969  85858  74747  4561
58585  69696  96969  85858  74747  4567  47474
69696  96969  85858  74747  4567  47474  58585
14725  36159  81972  58513  53619  75621  2378
15263  48597  45125  32838  97204  0314  58261
```

STEP 1   From the *Activities* menu, select *Activity 1 Spreadsheet Statistics.*

STEP 2   Select *Keypad Dexterity Drill* by either double-clicking on it or highlighting it and then selecting *OK.*

The display on your screen will be similar to that shown in Figure 1.3.

FIGURE 1.3

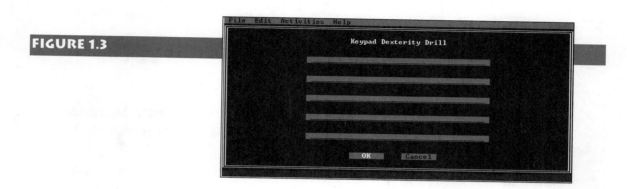

Note: If you do not want to continue with the drill at this time, either:

    A. Select *Cancel*. This pass will not be recorded

                OR

    B. Select *OK*. This pass will be labeled incomplete.

STEP 3   Enter the data for each line. Space between the groups of data where spaces appear on the screen. Press *enter* or *return* at the end of each line. This drill will be timed automatically, beginning when you strike the first number.

STEP 4   Select *OK* when you are finished key-entering. When you select OK, the timer stops automatically. Your accuracy score for each line will appear, along with the words per minute and strokes per hour.

STEP 5   Select *Review* to review any errors that were made. After reviewing your performance, select *OK.* You may generate a report of your performance. From the *File* menu, select *Open Report*, and highlight *Activity 1 Spreadsheet Statistics.* Select *Keypad Dexterity Drill* and select *Get Report.* When the report appears on your screen, from the *File* menu, select *Print.*

STEP 6   Repeat the Keypad Dexterity Drill as many times as instructed by your teacher. To repeat the drill:

A. Repeat Steps 1 and 2 above.

B.   If you completed the previous drill, select *New.* If you left a drill unfinished, select *Open,* and then complete the drill.

C.   Repeat Steps 3 through 5.

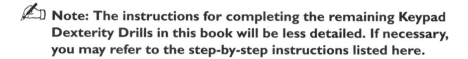 **Note: The instructions for completing the remaining Keypad Dexterity Drills in this book will be less detailed. If necessary, you may refer to the step-by-step instructions listed here.**

COMPLETE SPREADSHEET STATISTICS

STEP 1   Remove the **Wellingham, Inc., Corporate Softball League** statistics sheet that is located at the end of this activity.

(Hint: Key-enter means to key the data for a given field, and then press the enter, return, or tab key.)

STEP 2   From the *Activities* menu, select *Activity 1 Spreadsheet Statistics.*

STEP 3   Select *Spreadsheet* by double-clicking on it or by highlighting it and selecting *OK.*

The display on your screen will be similar to that shown in Figure 1.4.

FIGURE 1.4

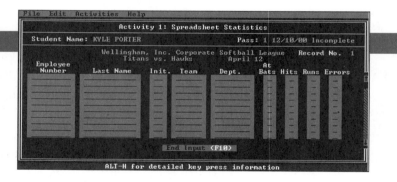

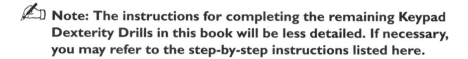 **Note: If you do not want to continue with the activity at this time, from the *File* menu select *Close.***

STEP 4   Key-enter the Employee Number (815257229 for the first record) in the first column. Each line on the form is a **record.** This is a numeric field. If you try to enter anything

other than a number, the computer will not accept the data and a beep will sound.

STEP 5 Key-enter the Last Name in the second column. This is an alphabetic field. If you try to enter a number or symbol, the computer will not accept the data and a beep will sound.

STEP 6 Key-enter the data for the remaining fields for the first record. After you have key-entered the data for the ERRORS field (0 for the first record), the cursor will advance to the first field of the second record.

STEP 7 Key-enter the data for the remaining records.

> **Note: Depending on how your teacher has set up the data correction in your software, you may be able to move to any field in any record at any time during the key-entering process to make a correction.**

> **Note: If you are interrupted before key-entering all of the records, you may stop by selecting *End Input*. Then select *Analyze*. Then select *OK*. This will save any data you have key-entered to that point. When you begin the next session to complete this activity, the cursor will be located in the first field of the first record that you entered. Use the appropriate keys to place the cursor in the proper record and field to begin key-entering data.**
>
> **To begin the next session:**
>
> - Repeat Steps 2 and 3.
> - Select *Open* from the menu.
> - Continue with Step 8 below.

STEP 8 After key-entering the data for all 24 records, select *End Input*. This will stop the timer. If you notice errors after you have selected End Input, select *Edit* and then move to the appropriate fields to key-enter the corrections. This will start the timer. After making the corrections, select *End Input* again. This will stop the timer. The timer is always running when you are key-entering data and making corrections.

Print the spreadsheet that is on the screen if instructed by your teacher. To do this, from the *File* menu, select *Print*.

STEP 9 Select *Analyze*. A box will appear as shown in Figure 1.5.

FIGURE 1.5

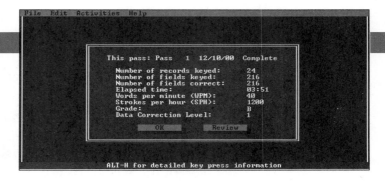

This box will show you:
- if you have completed entering all of the data for this activity
- the number of records keyed
- the number of fields keyed
- the number of fields that are correct
- elapsed time needed to complete the activity
- words per minute
- strokes per hour
- your grade
- data correction level

STEP 10 Select *Review.* Any errors will be highlighted. If instructed by your teacher, print the spreadsheet.

STEP 11 Select *Done.*

STEP 12 You may generate a report of your performance in this activity. To do this:

- From the *File* menu, select *Open Report* and select *Activity 1 Spreadsheet Statistics.*
- Select *Spreadsheet.*
- Select *Get Report.*
- From the *File* menu, select *Print.*
- Select *Print* again.
- Select *Done.*

Note: In a real work situation, you would strive for completely accurate records. Therefore, it is suggested that once you have completed all of the steps listed above, you should go back into the records and correct any errors. To do this:
- **From the *Activities* menu, select *Activity 1 Spreadsheet Statistics.***
- **Select *Spreadsheet.***
- **Select *Open.***

- Use the appropriate keys to locate the proper record and field and then key-enter the corrections.
- Select *End Input.*
- Select *Analyze Data.*
- Select *Review.*
- Select *Done.*
- Print the spreadsheet if instructed by your teacher. To do this, from the *File* menu select *Print.*

VOCABULARY

central processing unit (CPU)
concentric circles
control unit
data
data entry
directional arrows
disk
disk drive
diskette
electronic database
electronic spreadsheet
field
hard copy
hard disk
information
keyboard
key-enter
monitor (CRT)
numeric keypad
printer
read/write head
record
source documents
tracks

Activity 1 Study Guide

INTRODUCTION TO DATA ENTRY

PART 1

OBJECTIVES 1, 3, 4, 6, AND 7 (2 POINTS EACH)

✏️ **Match the vocabulary terms with the best definitions. Write the letter of the term in the space to the left of the definition. You will not use every vocabulary term.**

A. **concentric circles or tracks**
B. **CPU**
C. **disk drive**
D. **hard copy**
E. **home**
F. **monitor**
G. **numeric keypad**

_____ **1.** A name for a document printed from your printer.

_____ **2.** The set of keys located to the right of the main keyboard.

_____ **3.** The term that refers to the equipment used to display data as it is key-entered into the computer.

_____ **4.** Data is arranged on a disk in this manner.

_____ **5.** Part of the equipment often referred to as the brains of the computer system.

_____ **6.** The key that moves the cursor to the top of the screen.

PART 2

OBJECTIVES 1, 3, 4, 5, AND 7 (1 POINT EACH)

✏️ **Each of the following statements is either true or false. Indicate your choice by circling T for a true statement or F for a false statement.**

T   F   **1.** CPU is an abbreviation for central program unit.

T   F   **2.** Data is recorded on tracks on a disk.

T   F   **3.** When the "in-use" light of the disk drive is on, the disk should be removed from the drive.

T   F   **4.** The CPU is composed of a control unit, an arithmetic/logic unit and a memory unit.

PART 3

OBJECTIVES 1, 2, AND 3 (3 POINTS EACH)

Briefly answer each of the following items. Write your answers on the lines provided.

1. Define source document.

_____

_____

_____

2. Define data.

_____

_____

_____

3. Define information.

_____

_____

_____

_____

4. Define data entry.

_____

_____

_____

5. Define electronic spreadsheet.

_____

_____

6. Define electronic database.

_____

_____

7. List the basic components of a computer system.

_____

_____

_____

☛ **Remove the Activity 1 Study Guide from your
text-workbook and hand it to your instructor for
correcting.**

Total Points Possible	37
(Minus) Incorrect Points	_____
Total Points Earned	_____
Percent Correct	_____
Grade	_____

WELLINGHAM, INC. Corporate Softball League

Titans vs. Hawks   April 12

Employee Number	Last Name	Init.	Team	Dept.	At Bats	Hits	Runs	Errors
815257229	Groth	JT	Titans	Acct	4	2	0	0
296762059	Martinez	CR	Titans	Hmn Res	5	3	1	1
053660421	Neberman	JW	Titans	Mfg	5	2	1	0
919212641	Clemons	RF	Titans	Mfg	4	1	1	0
005820471	Brennen	CL	Titans	Research	3	0	0	0
690016579	Waldenberger	GL	Titans	Payroll	4	2	2	0
259765794	Przytarski	BA	Titans	Acct	2	0	0	1
097638347	Chang	ME	Titans	Research	3	1	1	0
915674259	Weinberg	FV	Titans	Adv	6	3	1	0
179555634	Price	CA	Titans	Mfg	4	2	1	0
465031858	Fleming	RK	Titans	Hmn Res	4	1	0	1
921578963	Campbell	OR	Titans	Acct	3	1	1	0
145776276	Romano	DL	Hawks	Adv	5	2	0	0
984270752	Zimmerman	TM	Hawks	Payroll	3	1	1	0
349146397	Beier	JJ	Hawks	Mfg	5	2	0	1
700602827	Johnston	CS	Hawks	Acct	4	1	1	0
539765491	Werner	JC	Hawks	Adv	3	0	0	1
760722951	Zaborowski	DM	Hawks	Research	2	0	0	0
907255221	Wuensch	JW	Hawks	Mfg	3	1	1	2
643646741	Brown	FL	Hawks	Payroll	5	2	0	0
089620035	Thao	DH	Hawks	Acct	2	1	0	0
950216837	Cunningham	ER	Hawks	Payroll	4	2	1	0
156641049	Smith	SS	Hawks	Hmn Res	5	2	0	1
164088189	Jonsgaard	KS	Hawks	Mfg	4	2	1	0

Activity 2

MERCHANDISE INVENTORY

09 13 32

→ **1** Define fiscal year inventory, perpetual inventory, periodic inventory, and Universal Product Code (UPC).

2 Describe the procedures used to establish and maintain a computerized inventory system.

3 Accurately key-enter data for an inventory system.

DATA ENTRY APPLICATION AND JOB DESCRIPTION

*S*elling merchandise generates a major source of revenue for businesses. In order to have sufficient merchandise to meet customer demands, businesses need to maintain an up-to-date inventory. **Inventory** refers to merchandise or goods on hand available for sale to customers.

In this activity you will key-enter inventory data for a wholesale company, Tyler Drug Store Supplies. Tyler Drug Store Supplies sells merchandise to drug stores. Examples of inventory for this wholesale distributor are cosmetics, non-prescription medicines, health aids, and hygiene products. To be successful, businesses need to know the size of the merchandise inventory to maintain. Too much or too little inventory can cause serious financial losses to businesses. Thus, it is very important that businesses maintain accurate merchandise inventory control.

Two methods of determining inventory commonly used are perpetual inventory and periodic inventory. Many businesses monitor their inventory levels on a continuous basis by recording the quantities of merchandise bought and sold after each transaction. This process is known as **perpetual inventory**, and it is either done manually or through the use of a computer. The perpetual inventory records show how many of each item are available for sale at any given time. When a computerized inventory system is used, each transaction is key-entered at a terminal. Any business using a computerized inventory system many employ data entry personnel.

Good accounting practices require businesses to actually count the items on hand once a year for auditing purposes. This process is called **periodic inventory**. A periodic inventory is a task that is usually performed at the end of a **fiscal year** (a yearly period established for accounting purposes). The purpose of taking a periodic inventory is to verify that the total items on hand actually agrees with the inventory records. It is common to find that there is actually more or less of a given item on hand than the inventory records show. In either case, an employee prepares a **discrepancy report** to notify management that there is an error on the inventory record. At Tyler Drug Store Supplies, information gathered during the physical inventory is recorded on forms known as the **inventory ticket,** which is attached to a storage bin, and the **inventory setup form.**

INVENTORY SETUP FORM

The **inventory setup form** for Tyler Drug Store Supplies is illustrated in Figure 2.1. The information recorded on this form is entered into the computer by a data entry operator. After the inventory file has been set up in the computer, it can be updated at any time by the data entry operator.

TYLER DRUG STORE SUPPLIES
INVENTORY SETUP FORM
June 30,

UPC NO.	DESCRIPTION	BIN NO.	UNIT	UNIT PRICE	VENDOR #1	VENDOR #2	QTY. ON HAND	REORDER POINT	REORDER QUANTITY

FIGURE 2.1 Inventory Setup Form

SALES TICKETS

Sales tickets are forms on which the Universal Product Code (UPC) number and the quantity of each item sold are recorded. The UPC is a bar code identifier assigned by the merchant or the product's manufacturer. When sales ticket data is key-entered into the computerized inventory system, the quantity on hand is adjusted automatically in the computer. As sales data for a certain product is key-entered, the quantity on hand for that product will automatically decrease. These fields will be explained further in the Input Fields section of this activity.

FIGURE 2.2 Sales Ticket

INVENTORY UPDATE FORM

Product information changes are recorded on the **inventory update form**. For example, changes in permanent information, such as unit, bin number, and reorder point are recorded on this form. This type of data seldom changes, but when changes do occur, they are recorded on the update form. In order to update the information in the computer, the data entry operator must first key-enter the UPC number to identify the specific item that must be updated. The operator then key-enters the change to the appropriate field.

TYLER DRUG STORE SUPPLIES
INVENTORY UPDATE FORM
June 30

UPC NO.	DESCRIPTION	BIN NO.	UNIT	UNIT PRICE	VENDOR #1	VENDOR #2	QTY. ON HAND	REORDER POINT	REORDER QUANTITY

FIGURE 2.3 Inventory Update Form

INPUT FIELDS

To set up the inventory system for Tyler Drug Store Supplies, you will key-enter the inventory data into the computer from the inventory setup form. You will then enter transaction data from 12 sales tickets to adjust the inventory levels to reflect the decreases in merchandise. Finally, you will update product information in the inventory system by entering changes from the inventory update form.

Three types of source documents are used to enter data into Tyler Drug Store Supplies' computerized inventory system—the inventory setup form, the sales tickets, and the inventory update form. Information from these forms is key-entered into fields on data entry screens.

INVENTORY SETUP AND UPDATE FIELDS

First you must "set up" the inventory file by key-entering all the data on the inventory setup form. Later, you must update this information by changing only the specific fields indicated on the inventory update form. Descriptions of the fields that you will use to set up and update the inventory are provided below.

UPC No. This identifier, a number assigned by the merchant or the product's manufacturer, is used primarily for accounting and tracking purposes. Each stock number within a company must be unique to identify each product without confusion. Imagine the problems with inventory records if a motor vehicle sales company assigned the same stock number to a bulldozer, a pickup truck, and a sports car. For this reason, many businesses use a standard numbering scheme called the **Universal Product Code (UPC) number**. The UPC number is a system of unique bar codes and digits encoded on each product by the manufacturer. The bar code can be read by computerized scanners at checkout counters. Bar codes can consist of various combinations of bars and digits. Bar codes consisting of ten numbers divided into two groups of five numbers are very common. The first five numbers identify a particular manufacturer or company. The last five numbers identify a particular product and package. In our example, Tyler Drug Store Supplies has chosen to use ten digit numbers as its stock numbers.

Description. This field contains a short name or phrase that describes each item of merchandise.

Bin No. This field contains the storage location of the items on hand in the storeroom of Tyler Drug Store Supplies.

Unit. This field is used to identify the unit of measure by which an item is stored. The unit of measure is typically one of the following: carton (crtn), case (case), dozen (dozn), or bottle (botl).

Unit Price. This field identifies the price of a unit of merchandise. Again, the unit can be a case, carton, dozen, or bottle.

Vendor #1. This field represents a unique number assigned to a particular vendor from whom Tyler's buys its merchandise. Merchants who wish to sell to Tyler's must have their names placed on an approved list.

Vendor #2. This field also represents a unique number assigned to a particular vendor from whom Tyler's buys its merchandise. This vendor is the backup or secondary source of supply.

Qty. on Hand. This field represents the amount of merchandise in stock.

Reorder Point. This field represents the minimum number of units allowed in stock. When this number is reached, reordering must take place.

Reorder Quantity. This field represents the number of units that will be purchased when the quantity on hand reaches the reorder point.

SALES TICKET FIELDS

The data entry screen used to key-enter the sales ticket information contains two input fields, the UPC number, and Quantity.

OBJECTIVE 3

GET READY

Follow the start-up procedures for your computer that are found in Appendix A.

COMPLETE ALPHA-NUMERIC DEXTERITY DRILL

```
123 2748 9816 2503 52511 36003 21224 472
7525 8261 COTTON 2112 11946 58918 263523
CASE 2364 96518 50 2541 17507 304021 100
16824 28713 8 741 46273 12063 47 2290 48
RAZORS 3348 57443 8020 11759 MUSK 3336 2
```

STEP 1   From the *Activities* menu, select *Activity 2 Merchandise Inventory.*

STEP 2   Select *Alpha-Numeric Dexterity Drill*.

STEP 3   Enter the data for each line. Press *enter* or *return* at the end of each line.

STEP 4   Select *OK* when you are finished key-entering. Review your score.

STEP 5   Select *Review* to review any errors that were made. After you have reviewed your performance, select *OK*.

STEP 6   Repeat the Alpha-Numeric Dexterity Drill as many times as instructed by your teacher. (See the detailed instructions in Activity 1, if necessary.)

COMPLETE KEYPAD DEXTERITY DRILL

```
41414  52525  63636  41014  63636  52525  4142
52525  63636  41014  63636  52525  41414  5252
63636  36363  25252  14141  5252  41414  52525
55201  51594  11419  32945  46253  01255  0896
68203  57765  28839  21374  37009  09065  4324
```

STEP 1   From the *Activities* menu, select *Activity 2 Merchandise Inventory*.

STEP 2   Select *Keypad Dexterity Drill*.

STEP 3   Enter the data for each line. Press *enter* or *return* at the end of each line.

STEP 4   Select *OK* when you have finished key-entering. Review your score.

STEP 5   Select *Review* to review any errors that were made. After reviewing your performance, select *OK*.

STEP 6   Repeat the Keypad Dexterity Drill as many times as instructed by your teacher. (See the detailed instructions listed in Activity 1, if necessary.)

COMPLETE MERCHANDISE INVENTORY SETUP FORM

STEP 1   Remove the inventory setup form for Tyler Drug Store that is located at the end of this activity.

STEP 2   From the *Activities* menu, select *Activity 2 Merchandise Inventory*.

STEP 3   Select *Inventory Setup Form*. Your screen will be similar to that shown in Figure 2.4.

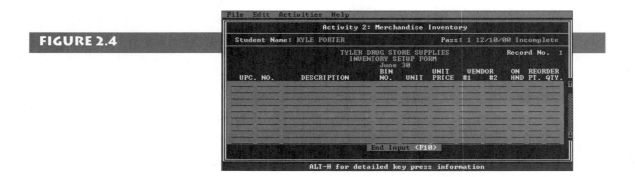

FIGURE 2.4

STEP 4   Key-enter the UPC number (76000 60600 for the first record) in the first field. Each line on the form is a **record.** You will key the first five digits, then the computer will automatically insert a space. Finish entering the UPC number by key-entering the last five digits.

STEP 5   Key-enter the Description (TOOTHPASTE 8.2 OZ for the first record) in the second field.

STEP 6   Key-enter the data for the remaining fields for the first record. After you have key-entered the Reorder Quantity (50) for the first record, the cursor will move to the first field of the second record.

STEP 7   Key-enter the data for all of the remaining records.

> **Note: Depending on how your teacher has set up the data correction in your software, you may be able to move to any field in any record at any time during the key-entering process to make a correction.**

> **Note: If you are interrupted before key-entering all of the records, you may stop by selecting *End Input*. Then select *Analyze*. Then select *OK*. This will save any data you have key-entered to that point. When you begin the next session to complete this activity, the cursor will be located in the first field of the first record that you entered. Use the appropriate keys to place the cursor in the proper record and field to begin key-entering data.**

> **To begin the next session:**
>   **- Repeat Steps 2 and 3.**
>   **- Select *Open* from the menu.**
>   **- Continue with Step 8.**

STEP 8   After key-entering the data for all 20 records, select *End Input*. This will stop the timer. If you notice errors after selecting End Input, select *Edit* and then move to the appropriate fields to key-enter the corrections. This will start the timer. After making the corrections, select *End Input* again. This will stop the timer. The timer is always running when you are key-entering data and making corrections.

While the spreadsheet is displayed on the screen, you may print the spreadsheet if instructed by your teacher. To do this, from the *File* menu, select *Print*.

STEP 9   Select *Analyze*. Review the information presented.

STEP 10   Select *Review*. Any errors will be highlighted. If instructed by your teacher, print the spreadsheet.

STEP 11   Select *Done*.

STEP 12   You may generate a report of your performance in this activity. To do so,

- From the *File* menu, select *Open Report* and select *Activity 2 Merchandise Inventory*.
- Select *Inventory Setup Form*.
- Select *Get Report*.
- From the *File* menu, select *Print*.
- Select *Print* again.
- Select *Done*.

 Note: In a real work situation, you would strive for completely accurate records. Therefore, it is suggested that once you have completed all of the steps listed above, you should go back into the records and correct any errors. To do this:

- **From the *Activities* menu, select *Activity 2 Merchandise Inventory*.**
- **Select *Inventory Setup Form*.**
- **Select *Open*.**
- **Use the appropriate keys to locate the proper record and field and then key-enter the correction.**
- **Select *End Input*.**
- **Select *Analyze*.**
- **Select *Review*.**
- **Select *Done*.**
- **Print the inventory setup form if instructed by your teacher.**

COMPLETE MERCHANDISE INVENTORY SALES TICKETS

STEP 1   Remove and separate all of the sales tickets for Tyler Drug Store that are located at the end of this activity. To keep track of the sales tickets, sort the tickets in numerical order, using the number in the upper right-hand corner of each ticket.

STEP 2   From the *Activities* menu, select *Activity 2 Merchandise Inventory.*

STEP 3   Select *Sales Ticket.* Your screen will be similar to that shown in Figure 2.5.

FIGURE 2.5

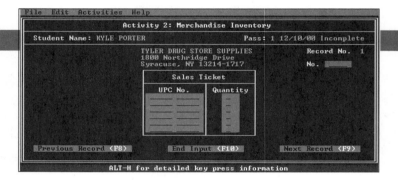

STEP 4   Key-enter the No. (0001 for the first record) in the first field. One entire sales ticket is considered a **record.**

STEP 5   Key-enter the UPC No.(40082 86106 for the first record) in the proper field.

STEP 6   Key-enter the Quantity (1 for the first record) in the proper field.

STEP 7   Key-enter the data in the appropriate fields for the entire record.

STEP 8   After key-entering the data for the first record (you will leave a blank line in this record and you may have blank lines in other records), select *Next Record.*

STEP 9   Key-enter the data for all of the remaining records.

> **Note: Depending on how your teacher has set up the data correction in your software, you may be able to move to any field in any record at any time during the key-entering process to make a correction.**

Note: If you are interrupted before key-entering all of the records, you may stop by selecting *End Input*. Then select *Analyze*. Then select *OK*. This will save any data you have key-entered to that point. When you begin the next session to complete this activity, the cursor will be located in the first field of the first record, in order of sales ticket number. Use the appropriate keys to place the cursor in the proper record and field to begin key-entering data.

To begin the next session:
- Repeat Steps 2 and 3.
- Select *Open* from the menu.
- Continue with Step 10 below.

STEP 10   After key-entering the data for all 12 sales invoices, select *End Input*. This will stop the timer. If you notice errors after you have selected *End Input*, select *Edit* and then move to the appropriate fields to key-enter the corrections. This will start the timer. After making the corrections, select *End Input* again. This will stop the timer.

Print the sales ticket that is on the screen if instructed by your teacher. To do this, from the *File* menu select *Print*.

STEP 11   Select *Analyze*. Review the information presented.

STEP 12   Select *Review*. Any errors will be highlighted. If instructed by your teacher, print the sales tickets. From the *File* menu, select *Print*.

STEP 13   Select *Done*.

STEP 14   You may generate a report of your performance in this activity. To do so,
- From the *File* menu, select *Open Report* and select *Activity 2 Merchandise Inventory*.
- Select *Spreadsheet*.
- Select *Get Report*.
- From the *File* menu, select *Print*.
- Select *Print* again.
- Select *Done*.

Note: In a real work situation, you would strive for completely accurate records. Therefore, it is suggested that once you have completed all of the steps listed above, you should go back into the records and correct any errors. To do this:

- From the *Activities* menu, select *Activity 2 Merchandise Inventory*.
- Select *Spreadsheet*.
- Select *Open*.
- Use the appropriate keys to locate the proper record and field and then key-enter the correction.
- Select *End Input*.

- Select *Analyze*.
- Select *Review*.
- Select *Done*.
- Print the inventory tickets if instructed by your teacher.

COMPLETE MERCHANDISE INVENTORY UPDATE FORM

STEP 1   Remove the inventory update form for Tyler Drug Store that is located at the end of this activity.

STEP 2   From the *Activities* menu, select *Activity 2 Merchandise Inventory*.

STEP 3   Select *Inventory Update Form*.

STEP 4   All of the correct data will appear on the screen. You must use the return, enter, or tab key to move to the first field that you wish to edit. You will want to find the record that corresponds to UPC number 15100 00370 and change the Reorder Point to 30 and the Reorder Quantity to 85.

> **Note: The UPC numbers will not be changed during this exercise. They are listed for your reference only.**

STEP 5   Key-enter the updated data for the remaining records. Be sure that you are in the correct fields for the appropriate records.

> **Note: Depending on how your teacher has set up the data correction in your software, you may be able to move to any field in any record at any time during the key-entering process to make a correction.**

> **Note: If you are interrupted before key-entering all of the records, you may stop by selecting *End Input*. Then select *Analyze*. Then select *OK*. This will save any data you have key-entered to that point. When you begin the next session to complete this activity, the cursor will be located in the first field of the first record. Use the appropriate keys to place the cursor in the proper record and field to begin key-entering data.**

> **To begin the next session:**
> - **Repeat Steps 2 and 3 above.**
> - **Select *Open* from the menu.**
> - **Continue with Step 6.**

STEP 6   After key-entering the data for all ten records, select *End Input*. This will stop the timer. If you notice errors after you have selected *End Input*, select *Edit* and then move to the appropriate fields to key-enter the corrections. This will start the timer. After making the corrections, select *End Input* again. This will stop the timer.

Print the inventory update form that is on the screen if instructed by your teacher.

STEP 7   Select *Analyze*. Review the information presented.

STEP 8   Select *Review*. Any errors will be highlighted. Print the update form if instructed by your teacher.

STEP 9   Select *Done*.

STEP 10   You may report of your performance in this activity. To do so,

- From the *File* menu, select *Open Report,* and select *Activity 2 Merchandise Inventory.*
- Select *Inventory Update Form.*
- Select *Get Report*.
- From the *File* menu, select *Print*.
- Select *Print* again.
- Select *Done*.

Note: In a real work situation, you would strive for completely accurate records. Therefore, it is suggested that once you have completed all of the steps listed above, you should go back into the records and correct any errors. To do this:

- **From the *Activities* menu, select *Activity 2 Merchandise Inventory*.**
- **Select *Inventory Update Form*.**
- **Select *Open*.**
- **Use the appropriate keys to locate the proper record and field and then key-enter the correction.**
- **Select *End Input*.**
- **Select *Analyze*.**
- **Select *Review*.**
- **Select *Done*.**
- **Print the inventory update form if instructed by your teacher.**

VOCABULARY

discrepancy report
fiscal year
inventory
inventory setup form
inventory ticket
inventory update form
periodic inventory
perpetual inventory
record
sales ticket
Universal Product Code (UPC number)

Activity 2 Study Guide

MERCHANDISE INVENTORY

PART 1

OBJECTIVES 1 AND 2 (2 POINTS EACH)

➥ **Match the vocabulary terms with the best definitions. Write the letter of the term in the space to the left of the definition. You will not use every vocabulary term.**

A. **bin number**
B. **discrepancy report**
C. **fiscal year**

D. **inventory ticket**
E. **inventory update form**

F. **sales ticket**
G. **Universal Product Code**

_____ 1. This shows if more or less merchandise is on hand than the inventory records show.

_____ 2. In a stockroom, an item's location is identified by this.

_____ 3. The Universal Product Code number and the quantity of each item sold are recorded on this.

_____ 4. Changes in permanent information, such as unit, bin number, and reorder point, are recorded on this.

_____ 5. When periodic inventory is taken, this is attached to a storage bin.

_____ 6. This unique number is assigned by the manufacturer to identify a particular product.

PART 2

OBJECTIVE 1 (1 POINT EACH)

➥ **Each of the following statements is either true or false. Indicate your choice by circling T for a true statement or F for a false statement.**

T   F   1. Inventory is the merchandise or goods on hand available for sale to customers.

T   F   2. Perpetual inventory is used by a business to monitor its inventory only once a year.

T   F   3. Periodic inventory is the process whereby the number of items on hand are actually counted.

T   F   4. Universal Product Code numbers are used to distinguish one item from another item.

OBJECTIVE 1 (3 POINTS EACH)

➥ **Briefly answer each of the following items. Write your answers on the lines provided.**

1. Define inventory.

_____

_____

_____

2. Define perpetual inventory.

_____

_____

_____

_____

3. Define periodic inventory.

_____

_____

_____

_____

☞ **Remove the Activity 2 Study Guide from your text-workbook and hand it to your instructor for correcting.**

Total Points Possible	25
(Minus) Incorrect Points	_____
Total Points Earned	_____
Percent Correct	_____
Grade	_____

TYLER DRUG STORE SUPPLIES
INVENTORY SETUP FORM
June 30

UPC NO.	DESCRIPTION	BIN NO.	UNIT	UNIT PRICE	VENDOR #1	VENDOR #2	QTY. ON HAND	REORDER POINT	REORDER QUANTITY
76000 60600	Toothpaste 8.2 oz	13284	carton	27.48	19689	74151	26	20	50
05251 13600	Mouthwash 32 oz	21224	carton	47.28	42751	30420	65	25	55
40028 26106	Cotton Swabs/375	99052	case	21.12	11946	81085	26	35	23
78089 49101	Deodorant 1.75 oz	00199	case	23.64	96518	98603	41	50	25
21000 63040	Dental Floss 100 yds	60578	case	26.64	16834	28733	13	13	8
16000 00320	Hair Spray 7 oz	91240	carton	17.88	19689	74151	32	27	15
38000 02290	Shaving Cream 12 oz	97458	carton	29.16	47887	12063	48	30	100
38520 85020	Razors/10	35249	case	33.48	00370	34475	84	20	80
30000 01090	Musk Cologne 2 oz	38980	carton	68.82	50993	30420	41	15	68
21000 68583	Shampoo 15 oz	10750	case	35.64	06483	11759	10	17	33
26000 43180	Cream Rinse 15 oz	36247	carton	33.36	18312	04315	46	43	63
41000 16850	Vitamin C/250	70994	carton	85.64	14229	38749	55	21	45
15100 00370	Toothbrush	99638	carton	23.88	38646	73598	15	15	78
38000 08100	Bubble Bath 15 oz	72055	case	23.28	47887	12063	41	30	65
16000 00040	Aspirin/100	24038	case	47.88	19689	74151	117	40	148
36200 14006	Cough Syrup 8 oz	74976	carton	80.28	46600	38646	65	20	50
26000 38040	Contact Sol. 1 oz	35553	case	43.08	18312	30420	28	10	20
38000 10260	Hairbrush	35676	case	44.04	47887	12063	31	24	48
58400 60600	Bandages/30	74815	carton	23.88	52745	99744	48	20	35
46000 40510	Moist. Lotion 13 oz	45246	carton	76.44	18312	03883	34	15	36

No. __0004__

TYLER DRUG STORE SUPPLIES
1800 Northridge Drive
Syracuse, NY 13214-1717
(315) 555-1687
Sales Ticket

UPC No.	Quantity
05251 13600	2
16000 00320	1
58400 60600	5
40028 26106	2

No. __0006__

TYLER DRUG STORE SUPPLIES
1800 Northridge Drive
Syracuse, NY 13214-1717
(315) 555-1687
Sales Ticket

UPC No.	Quantity
78089 49101	2
76000 60600	1
21000 63040	1
38000 02290	2

No. __0002__

TYLER DRUG STORE SUPPLIES
1800 Northridge Drive
Syracuse, NY 13214-1717
(315) 555-1687
Sales Ticket

UPC No.	Quantity
38520 85020	2
21000 68583	1
26000 43180	4

No. __0010__

TYLER DRUG STORE SUPPLIES
1800 Northridge Drive
Syracuse, NY 13214-1717
(315) 555-1687
Sales Ticket

UPC No.	Quantity
30000 01090	1
41000 16850	3
05251 13600	2
38000 08100	1
36200 14006	2
78089 49101	4

No. __0008__

TYLER DRUG STORE SUPPLIES
1800 Northridge Drive
Syracuse, NY 13214-1717
(315) 555-1687
Sales Ticket

UPC No.	Quantity
46000 40510	1
26000 38040	4
05251 13600	3
26000 38040	1
38000 02290	2

No. __0005__

TYLER DRUG STORE SUPPLIES
1800 Northridge Drive
Syracuse, NY 13214-1717
(315) 555-1687
Sales Ticket

UPC No.	Quantity
16000 00040	3
26000 38040	2
36200 14006	2
78089 49101	6
46000 40510	3

No. __0007__

TYLER DRUG STORE SUPPLIES
1800 Northridge Drive
Syracuse, NY 13214-1717
(315) 555-1687
Sales Ticket

UPC No.	Quantity
15100 00370	8
16000 00320	2
16000 00040	3
36200 14006	2

No. __0012__

TYLER DRUG STORE SUPPLIES
1800 Northridge Drive
Syracuse, NY 13214-1717
(315) 555-1687
Sales Ticket

UPC No.	Quantity
76000 60600	2
38000 08890	6
21000 68583	2

No. __0009__

TYLER DRUG STORE SUPPLIES
1800 Northridge Drive
Syracuse, NY 13214-1717
(315) 555-1687
Sales Ticket

UPC No.	Quantity
41000 16850	1
16000 00040	3
26000 38040	4

No. __0001__

TYLER DRUG STORE SUPPLIES
1800 Northridge Drive
Syracuse, NY 13214-1717
(315) 555-1687
Sales Ticket

UPC No.	Quantity
40082 86106	1
21000 68583	2
58400 60600	8
76000 60600	3
38000 10260	1

No. __0011__

TYLER DRUG STORE SUPPLIES
1800 Northridge Drive
Syracuse, NY 13214-1717
(315) 555-1687
Sales Ticket

UPC No.	Quantity
38520 85020	2
38000 08890	5
05251 13600	1
21000 63040	3
26000 43180	4

No. __0003__

TYLER DRUG STORE SUPPLIES
1800 Northridge Drive
Syracuse, NY 13214-1717
(315) 555-1687
Sales Ticket

UPC No.	Quantity
46000 40510	6
38520 85020	3
36200 14006	4

TYLER DRUG STORE SUPPLIES
INVENTORY UPDATE FORM
June 30

UPC NO.	DESCRIPTION	BIN NO.	UNIT	UNIT PRICE	VENDOR #1	VENDOR #2	QTY. ON HAND	REORDER POINT	REORDER QUANTITY
76000 60600						71945			
78089 49101								30	20
38000 02290		62757							
38520 85020					97161				
21000 68583									
41000 16850		32305			83991			20	35
15100 00370									
36200 14006		21361						30	85
58400 60600						26759			
46000 40510								20	40

Activity 3

POINT OF SALE

LEARNING OBJECTIVES

Upon completion of this activity, you will be able to:

→ **1** *Define electronic cash register, point-of-sale terminal, and scanner.*

2 *Identify the functions of an electronic cash register.*

3 *Recognize the differences between point-of-sale terminals and electronic cash registers.*

4 *Key-enter data for a sales transaction.*

DATA ENTRY APPLICATION AND JOB DESCRIPTION

*I*n this activity you will key-enter sales data for an office supply store. Office supply stores sell a wide variety of merchandise, from paper clips to office furniture. These stores must keep a running inventory of what is on hand and what has to be ordered for future use. To organize its inventory, an office supply store must divide its merchandise stock numbers into categories according to the type of product. To keep track of how much was sold during any given period, the store must keep records for cash sales as well as credit card sales.

In cash transactions, most retail stores use cash registers or point-of-sale terminals to temporarily store money exchanged for merchandise purchased by customers. An **electronic cash register** is composed of electronic circuit devices. It displays the price of each item and the total purchase price in a lighted digital format. Most stores, including those in small neighborhood shops or stores in large shopping centers, use electronic cash registers.

Another popular type of cash register is the point-of-sale (POS) terminal. A **point-of-sale terminal** uses an electronic **bar scanner** to "read" the merchandise product bar code (Universal Product Code). The bar scanner eliminates the need to enter a product's stock number and price manually. Thus, the chance for human error in data entry is greatly reduced and businesses are able to operate more efficiently. Unlike electronic cash registers, the POS terminal is connected to a computer. Many stores now use point-of-sale terminals because of their increased capabilities. Point-of-sale terminals are capable of increasing the speed and accuracy of checkouts, updating inventory records, keeping sales records for each product, and preparing purchase orders when more stock is needed. The speed and efficiency of these machines help provide significant and timely information needed by management.

Sales may be recorded in one of two ways. When an electronic cash register is used, the quantity, stock number, and description of an item are written on a sales slip; and the price of the merchandise is entered on the cash register keyboard every time a sale is made. The cash register then prints a tape of the transaction, which is given to the customer as a receipt. Later, the sales slip data may be key-entered into the computerized sales system. In this activity you will key-enter sales slip data for Granger Office Supplies. A sample sales slip for Granger Office Supplies is illustrated in Figure 3.1.

FIGURE 3.1 Sales Slip

When a point-of-sale terminal is used, the electronic bar scanner automatically reads and stores the product number in the computer. The point-of-sale terminal then prints a tape of the transaction, which is given to the customer as a receipt. At the end of the day, a report containing the total sales for each department is printed. Each department's total is combined to give the total sales for the day.

INPUT FIELDS

*I*n this activity you will be working for Granger Office Supplies, which has just started computerizing its sales records. Sales information is recorded by hand on a sales slip at the time of the sales transaction. Your job will be to key-enter data from the sales slip into the computerized sales system.

Information from the sales slips used at Granger Office Supplies is key-entered into five fields on the data-entry screen. A brief description of each field is provided below.

Sales Slip Number. This four-digit field represents the number of the sales ticket and is used as a reference number.

Date. This six-digit field represents the date the sales ticket was prepared.

Quantity. This three-character field represents the number of items of a particular product that were sold to the buyer.

Stock Number. This six-character field represents the unique code assigned to each article in inventory. No two items have the same stock number.

Description. This field contains a description of the item being sold. An even shorter version often appears on the receipt produced by the cash register. This receipt is given to the customer at the end of the transaction.

Step-by-Step Instructions

GET READY

Follow the start-up procedures for your computer that are found in Appendix A.

COMPLETE ALPHA-NUMERIC DEXTERITY DRILL

```
2104 DESK SET 31 1 LC3035 2116 03021 217
KC3290 212250 TP8122 LEAD PENCIL 0201 24
0112 AS9878 10 DISKETTE TRAY 1128 0303 9
STIFF COVER BINDER BT0965 3529964 050 70
708020 1110 631798 SIDE ARM CHAIR CM6897
```

STEP 1   From the *Activities* menu, select *Activity 3 Sales Analysis.*

STEP 2   Select *Alpha-Numeric Dexterity Drill.*

STEP 3   Enter the data for each line. Press *enter* or *return* at the end of each line.

STEP 4   Select *OK* when you are finished key-entering. Review your scores.

STEP 5   Select *Review* to review any errors that were made. After you have reviewed your performance, select *OK.*

Repeat the Alpha-Numeric Dexterity Drill as many times as instructed by your teacher. (See the detailed instructions in Activity 1, if necessary.)

COMPLETE KEYPAD DEXTERITY DRILL

```
10012  20023  30034  40045  50056  60067  7003
80089  90090  21212  31232  42345  53456  7456
56789  67890  78901  89012  90123  01234  0011
29057  28331  56123  50697  76852  34719  8476
28025  66782  86672  47104  58191  68954  5414
```

STEP 1   From the *Activities* menu, select *Activity 3 Sales Analysis.*

STEP 2   Select *Keypad Dexterity Drill.*

STEP 3   Enter the data for each line. Press *enter* or *return* at the end of each line.

STEP 4   Select *OK* when you are finished key-entering. Review your score.

STEP 5   Select *Review* to review any errors that were made. After reviewing your performance, select *OK.*

Repeat the Keypad Dexterity Drill as many times as instructed by your teacher. (See the detailed instructions in Activity 1, if necessary.)

COMPLETE SALES SLIPS

STEP 1   Remove and separate all of the sales slips for Granger Office Supplies that are located at the end of this activity. It is not necessary to sort the slips since the computer will accept data in any order. However, if you need to keep track of the sales slips, sort them in numerical order.

STEP 2 From the *Activities* menu, select *Activity 3 Sales Analysis*.

STEP 3 Select *Sales Slip*. The display on your screen will be similar to that shown in Figure 3.2.

FIGURE 3.2

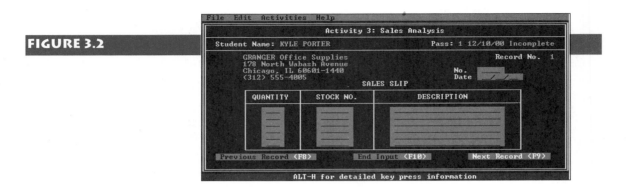

STEP 4 Key-enter the No. (2104 for the first record shown in the book) in the first field. Each sales slip is considered a **record.**

STEP 5 Key-enter the Date in the appropriate field. Key the first two digits of the date, then key the next two digits of the date. Key-enter the last two digits of the current year. The slashes are already displayed on the screen, so you do not need to key the slashes.

STEP 6 Key-enter the Quantity (1), Stock Number (SH7022), and the Description (DESK SET) in the appropriate fields.

STEP 7 Key-enter the data for the entire record in the appropriate fields.

STEP 8 After you have completed key-entering the data for the first record (you will leave blank lines in the first record and you may have blank lines in other records), select *Next Record*.

STEP 9 Key-enter the remaining records.

Note: Depending on how your teacher has set up the data correction in your software, you may be able to move to any field in any record at any time during the key-entering process to make a correction.

Note: If you are interrupted before key-entering all of the records, you may stop by selecting *End Input*. Then select *Analyze*. Then select *OK*. This will save any data you have key-entered to that point. When you begin the next session to complete this activity, the cursor will be located in the first field of the first record that you entered. Use the appropriate

keys to place the cursor in the proper record and field to begin key-entering data.

To begin the next session:

- **Repeat Steps 2 and 3.**
- **Select *Open* from the menu.**
- **Continue with Step 10 below.**

STEP 10   After you have key-entered the data for all 24 sales slips, select *End Input*. This will stop the timer. If you notice errors after you have selected End Input, select *Edit* and then move to the appropriate fields to key-enter the corrections. This will start the timer. After making the corrections, select *End Input* again. This will stop the timer. The timer is always running when you are key-entering data and making corrections.

✎ **Note: This description regarding starting and stopping the timer will not appear in the remaining activities in this book. You may refer back to these directions if necessary.**

Print the sales slip that is on the screen if instructed by your teacher.

STEP 11   Select *Analyze*. Review the information presented.

STEP 12   Select *Review*. Any errors will be highlighted. Print the sales slips if instructed by your teacher.

STEP 13   Select *Done*.

STEP 14   You may generate a report of your performance in this activity. To do so,

- From the *File* menu, select *Open Report* and select *Activity 3 Sales Analysis*.
- Select *Sales Slip*.
- Select *Get Report*.
- From the *File* menu, select *Print*.
- Select *Print* again.
- Select *Done*.

✎ **Note: In a real work situation, you would strive for completely accurate records. Therefore, it is suggested that once you have completed all of the steps listed here, you should go back into the records and correct any errors. To do this:**

- **From the *Activities* menu, select *Activity 3 Sales Analysis*.**
- **Select *Sales Slip*.**

- Select *Open*.
- Use the appropriate keys to locate the proper record and field and then key-enter the correction.
- Select *End Input*.
- Select *Analyze*.
- Select *Review*.
- Select *Done*.
- Print the sales slips if instructed by your teacher.

VOCABULARY

bar scanner
electronic cash register
point-of-sale terminal
record

Activity 3 Study Guide

POINT OF SALE

PART 1

OBJECTIVES 1, 2, AND 3 (2 POINTS EACH)

●━◆ **Match the vocabulary terms with the best definitions. Write the letter of the term in the space to the left of the definition.**

A. **bar scanner**
B. **electronic cash register**

C. **point-of-sale terminal**
D. **stock number**

E. **Universal Product Code**

_____ **1.** A unique number assigned to each inventory item.

_____ **2.** This device reads product bar codes electronically, thus eliminating the need to key-enter data manually.

_____ **3.** Uses a scanner to "read" the merchandise product bar code.

_____ **4.** Another name for a product bar code.

_____ **5.** A device composed of electronic circuit devices for displaying the price of each item and the total purchase price in lighted digital format.

PART 2

OBJECTIVES 1, 2, AND 3 (1 POINT EACH)

●━◆ **Each of the following statements is either true or false. Indicate your choice by circling T for a true statement or F for a false statement.**

T   F   **1.** Bar scanners make product bar codes.

T   F   **2.** Each stock item has a different stock number.

T   F   **3.** Point-of-sale terminals can prepare purchase orders when more stock is needed.

T   F   **4.** Credit card sales are not treated the same as cash sales.

T   F   **5.** Many stores now use point-of-sale terminals instead of mechanical or electronic cash registers.

T   F   **6.** A description of a purchased item is never printed on
                  the receipt that is given to the customer.

T   F   **7.** Point-of-sale terminals do not reduce errors in the
                  checkout process.

PART 3

OBJECTIVES 1 AND 3 (3 POINTS EACH)

☞ **Briefly answer each of the following items. Write your answers on the lines provided.**

1. Define point-of-sale terminal.

_____

_____

2. What are the two common pieces of equipment a store may use to process cash sales?

_____

_____

3. List the capabilities of a point-of-sale terminal.

_____

_____

☞ **Remove the Activity 3 Study Guide from your text-workbook and hand it to your instructor for correcting.**

Total Points Possible	26
(Minus) Incorrect Points	_____
Total Points Earned	_____
Percent Correct	_____
Grade	_____

GRANGER Office Supplies

178 North Wabash Avenue
Chicago, IL 60601-1440
(312) 555-4005

No. 2104
Date: 02/25

SALES SLIP

QUANTITY	STOCK NUMBER	DESCRIPTION
1	SH7022	Desk Set
31	KC3035	Mailing Tube

GRANGER Office Supplies

178 North Wabash Avenue
Chicago, IL 60601-1440
(312) 555-4005

No. 2116
Date: 03/02

SALES SLIP

QUANTITY	STOCK NUMBER	DESCRIPTION
1	XU7033	Electric Stapler

GRANGER Office Supplies

178 North Wabash Avenue
Chicago, IL 60601-1440
(312) 555-4005

No. 2107
Date: 02/27

SALES SLIP

QUANTITY	STOCK NUMBER	DESCRIPTION
6	KC6499	Bookends
6	KC2484	Desk Organizer
6	KC3290	Card File

GRANGER Office Supplies

178 North Wabash Avenue
Chicago, IL 60601-1440
(312) 555-4005

No. 2122
Date: 03/04

SALES SLIP

QUANTITY	STOCK NUMBER	DESCRIPTION
50	TP8122	#2 Lead Pencil

GRANGER Office Supplies

178 North Wabash Avenue
Chicago, IL 60601-1440
(312) 555-4005

No. 2101
Date: 02/24

SALES SLIP

QUANTITY	STOCK NUMBER	DESCRIPTION
2	HN8484	4-Drawer File Cabinet
8	HN3290	Hanging Folder Support

GRANGER Office Supplies

178 North Wabash Avenue
Chicago, IL 60601-1440
(312) 555-4005

No. 2110
Date: 02/28

SALES SLIP

QUANTITY	STOCK NUMBER	DESCRIPTION
10	AS9878	Diskette Tray

GRANGER Office Supplies
178 North Wabash Avenue
Chicago, IL 60601-1440
(312) 555-4005

No. 2118
Date: 03/03

SALES SLIP

QUANTITY	STOCK NUMBER	DESCRIPTION
1	UC4689	Side Arm Chair
1	UC6317	Double Pedestal Desk

GRANGER Office Supplies
178 North Wabash Avenue
Chicago, IL 60601-1440
(312) 555-4005

No. 2124
Date: 03/05

SALES SLIP

QUANTITY	STOCK NUMBER	DESCRIPTION
35	BT0122	Stiff Cover Binder
20	BT0648	View Binder
C 50	CM6833	Report Cover
50	CM1436	Portfolio

GRANGER Office Supplies
178 North Wabash Avenue
Chicago, IL 60601-1440
(312) 555-4005

No. 2123
Date: 03/02

SALES SLIP

QUANTITY	STOCK NUMBER	DESCRIPTION
48	BC1565	Ball Point Pen

GRANGER Office Supplies
178 North Wabash Avenue
Chicago, IL 60601-1440
(312) 555-4005

No. 2120
Date: 03/03

SALES SLIP

QUANTITY	STOCK NUMBER	DESCRIPTION
1	VY2906	50-Sheet Punch
5	HW8267	Letter Sorter
5	HW2583	Pencil Cup
5	HW9630	Memo Holder

GRANGER Office Supplies
178 North Wabash Avenue
Chicago, IL 60601-1440
(312) 555-4005

No. 2105
Date: 02/25

SALES SLIP

QUANTITY	STOCK NUMBER	DESCRIPTION
10	KG7807	White Board Marker Set
1	TC8627	Presentation Board

GRANGER Office Supplies
178 North Wabash Avenue
Chicago, IL 60601-1440
(312) 555-4005

No. 2102
Date: 02/24

SALES SLIP

QUANTITY	STOCK NUMBER	DESCRIPTION
100	MG4543	Account. Worksheet Pad
30	BT3293	Elliptical Ring Binder

GRANGER Office Supplies
178 North Wabash Avenue
Chicago, IL 60601-1440
(312) 555-4005

No. 2119
Date: 03/03

SALES SLIP

QUANTITY	STOCK NUMBER	DESCRIPTION
15	FM0037	Magazine File
40	FM4788	Manila File Pocket

GRANGER Office Supplies
178 North Wabash Avenue
Chicago, IL 60601-1440
(312) 555-4005

No. 2108
Date: 02/27

SALES SLIP

QUANTITY	STOCK NUMBER	DESCRIPTION
12	YW5099	Tape Dispenser
1	YW0648	Envelope Moistener
300	SS1831	Shipping Carton

GRANGER Office Supplies
178 North Wabash Avenue
Chicago, IL 60601-1440
(312) 555-4005

No. 2117
Date: 03/03

SALES SLIP

QUANTITY	STOCK NUMBER	DESCRIPTION
15	TT1422	Colored Highlighter Set
2	PS1683	Rotary Card File

GRANGER Office Supplies
178 North Wabash Avenue
Chicago, IL 60601-1440
(312) 555-4005

No. 2111
Date: 03/01

SALES SLIP

QUANTITY	STOCK NUMBER	DESCRIPTION
1	KG2122	Double Letter Tray

GRANGER Office Supplies
178 North Wabash Avenue
Chicago, IL 60601-1440
(312) 555-4005

No. 2115
Date: 03/02

SALES SLIP

QUANTITY	STOCK NUMBER	DESCRIPTION
7	SP5575	Secretarial Chair
2	VS0778	Mobile Computer Cart

GRANGER Office Supplies
178 North Wabash Avenue
Chicago, IL 60601-1440
(312) 555-4005

No. 2103
Date: 02/25

SALES SLIP

QUANTITY	STOCK NUMBER	DESCRIPTION
12	YE2815	Dictionary

GRANGER Office Supplies
178 North Wabash Avenue
Chicago, IL 60601-1440
(312) 555-4005

No. 2121
Date: 03/04

SALES SLIP

QUANTITY	STOCK NUMBER	DESCRIPTION
4	HG6565	Sorting Rack
8	HG1214	Stationery Rack
7	KG5761	Desk Lamp

GRANGER Office Supplies
178 North Wabash Avenue
Chicago, IL 60601-1440
(312) 555-4005

No. 2106
Date: 02/26

SALES SLIP

QUANTITY	STOCK NUMBER	DESCRIPTION
7	MF5262	Computer Table
7	MF0263	Printer Table

GRANGER Office Supplies
178 North Wabash Avenue
Chicago, IL 60601-1440
(312) 555-4005

No. 2113
Date: 03/05

SALES SLIP

QUANTITY	STOCK NUMBER	DESCRIPTION
48	FR8121	Retractable Pen
64	FR3705	Stick Pen
24	PA6210	Metal Roller Pen
12	DC3035	Message Form

GRANGER Office Supplies
178 North Wabash Avenue
Chicago, IL 60601-1440
(312) 555-4005

No. 2109
Date: 02/28

SALES SLIP

QUANTITY	STOCK NUMBER	DESCRIPTION
1	TM7883	Magnetic In-Out Board

GRANGER Office Supplies
178 North Wabash Avenue
Chicago, IL 60601-1440
(312) 555-4005

No. 2114
Date: 02/28

SALES SLIP

QUANTITY	STOCK NUMBER	DESCRIPTION
5	KZ1616	Desktop Calculator
12	JM2079	Appointment Book
12	JM2950	Desktop Calendar

GRANGER Office Supplies
178 North Wabash Avenue
Chicago, IL 60601-1440
(312) 555-4005

No. 2112
Date: 03/01

SALES SLIP

QUANTITY	STOCK NUMBER	DESCRIPTION
1	BK8272	Conference Table

Quiz 1

PART 1

(2 POINTS EACH)

➥ Match the vocabulary terms with the best definitions. Write the letter of the term in the space to the left of the definition. You will not use every vocabulary term.

A. **bar scanner**
B. **bin number**
C. **concentric circles**
D. **CPU**
E. **data**

F. **disk**
G. **electronic database**
H. **electronic spreadsheet**
I. **information**

J. **inventory**
K. **periodic inventory**
L. **perpetual inventory**
M. **point-of-sale terminal**
N. **source document**

_____ 1. A software application that displays data in a series of rows and columns that form a grid.

_____ 2. Part of the equipment that is often referred to as the brains of the computer system.

_____ 3. Goods on hand or merchandise available for sale to customers.

_____ 4. Data that has been processed to produce usable, meaningful report formats.

_____ 5. The process whereby an actual count is taken of items on hand.

_____ 6. A form on which data is originally recorded, then key-entered into a microcomputer.

_____ 7. The process of continually monitoring the inventory levels by recording the quantities of merchandise bought and sold after each transaction.

_____ 8. In a stockroom, an item's location is identified by this number.

_____ 9. The raw facts that are processed by the microcomputer.

_____ 10. This device reads product bar codes electronically.

_____ 11. A software application that is used to create electronic files.

_____ 12. Uses an electronic bar scanner to "read" the merchandise product bar code.

65

(1 POINT EACH)

●✦ **Each of the following statements is either true or false. Indicate your choice by circling T for a true statement or F for a false statement.**

T   F   **1.** Credit card sales are treated the same as cash sales.

T   F   **2.** On a disk, data is arranged in concentric circles.

T   F   **3.** It is okay to remove a disk from a disk drive when the "in-use" light of the disk drive is on.

T   F   **4.** Perpetual inventory permits businesses to monitor inventory on a continuous basis.

T   F   **5.** Changes in permanent information, such as unit, bin number, and reorder point, are recorded on an inventory update form.

(3 POINTS EACH)

●✦ **Briefly answer each of the following items. Write your answers on the lines provided.**

1. What is a Universal Product Code?

_____

_____

2. Define discrepancy report.

_____

_____

3. What is a stock number?

_____

_____

4. Define hard copy.

_____

_____

5. Define data entry.

_____

_____

6. What are the two common pieces of equipment a store may use to process cash sales?

_____

_____

7. List the capabilities of a point-of-sale terminal.

_____

☞ **Remove Quiz 1 from your text-workbook and hand it to your instructor for correcting.**

Total Points Possible	**50**
(Minus) Incorrect Points	_____
Total Points Earned	_____
Percent Correct	_____
Grade	_____

Activity 4

ACCOUNTS RECEIVABLE

LEARNING OBJECTIVES

Upon completion of this activity, you will be able to:

→ 1 Define cash sale, sale on account, sales invoice, extension, statement, and accounts receivable ledger.
2 Explain the process of making extensions on an invoice.
3 Identify the two parts of a sales invoice.
4 Key-enter data for an accounts receivable system.

DATA ENTRY APPLICATION AND JOB DESCRIPTION

*E*xpress Home Cuisine is a home delivery food service that delivers frozen food products such as seafood, vegetables, meats, and desserts directly to each customer's door. The type of delivery service is ideal for anyone who doesn't have the time to go grocery shopping or doesn't like the task of shopping in crowded supermarkets. Every other week a salesperson goes to each customer's door with a product brochure from which the customer selects the desired food items. Once an order is taken, the salesperson goes back to the delivery truck, gets the selected items, and gives them to the customer.

The salesperson must keep a record of all sales to ensure accurate accounting and inventory records. Two types of sales transactions may occur: cash sales and sales on account.

In a **cash sale** transaction, the seller receives cash from the customer when a sale is made. A receipt is then given to the customer as a proof of purchase. Total cash sales for a given day are recorded as one entry in the business's accounting records.

Another type of sale is the **sale on account**. For this type of sale, the customer can buy merchandise now and pay for it later. Sales on account, or charge sales, are made by both individuals and businesses. Frequently, a **credit card** is issued to a customer. This small plastic card identifies the customer as having a charge account with a company. Credit cards are commonly issued by stores, oil companies, banks, and credit card companies. When using a credit card, a customer agrees to pay for any charged purchases within a certain time period.

Customers who purchase merchandise on account are known as **charge customers**. Each time a charge customer purchases merchandise, the seller completes a **sales invoice.** A sales invoice for Express Home Cuisine is illustrated in Figure 4.1. The original copy of the invoice is kept by the company, and a copy is given to the customer as a receipt when the sale is made.

The invoice for Express Home Cuisine is divided into two parts—the heading division and the detail division. The customer number, the customer name and address, and the

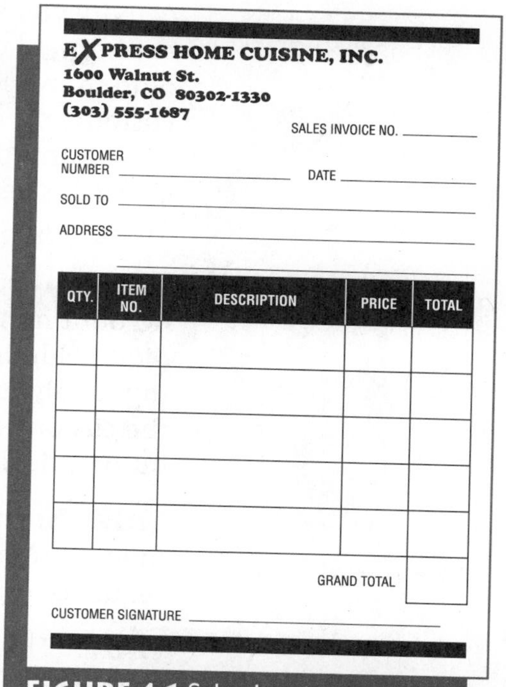
EXPRESS HOME CUISINE, INC.
1600 Walnut St.
Boulder, CO 80302-1330
(303) 555-1687

SALES INVOICE NO. ______

CUSTOMER NUMBER ______ DATE ______

SOLD TO ______

ADDRESS ______

QTY.	ITEM NO.	DESCRIPTION	PRICE	TOTAL
			GRAND TOTAL	

CUSTOMER SIGNATURE ______

FIGURE 4.1 Sales Invoice

date of the sale are recorded in the heading division. The quantity, item number, description, and price of each item sold are recorded in the detail division. The total for each item is calculated by multiplying the price of an item by the quantity sold. This total is also known as the **extension.** After all items have been recorded on the invoice, the grand total is calculated by adding the extensions for each item. On some sales invoices, shipping charges, handling charges, and sales tax are also recorded in the detail division, depending on the business's needs.

A **statement** is sent to each charge customer on a monthly basis. This statement shows all items purchased during the month, the dates the items were purchased, the amount of all payments received during the month, and the total amount owed. The total amount owed to the company by all of its charge customers is recorded in the **accounts receivable** account in the general ledger. The company also keeps a record of its charge customers and the amounts they owe in a subsidiary ledger known as the **accounts receivable ledger.** This ledger is arranged alphabetically by customer name.

INPUT FIELDS

When charge customers purchase merchandise from Express Home Cuisine, the salesperson prepares a sales invoice. At the end of each day, all sales invoices are forwarded to the accounts receivable department. In this activity you will be working in the accounts receivable department of Express Home Cuisine. You will key-enter data from the sales invoices (source documents) for twenty customers.

Information from sales invoices of Express Home Cuisine is key-entered into fields on the data entry screen. These fields are described below.

Customer Number. This six-digit field represents the account number assigned to the customer. With this six-digit field, the computer system is capable of accommodating nearly one million different customer numbers. When the customer number is key-entered, the computer will automatically display the customer name and address.

Sales Invoice No. This five-digit field contains the sales invoice number. The invoice number is preprinted in sequence on the sales invoices.

Date. This field represents the date the sales invoice was prepared.

Qty. This field represents the number of units of an item purchased by the customer. This information is important in determining how much the customer owes and for keeping inventory records accurate. If a perpetual inventory is maintained, the number of units sold is subtracted from the number of units available in the inventory, thereby updating the quantity on hand.

Item No. This six-digit field represents the unique stock number assigned to a particular item. After the item number is key-entered, the computer automatically displays the description of the item. You should check this description against the one written on the sales invoice. If the description does not match the one on the sales invoice, check to make sure the item number was entered correctly.

Price. This field represents the amount charged for one unit purchased. After the price is key-entered, the computer will automatically multiply the quantity ordered by the price and display the total (extension) for that item.

(OBJECTIVE 4)

GET READY

Follow the start-up procedures for your computer that are found in Appendix A.

COMPLETE ALPHA-NUMERIC DEXTERITY DRILL

```
9193385  635852  117082  CORN  695750  825280
LASAGNA  390449  491978  42312  38285  762  78
69641  6822  4491  PEAS  1890  98006  4  ORANGE
72673  348501  STUFFED  SHRIMP  1850  395  725
112577  HAM  STEAKS  10045  8290  287228  1195
```

STEP 1   From the *Activities* menu, select *Activity 4 Accounts Receivable*.

STEP 2   Select *Alpha-Numeric Dexterity Drill*.

STEP 3   Enter the data for each line. Press *enter* or *return* at the end of each line.

STEP 4   Select *OK* when you are finished key-entering. Review your score.

STEP 5   Select *Review* to review any errors that were made. After you have reviewed your performance, select *OK*.

Repeat the Alpha-Numeric Dexterity Drill as many times as instructed by your teacher.

COMPLETE KEYPAD DEXTERITY DRILL

```
72875  65806  30543  48745  30458  37227  4034
81833  72285  49487  02825  97153  94439  4474
80780  25618  70948  40683  50309  55314  8166
52522  97783  11104  55898  08553  95523  2764
54271  12909  12266  00196  44104  14188  9051
```

STEP 1 From the *Activities* menu, select *Activity 4 Accounts Receivable*.

STEP 2 Select *Keypad Dexterity Drill*.

STEP 3 Enter the data for each line. Press *enter* or *return* at the end of each line.

STEP 4 Select *OK* when you are finished key-entering. Review your score.

STEP 5 Select *Review* to review any errors that were made. After reviewing your performance, select *OK*.

Repeat the Keypad Dexterity Drill as many times as instructed by your teacher.

COMPLETE SALES INVOICES

STEP 1 Remove and separate the 20 sales invoices for Express Home Cuisine, Inc., that are located at the end of this activity. You may sort them by invoice number if you wish.

STEP 2 From the *Activities* menu, select *Activity 4 Accounts Receivable*.

STEP 3 Select *Sales Invoice*. Your screen will be similar to that shown in Figure 4.2.

FIGURE 4.2

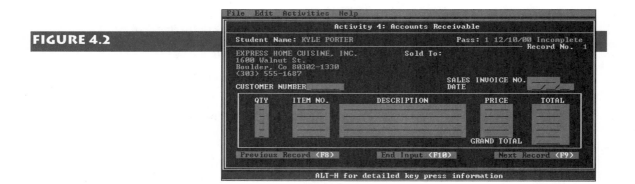

STEP 4 Key-enter the Customer Number for the first record in the first field. Each sales invoice is a record. After you have entered that number, the customer's name and address will appear automatically on the screen.

STEP 5 Key-enter the Sales Invoice No. for the first record.

STEP 6 Key-enter the Date in the appropriate field. Enter the current year in the last two digits.

STEP 7 Key-enter the Qty. in the appropriate field.

STEP 8 Key-enter the Item No. in the appropriate field. After you have entered the item number, the description will appear automatically on the screen.

STEP 9   Key-enter the Price in the appropriate field. This is the price for one item. The computer will calculate the Total, multiplying quantity times price.

STEP 10   Key-enter the data for the entire record. The computer will calculate the Grand Total, adding the totals for the items key-entered.

          After you have key-entered the data for the first record, select *Next Record*.

STEP 11   Key-enter the remaining records.

✎ **Note: If you are interrupted before key-entering all of the records, you may stop by selecting *End Input*. Then select *Analyze*. Then select *OK*. This will save any data you have key-entered to that point. When you begin the next session to complete this activity, the cursor will be located in the first field of the first record that you entered. Use the appropriate keys to place the cursor in the proper record and field to begin key-entering data.**

To begin the next session:

      - Repeat Steps 2 and 3.

      - Select *Open* from the menu.

      - Continue with Step 12 below.

✎ **Note: This description regarding how to begin a session will not appear in the remaining activities in this book. You may refer back to these instructions if necessary.**

STEP 12   After key-entering all 20 sales invoices, select *End Input*. If you notice errors after you have selected End Input, select *Edit* and then move to the appropriate fields to key-enter the corrections. After making the corrections, select *End Input* again.

          Print the sales invoice that is on the screen if instructed by your teacher.

STEP 13   Select *Analyze*. Review the information presented.

STEP 14   Select *Review*. Any errors will be highlighted. Print the sales invoices if instructed by your teacher.

STEP 15   Select *Done*.

STEP 16   You may generate a report of your performance in this activity. To do so,

      - From the File menu, select *Open Report* and select *Activity 4 Accounts Receivable*.

- Select *Sales Invoice.*

- Select *Get Report.*

- From the *File* menu, select *Print.*

- Select *Print* again.

- Select *Done.*

Note: In a real work situation, you would strive for completely accurate records. Therefore, it is suggested that once you have completed all of the steps listed here, you should go back into the records and correct any errors. To do this:

- **From the *Activities* menu, select *Activity 4 Accounts Receivable.***

- **Select *Sales Invoice.***

- **Select *Open.***

- **Use the appropriate keys to locate the proper record and field and then key-enter the correction.**

- **Select *End Input.***

- **Select *Analyze.***

- **Select *Review.***

- **Select *Done.***

- **Print the sales invoices if instructed by your teacher.**

VOCABULARY

accounts receivable
accounts receivable ledger
cash sale
charge customers
credit card
extension
sale on account
sales invoice
statement

Activity 4 Study Guide

PART 1

OBJECTIVES 1, 2, AND 3 (2 POINTS EACH)

➤ **Match the vocabulary terms with the best definitions. Write the letter of the term in the space to the left of the definition. You will not use every vocabulary term.**

A. **accounts receivable ledger**
B. **cash sale**
C. **charge customers**
D. **credit card**
E. **extension**
F. **price**
G. **quantity**
H. **sales invoice**
I. **statement**
J. **sale on account**

_____ 1. This record of all customers and the amount they owe is arranged alphabetically.

_____ 2. This form shows all items purchased, the amount of all payments, and the total amount owed.

_____ 3. This field represents the number of units purchased.

_____ 4. This field represents the amount charged per unit.

_____ 5. Each time a charge customer purchases merchandise, the seller completes this form.

_____ 6. When a customer has an account with a store, this card identifies the charge customer.

_____ 7. During this type of sale, the seller receives cash from the customer.

_____ 8. This total is calculated by multiplying price by quantity.

_____ 9. This type of sale occurs when a customer buys merchandise now but pays for it at a later date.

OBJECTIVES 1, 2, AND 3 (1 POINT EACH)

➥ **Each of the following statements is either true or false. Indicate your choice by circling T for a true statement or F for a false statement.**

T　　　F　　**1.** A credit card identifies a charge customer.

T　　　F　　**2.** All sales of merchandise are on a cash basis.

T　　　F　　**3.** Sales invoices are numbered in sequential order.

T　　　F　　**4.** The names of all charge customers and the amounts they owe are recorded in a company's accounts receivable ledger.

T　　　F　　**5.** The quantity and price are recorded in the heading section of a sales invoice.

OBJECTIVES 2 AND 3 (3 POINTS EACH)

➥ **Briefly answer each of the following items. Write your answers on the lines provided.**

1. Explain how the computer determines the extension for each item on the sales invoice.

_____

_____

2. Describe the two parts of a sales invoice.

_____

_____

☞ **Remove the Activity 4 Study Guide from your text-workbook and hand it to your instructor for correcting.**

Total Points Possible	29
(Minus) Incorrect Points	_____
Total Points Earned	_____
Percent Correct	_____
Grade	_____

E✗PRESS HOME CUISINE, INC.

1600 Walnut St.
Boulder, CO 80302-1330
(303) 555-1687

SALES INVOICE NO. 37621

DATE 10/27

CUSTOMER NUMBER 491978

SOLD TO Martin Taylor

ADDRESS 1706 Spruce Ct.

Boulder, CO 80302-1265

QTY.	ITEM NO.	DESCRIPTION	PRICE	TOTAL
2	390449	Vegetable Lasagna (3 lbs)	11.95	23.90
3	825280	Corn (2.5 lbs)	2.95	8.85
1	876630	Peas (2.5 lbs)	2.95	2.95
2	469618	American Cheese (3 lbs)	9.45	18.90
2	988006	Orange Roughy (2.5 lbs)	21.65	43.30
			GRAND TOTAL	97.90

CUSTOMER SIGNATURE _Martin Taylor_

E✗PRESS HOME CUISINE, INC.

1600 Walnut St.
Boulder, CO 80302-1330
(303) 555-1687

SALES INVOICE NO. 37626

DATE 10/30

CUSTOMER NUMBER 765179

SOLD TO Ann Kaminski

ADDRESS 915 Adams Cir.

Boulder, CO 80303-1477

QTY.	ITEM NO.	DESCRIPTION	PRICE	TOTAL
2	365725	Breaded Chicken (5 lbs)	11.70	23.40
1	825280	Corn (2.5 lbs)	2.95	2.95
2	390536	Frozen Bread Dough (6)	3.75	7.50
			GRAND TOTAL	33.85

CUSTOMER SIGNATURE _Ann Kaminski_

E✗PRESS HOME CUISINE, INC.
1600 Walnut St.
Boulder, CO 80302-1330
(303) 555-1687

SALES INVOICE NO. 37631

CUSTOMER NUMBER 112577   DATE 10/04

SOLD TO Paul Kelley

ADDRESS 304 Juniper Ave.

Boulder, CO 80302-6613

QTY.	ITEM NO.	DESCRIPTION	PRICE	TOTAL
2	287338	Shrimp Egg Rolls (16)	10.95	21.90
1	920468	Ham Steaks (2.5 lbs)	9.95	9.95
2	082062	California Blend (2 lbs)	2.60	5.20
1	145706	Beef Lasagna (3 lbs)	11.95	11.95
1	569348	Turkey Breast (3 lbs)	15.30	15.30
			GRAND TOTAL	64.30

CUSTOMER SIGNATURE _Paul Kelley_

E✗PRESS HOME CUISINE, INC.
1600 Walnut St.
Boulder, CO 80302-1330
(303) 555-1687

SALES INVOICE NO. 37627

CUSTOMER NUMBER 977603   DATE 10/30

SOLD TO Norman Meadows

ADDRESS 769 Orin Dr.

LaFayette, CO 80026-9606

QTY.	ITEM NO.	DESCRIPTION	PRICE	TOTAL
1	748501	Stuffed Shrimp (2 lbs)	18.50	18.50
1	395725	Breaded Chicken (5 lbs)	11.70	11.70
2	303547	Baby Carrots (2 lbs)	2.40	4.80
1	788050	Hot Wings (2.5 lbs)	7.90	7.90
1	673211	Sundae Cones (12)	5.50	5.50
			GRAND TOTAL	48.40

CUSTOMER SIGNATURE _Norman Meadows_

E𝗫PRESS HOME CUISINE, INC.

1600 Walnut St.
Boulder, CO 80302-1330
(303) 555-1687

SALES INVOICE NO. 37625

CUSTOMER NUMBER ___ 978197 ___ DATE ___ 10/29

SOLD TO ___ Daniel Fuller

ADDRESS ___ 1201 Lydia Dr.

LaFayette, CO 80026-4206

QTY.	ITEM NO.	DESCRIPTION	PRICE	TOTAL
2	145709	Beef Lasagna (3 lbs)	11.95	23.90
2	266794	Flautas (2.5 lbs)	7.70	15.40
1	469618	American Cheese (3 lbs)	9.45	9.45
1	197809	Straw. Ice Ceam (1 gal)	5.40	5.40
			GRAND TOTAL	54.15

CUSTOMER SIGNATURE ___ Daniel Fuller

E𝗫PRESS HOME CUISINE, INC.

1600 Walnut St.
Boulder, CO 80302-1330
(303) 555-1687

SALES INVOICE NO. 37633

CUSTOMER NUMBER ___ 904017 ___ DATE ___ 11/05

SOLD TO ___ Steven Boyle

ADDRESS ___ 2011 Goss Clr.

Boulder, CO 80302-9316

QTY.	ITEM NO.	DESCRIPTION	PRICE	TOTAL
2	876630	Peas (2.5 lbs)	2.95	5.90
2	133008	Beef Tortellini (3 lbs)	6.15	12.30
1	841546	Sausage Patties (3 lbs)	8.75	8.75
2	788050	Hot Wings (2.5 lbs)	7.90	15.80
1	050887	Beef Teriyaki (12 oz)	2.79	2.79
			GRAND TOTAL	45.54

CUSTOMER SIGNATURE ___ Steven Boyle

E✗PRESS HOME CUISINE, INC.

1600 Walnut St.
Boulder, CO 80302-1330
(303) 555-1687

SALES INVOICE NO. 37635

CUSTOMER NUMBER 114583 DATE 11/06

SOLD TO Lisa Wilson

ADDRESS 607 Quail Dr.

Boulder, CO 80303-6977

QTY.	ITEM NO.	DESCRIPTION	PRICE	TOTAL
2	781788	Turkey Roll (4.5 lbs)	11.85	23.70
1	092277	Broccoli Spears (2 lbs)	3.15	3.15
2	569348	Turkey Breast (3 lbs)	15.30	30.60
3	266794	Flautas (2.5 lbs)	7.70	23.10
1	287538	Shrimp Egg Rolls (16)	10.95	10.95
			GRAND TOTAL	91.50

CUSTOMER SIGNATURE _Lisa Wilson_

E✗PRESS HOME CUISINE, INC.

1600 Walnut St.
Boulder, CO 80302-1330
(303) 555-1687

SALES INVOICE NO. 37620

CUSTOMER NUMBER 019120 DATE 10/27

SOLD TO Edward Baker

ADDRESS 705 Applewood Dr.

Castle Rock, CO 80140-5992

QTY.	ITEM NO.	DESCRIPTION	PRICE	TOTAL
1	651900	BBQ Beef (3 lbs)	14.50	14.50
1	597596	Beef Ravioli (3 lbs)	6.65	6.65
2	018062	California Blend (2 lbs)	2.60	5.20
1	303547	Baby Carrots (2 lbs)	2.40	2.40
			GRAND TOTAL	28.75

CUSTOMER SIGNATURE _Edward Baker_

EXPRESS HOME CUISINE, INC.

1600 Walnut St.
Boulder, CO 80302-1330
(303) 555-1687

SALES INVOICE NO. 37630

DATE 11/03

CUSTOMER NUMBER 704082

SOLD TO Greg Wheeler

ADDRESS 308 Forest Ave.

Boulder, CO 80302-8485

QTY.	ITEM NO.	DESCRIPTION	PRICE	TOTAL
2	092277	Broccoli Spears (2 lbs)	3.15	6.30
1	781788	Turkey Roll (4.5 lbs)	11.85	11.85
1	133008	Beef Tortellini (3 lbs)	6.15	6.15
2	673211	Sundae Cones (12)	5.50	11.00
2	841546	Sausage Patties (3 lbs)	8.75	17.50
			GRAND TOTAL	52.80

CUSTOMER SIGNATURE _Greg Wheeler_

EXPRESS HOME CUISINE, INC.

1600 Walnut St.
Boulder, CO 80302-1330
(303) 555-1687

SALES INVOICE NO. 37637

DATE 11/10

CUSTOMER NUMBER 680388

SOLD TO Sylvia Holmes

ADDRESS 616 Skylark Dr.

LaFayette, CO 80026-4168

QTY.	ITEM NO.	DESCRIPTION	PRICE	TOTAL
1	185653	Garden Blend (2 lbs)	2.60	2.60
2	597596	Beef Ravioli (3 lbs)	6.65	13.30
1	145709	Beef Lasagna (3 lbs)	11.95	11.95
			GRAND TOTAL	27.85

CUSTOMER SIGNATURE _Sylvia Holmes_

EXPRESS HOME CUISINE, INC.

1600 Walnut St.
Boulder, CO 80302-1330
(303) 555-1687

SALES INVOICE NO. 37638

| CUSTOMER NUMBER | 232336 | DATE | 11/10 |

SOLD TO __George Knox__

ADDRESS __173 Huron Ct.__

__Boulder, CO 80303-1547__

QTY.	ITEM NO.	DESCRIPTION	PRICE	TOTAL
1	202338	Chicken Kiev (8)	16.35	16.35
2	498289	Ocean Perch (5 lbs)	20.20	40.40
1	185653	Garden Blend (2 lbs)	2.60	2.60
			GRAND TOTAL	59.35

CUSTOMER SIGNATURE ___George Knox___

EXPRESS HOME CUISINE, INC.

1600 Walnut St.
Boulder, CO 80302-1330
(303) 555-1687

SALES INVOICE NO. 37624

| CUSTOMER NUMBER | 174569 | DATE | 10/29 |

SOLD TO __Alice Collins__

ADDRESS __616 Sparta Dr.__

__LaFayette, CO 80026-0200__

QTY.	ITEM NO.	DESCRIPTION	PRICE	TOTAL
2	390449	Vegetable Lasagna (3 lbs)	11.95	23.90
1	018062	California Blend (2 lbs)	2.60	2.60
1	287338	Shrimp Egg Rolls (16)	10.95	10.95
1	876630	Peas (2.5 lbs)	2.95	2.95
			GRAND TOTAL	40.40

CUSTOMER SIGNATURE ___Alice Collins___

EXPRESS HOME CUISINE, INC.
1600 Walnut St.
Boulder, CO 80302-1330
(303) 555-1687

SALES INVOICE NO. 37628

DATE 10/31

CUSTOMER NUMBER 907702

SOLD TO Janet Alonso

ADDRESS 761 Laurel Ave.

Boulder, CO 80303-4951

QTY.	ITEM NO.	DESCRIPTION	PRICE	TOTAL
1	092277	Broccoli Spears (2 lbs)	3.15	3.15
2	144437	Enchiladas (2.5 lbs)	7.25	14.50
2	185653	Garden Blend (2 lbs)	2.60	5.20
		GRAND TOTAL		22.85

CUSTOMER SIGNATURE _Janet Alonso_

EXPRESS HOME CUISINE, INC.
1600 Walnut St.
Boulder, CO 80302-1330
(303) 555-1687

SALES INVOICE NO. 37634

DATE 11/06

CUSTOMER NUMBER 478210

SOLD TO Melissa Fox

ADDRESS 1440 Marine St.

Boulder, CO 80302-4841

QTY.	ITEM NO.	DESCRIPTION	PRICE	TOTAL
1	543040	Flounder Fillets (5 lbs)	23.40	23.40
2	191202	Stuffed Scrod (2.5 lbs)	13.95	27.90
2	920468	Ham Steaks (2.5 lbs)	9.95	19.90
1	197809	Straw. Ice Cream (1 gal)	5.40	5.40
1	625407	Cheese Tortellini (3 lbs)	6.15	6.15
		GRAND TOTAL		82.75

CUSTOMER SIGNATURE _Melissa Fox_

E✗PRESS HOME CUISINE, INC.

1600 Walnut St.
Boulder, CO 80302-1330
(303) 555-1687

SALES INVOICE NO. 37639

| CUSTOMER NUMBER | 002689 | DATE | 11/11 |

SOLD TO Marilyn White

ADDRESS 620 Dover Ave.

LaFayette, CO 80026-7000

QTY.	ITEM NO.	DESCRIPTION	PRICE	TOTAL
1	543040	Flounder Fillets (5 lbs)	23.40	23.40
1	781788	Turkey Roll (4.5 lbs)	11.85	11.85
2	876630	Peas (2.5 lbs)	2.95	5.90
1	498284	Ocean Perch (5 lbs)	20.20	20.20
		GRAND TOTAL		61.35

CUSTOMER SIGNATURE _Marilyn White_

E✗PRESS HOME CUISINE, INC.

1600 Walnut St.
Boulder, CO 80302-1330
(303) 555-1687

SALES INVOICE NO. 37623

| CUSTOMER NUMBER | 224678 | DATE | 10/29 |

SOLD TO Carl Flanagan

ADDRESS 121 Edgewood Dr.

Boulder, CO 80303-4558

QTY.	ITEM NO.	DESCRIPTION	PRICE	TOTAL
1	525499	Polish Sausage (4 lbs)	14.95	14.95
1	202338	Chicken Kiev (8)	16.35	16.35
1	498289	Ocean Perch (5 lbs)	20.20	20.20
1	266794	Flautas (2.5 lbs)	7.70	7.70
1	187280	Bratwurst (3 lbs)	10.25	10.25
		GRAND TOTAL		69.45

CUSTOMER SIGNATURE _Carl Flanagan_

E✕PRESS HOME CUISINE, INC.

1600 Walnut St.
Boulder, CO 80302-1330
(303) 555-1687

SALES INVOICE NO. 37632

CUSTOMER NUMBER 953317   DATE 11/05

SOLD TO Charles House

ADDRESS 70 Pima Ct.

Boulder, CO 80303-9618

QTY.	ITEM NO.	DESCRIPTION	PRICE	TOTAL
1	825280	Corn (2.5 lbs)	2.95	2.95
3	303547	Baby Carrots (2 lbs)	2.40	7.20
2	092277	Broccoli Spears (2 lbs)	3.15	6.30
2	569348	Turkey Breast (3 lbs)	15.30	30.60
			GRAND TOTAL	47.05

CUSTOMER SIGNATURE Charles House

E✕PRESS HOME CUISINE, INC.

1600 Walnut St.
Boulder, CO 80302-1330
(303) 555-1687

SALES INVOICE NO. 37636

CUSTOMER NUMBER 777868   DATE 11/07

SOLD TO Teresa Williams

ADDRESS 169 Sandler Dr.

LaFayette, CO 80026-9488

QTY.	ITEM NO.	DESCRIPTION	PRICE	TOTAL
1	651900	BBQ Beef (3 lbs)	14.50	14.50
2	202338	Chicken Kiev (8)	16.35	32.70
2	206000	Red Raspberries (5 lbs)	13.05	26.10
2	185653	Garden Blend (2 lbs)	2.60	5.20
			GRAND TOTAL	78.50

CUSTOMER SIGNATURE Teresa Williams

E✗PRESS HOME CUISINE, INC.

1600 Walnut St.
Boulder, CO 80302-1330
(303) 555-1687

SALES INVOICE NO. 37622

DATE 10/28

CUSTOMER NUMBER 505583

SOLD TO Loretta Fernandez

ADDRESS 415 Manhattan Dr.

Boulder, CO 80305-1436

QTY.	ITEM NO.	DESCRIPTION	PRICE	TOTAL
1	651900	BBQ Beef (3 lbs)	14.50	14.50
1	781788	Turkey Roll (4.5 lbs)	11.85	11.85
1	202338	Chicken Kiev (8)	16.35	16.35
2	876630	Peas (2.5 lbs)	2.95	5.90
2	350515	Blueberries (5 lbs)	13.65	27.30
			GRAND TOTAL	75.90

CUSTOMER SIGNATURE _Loretta Fernandez_

E✗PRESS HOME CUISINE, INC.

1600 Walnut St.
Boulder, CO 80302-1330
(303) 555-1687

SALES INVOICE NO. 37629

DATE 11/03

CUSTOMER NUMBER 701643

SOLD TO Cindy Schwab

ADDRESS 451 Utica Ave.

Boulder, CO 80312-3011

QTY.	ITEM NO.	DESCRIPTION	PRICE	TOTAL
1	390449	Vegetable Lasagna (3 lbs)	9.45	9.45
1	920468	Ham Steaks (2.5 lbs)	9.95	9.95
			GRAND TOTAL	19.40

CUSTOMER SIGNATURE _Cindy Schwab_

Activity 5

ACCOUNTS PAYABLE

→ **1** Define vendor, purchase on account, creditor, packing slip, purchase order, sales invoice, and accounts payable.

2 Explain the relationship between a purchase order and a sales invoice.

3 Enter data for an accounts payable system.

DATA ENTRY APPLICATION AND JOB DESCRIPTION

*I*n Activity Two the beginning inventory for Tyler Drug Store Supplies was set up and updated. Now Tyler Drug Store Supplies must purchase from suppliers the merchandise that it sells to its customers. These suppliers are known as **vendors.** The most widely used method of purchasing merchandise for resale is known as **purchase on account**. In this type of purchase, the goods are delivered before the payment occurs. In order to use this method, Tyler Drug Store Supplies had to establish a credit relationship with each of its vendors. Vendors who agree to sell merchandise on account are known as **creditors.** The total amount Tyler's owes to its creditors for purchases is recorded in the company's **accounts payable** general ledger. The amount owed to each creditor is recorded in the individual creditor account in the **accounts payable ledger**, which is arranged alphabetically by creditor name.

When Tyler's wishes to purchase merchandise, a **purchase order** must first be completed. The purchase order is prepared by the buyer and lists the description, quantity, and price of the goods to be purchased. Figure 5.1 illustrates a purchase order prepared by Tyler Drug Store Supplies.

Purchase Order

DATE:			PURCHASE ORDER NO:	
BILL TO:			SHIP TO:	
VENDOR:				

TYLER DRUG STORE SUPPLIES

QTY	UPC NO.	ITEM DESCRIPTION	UNIT PRICE	EXTENDED AMOUNT

AUTHORIZED SIGNATURE_____			TOTAL AMOUNT	

THIS PURCHASE ORDER IS VOID IF IT DOES NOT HAVE A PURCHASE ORDER NUMBER AND PURCHASING SIGNATURE

FIGURE 5.1 Purchase Order

Upon receipt of the purchase order, the vendor completes a **sales invoice**. A sales invoice also lists the description, quantity, and price of the goods being sold. Once the sales invoice has been prepared, the creditor's shipping department packages the merchandise for shipment. A copy of the sales invoice is sent with the merchandise to the buyer. When the merchandise reaches the buyer's receiving department, a copy of the buyer's purchase order and a copy of the creditor's sales invoice are used to check the arriving merchandise. Some companies also send a **packing slip** along with the merchandise. A packing slip contains the amount ordered, the amount shipped, and a description of the items. Prices usually do not appear on a packing slip. This check is to ensure that the proper items and quantities have been delivered. Figure 5.2 illustrates a sales invoice prepared by one of Tyler's creditors based on the purchase order illustrated in Figure 5.1.

DAMIEN DISTRIBUTORS, INC.
736 Onondaga Blvd. • Syracuse, NY 13213-1436

SALES INVOICE

SOLD TO:

VENDOR NUMBER:
TERMS:
INVOICE NUMBER:
DATE:

QTY	UPC NO.	DESCRIPTION	PRICE	EXTENDED AMOUNT
			GRAND TOTAL	

FIGURE 5.2 Sales Invoice

The copy of the sales invoice is forwarded to the buyer's accounting department. The accounting department checks this verified copy for accuracy in all the extended amounts and totals. If an error has been found in the items shipped or in the amounts listed on the invoice, the vendor is notified so that the error may be corrected. The payment is sent at the time designated by the **terms** shown on the invoice. The terms state how and when the invoice should be paid. Customers often receive a discount if their bills are paid before the due date. For example, "2/10, N/30" means that a two percent discount may be taken if the bill is paid within 10 days. The entire net amount is due within 30 days. The percentage of the discount and the time period for payment may vary from vendor to vendor.

INPUT FIELDS

*I*n this activity you will key-enter data from 20 sales invoices into the computerized accounts payable system. The data pertains to invoices involving merchandise purchased on account by Tyler Drug Store Supplies. Make sure that the quantity and price you entered are correct and that the amount on the computer is identical to that shown on the sales invoices.

Various vendors have sent sales invoices to Tyler Drug Store Supplies. Information from these sales invoices are key-entered into fields on the data entry screen. These fields are described below.

Vendor Number. This five-character field contains the identification number that Tyler's assigns to each of its vendors.

Invoice Number. This is a five-character field containing the vendor's invoice number. The invoice number is a unique identifying number printed on the vendor's invoices that distinguishes one invoice from another. Any reference to the merchandise listed on the invoice is usually identified by this number.

Date. This six-character field contains the date on which the vendor sent the goods and the invoice.

Qty. This field is a maximum of two characters in length and identifies how many units of each item have been shipped.

UPC No. This ten-character field is a unique code number assigned to a particular product or package by a manufacturer. The first five numbers of the UPC number are assigned to a particular manufacturer or company. The second group of five numbers is uniquely assigned by the manufacturer to designate a particular product or package.

Price. This field is a maximum of five characters in length and identifies the cost of one unit of an item.

(OBJECTIVE 3)

GET READY

Follow the start-up procedures for your computer that are found in Appendix A.

COMPLETE ALPHA-NUMERIC DEXTERITY DRILL

```
1321436 56109 TOOTHPASTE 788468 299 1966
47883 EYE DROPS 658-51 33400 16750 39748
539695 037802 BABY OIL 139 41143 02 3296
DEODORANT 77639 10500 16830 EMERY BOARDS
25669 123735 34 891126 MOUTHWASH 24 8670
```

STEP 1   From the *Activities* menu, select *Activity 5 Accounts Payable.*

STEP 2   Select *Alpha-Numeric Dexterity Drill.*

STEP 3   Enter the data for each line. Press *enter* or *return* at the end of each line.

STEP 4   Select *OK* when you are finished key-entering. Review your scores.

STEP 5   Select *Review* to review any errors that were made. After you have reviewed your performance, select *OK*.

Repeat the Alpha-Numeric Dexterity Drill as many times as instructed by your teacher.

COMPLETE KEYPAD DEXTERITY DRILL

```
51549 67365 35341 35353 08796 53657 9325
84575 29637 78333 42318 00231 16342 3526
08972 38079 28298 97705 82221 27444 7554
83375 46276 62315 97951 43925 71004 7496
50939 28257 30997 02215 30175 53353 5230
```

STEP 1 From the *Activities* menu, select *Activity 5 Accounts Payable.*

STEP 2 Select *Keypad Dexterity Drill.*

STEP 3 Enter the data for each line. Press *enter* or *return* at the end of each line.

STEP 4 Select *OK* when you are finished key-entering. Review your score.

STEP 5 Select *Review* to review any errors that were made. After reviewing your performance, select *OK.*

Repeat the Keypad Dexterity Drill as many times as instructed by your teacher.

COMPLETE SALES INVOICES

STEP 1 Remove all of the sales invoices that are located at the end of this activity. The invoices may be key-entered in any order.

STEP 2 From the *Activities* menu, select *Activity 5 Accounts Payable.*

STEP 3 Select *Sales Invoice.* The display on your screen will be similar to that shown in Figure 5.3

FIGURE 5.3

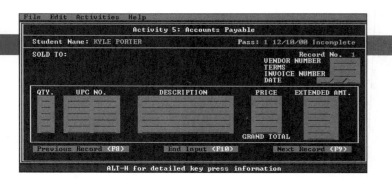

STEP 4 Key-enter the Vendor Number for your first record in the first field. The vendor's name and address and the terms of the sale will appear automatically on your screen.

STEP 5 Key-enter the Sales Invoice No. in the appropriate field.

STEP 6 Key-enter the Date in the appropriate field. Use the last two digits of the current year.

STEP 7 Key-enter the Qty. in the appropriate field.

STEP 8 Key-enter the UPC number in the appropriate field. The product description will appear automatically.

STEP 9 Key-enter the Price in the appropriate field. This is the price for one item. The computer will calculate the Extended Amount, multiplying quantity times price.

STEP 10   Key-enter the data for the entire record. The computer will calculate the Grand Total, automatically adding the Extended Amounts. After key-entering the data for the first record, select Next Record.

STEP 11   Key-enter the remaining records.

✍ **Note: If you are interrupted before key-entering all of the records, follow the necessary procedures to end your input and to begin the next session. Refer to the detailed instructions for this procedure in Activity 4, if necessary.**

STEP 12   After key-entering all 20 sales invoices, select *End Input*. If you notice errors after you have selected End Input, select *Edit* and then move to the appropriate fields to key-enter the corrections. After making the corrections, select *End Input* again.

Print the sales invoice that is on the screen if instructed by your teacher.

STEP 13   Select *Analyze*. Review the information presented.

STEP 14   Select *Review.* Any errors will be highlighted. Print the sales invoices if instructed by your teacher.

STEP 15   Select *Done.*

STEP 16   You may generate a report of your performance in this activity. To do so,

> - From the *File* menu, select *Open Report.*
>
> - From the *Activities* menu, Select *Activity 5 Accounts Payable.*
>
> - Select *Sales Invoice.*
>
> - Select *Get Report.*
>
> - From the *File* menu, select *Print.*
>
> - Select *Print* again.
>
> - Select *Done.*

✍ **Note: In a real work situation, you would strive for completely accurate records. Therefore, it is suggested that once you have completed all of the steps listed here, you should go back into the records and correct any errors. To do this:**

> - **From the *Activities* menu, Select *Activity 5 Accounts Payable.***

- Select *Sales Invoice*.

- Select *Open*.

- Use the appropriate keys to locate the proper record and field and then key-enter the correction.

- Select *End Input*.

- Select *Analyze*.

- Select *Review*.

- Select *Done*.

- Print the sales invoices if instructed by your teacher.

VOCABULARY

accounts payable
accounts payable ledger
creditors
packing slip
purchase on account
purchase order
sales invoice
terms
vendors

Activity 5 Study Guide

ACCOUNTS PAYABLE

PART 1

OBJECTIVES 1 AND 2 (2 POINTS EACH)

✏ **Match the vocabulary terms with the best definitions. Write the letter of the term in the space to the left of the definition. You will not use every vocabulary term.**

A. **accounts payable**
B. **accounts payable ledger**
C. **creditors**
D. **invoice number**

E. **packing slip**
F. **purchase on account**

G. **purchase order**
H. **sales invoice**
I. **vendors**

_____ 1. These companies sell merchandise that is often purchased on account.

_____ 2. The total amount a company owes all of its vendors due to purchases on account is recorded in this account.

_____ 3. This is the most widely used method for purchasing merchandise for resale. Goods are delivered before payment.

_____ 4. All of a company's creditors and the amount owed to each creditor are listed alphabetically here.

_____ 5. This document is prepared by the buyer and lists the description, quantity, and price of the goods to be purchased.

_____ 6. This unique identifying number distinguishes one invoice from another.

_____ 7. This document is prepared by the seller and lists the description, quantity, and price of the goods being sold.

PART 2

OBJECTIVES 1 AND 2 (1 POINT EACH)

●✧ **Each of the following statements is either true or false. Indicate your choice by circling T for a true statement or F for a false statement.**

T   F   **1.** The terms listed on a sales invoice state the expected date of delivery.

T   F   **2.** Merchandise purchased on account is paid for after delivery.

T   F   **3.** An invoice should be checked against its corresponding purchase order to verify that the merchandise sent is the same as ordered.

T   F   **4.** Invoices should always be checked carefully before payment.

T   F   **5.** The accounts payable ledger lists the amounts that customers owe a business.

T   F   **6.** If an invoice is not paid within the discount period, it is still permissible to take the discount.

T   F   **7.** It is not necessary to verify receipt of all the items listed on an invoice.

T   F   **8.** A purchase order is completed by the supplier of the goods.

T   F   **9.** A vendor uses information contained on an invoice when preparing a purchase order.

(3 POINTS EACH)

●✧ **Briefly answer each of the following items. Write your answers on the lines provided.**

1. Explain the steps that take place from the time a buyer decides to purchase goods to the time the goods arrive from the seller.

_____

_____

2. Explain the steps that occur once the merchandise that was ordered reaches the receiving department of the buyer.

_____

_____

_____

3. What steps should be taken if the extended amount on the seller's invoice is incorrect?

_____

_____

_____

☛ **Remove the Activity 5 Study Guide from your text-workbook and hand it to your instructor for correcting.**

Total Points Possible	32
(Minus) Incorrect Points	_____
Total Points Earned	_____
Percent Correct	_____
Grade	_____

DAMIEN DISTRIBUTORS, INC.
736 Onondaga Blvd. • Syracuse, NY 13213-1436

SALES INVOICE

SOLD TO: Tyler Drug Store Supplies
1800 Northridge Dr.
Syracuse, NY
13214-1717

VENDOR NUMBER: **19689**
TERMS: **N/30**
INVOICE NUMBER: **51602**
DATE: **02/13**

QTY	UPC NO.	DESCRIPTION	PRICE	EXTENDED AMOUNT
12	76000 60600	Toothpaste 8.2 oz	2.29	27.48
12	16000 00320	Hair Spray 7 oz	1.49	17.88
12	16000 00040	Aspirin/100	3.99	47.88

GRAND TOTAL **93.24**

SALES INVOICE

Wilson Pharmaceuticals
1300 East Genessee Street / Fayetteville, NY 13066-8928

Sold To: Tyler Drug Store Supplies
1800 Northridge Dr.
Syracuse, NY
13214-1717

Vendor Number: **04839**
Terms: **2/20**
Invoice Number: **63904**
Date: **03/30**

QTY.	UPC NO.	DESCRIPTION	PRICE	EXTENDED AMOUNT
32	21000 64501	Roll-on Deo. 1.7 oz	1.99	63.68
40	43000 22080	Mint Tooth. 4.6 oz	1.79	71.60
20	39000 07400	Child. Aspirin/30	3.29	65.80
16	21100 65041	Plaque Rinse 24 oz	4.49	71.84
24	33400 16750	Eye Drops 1 oz	5.19	124.56

GRAND TOTAL _____ 397.48

Oper Door

TITAN MANUFACTURING

2315 JAMES ST.
SYRACUSE, NY 13206-6935

SALES INVOICE

SOLD TO: Tyler Drug Store Supplies
1800 Northridge Dr.
Syracuse, NY
13214-1717

VENDOR NUMBER: 68086
TERMS: 1/15, N/30
INVOICE NUMBER: 13241
DATE: 02/03

QTY	UPC NO.	DESCRIPTION	PRICE	EXTENDED AMOUNT
24	03780 29615	Baby Oil 9 oz	3.59	86.16
70	36000 00830	Cherry Lip Balm	1.39	97.30
50	41143 02542	Comb	2.39	119.50
			GRAND TOTAL	302.96

PROFESSIONAL SUPPLIERS, INC.

1103 MAIN ST. | TULLY, NY 13159-1724

SALES INVOICE

SOLD TO: Tyler Drug Store Supplies
1800 Northridge Dr.
Syracuse, NY
13214-1717

VENDOR NUMBER: 39034
TERMS: N/30
INVOICE NUMBER: 77638
DATE: 02/10

QTY	UPC NO.	DESCRIPTION	PRICE	EXTENDED AMOUNT
40	38100 10201	Solid Deodorant 2 oz	1.99	79.60
30	38100 10500	Spray Deodorant 4 oz	1.99	59.70
30	30000 05300	Bath Beads 15 oz	1.59	47.70
24	52100 11205	Dandruff Shamp. 8 oz	8.09	194.16
50	01020 30000	Emery Boards/10	1.20	60.00
			GRAND TOTAL ▶	441.16

Nodine, Inc.

813 West Belden Avenue / Syracuse, NY 13204-4822

SALES INVOICE

Sold To: Tyler Drug Store Supplies
1800 Northridge Dr.
Syracuse, NY
            13214-1717

Vendor Number: **25669**
Terms: **N/30**
Invoice Number: **80612**
Date: **03/10**

QTY	UPC NO.	DESCRIPTION	PRICE	EXTENDED AMOUNT
70	14100 44300	Hair Condit. 13 oz	1.69	118.30
35	07488 12373	Tooth Powder 4 oz	2.39	83.65
12	01441 24000	Shoe Insoles/2	1.89	22.68
24	48001 11071	Skin Cream 14 oz	3.59	86.16
30	26516 11230	Mint Mouthwash 18 oz	2.89	86.70
		GRAND TOTAL		397.49

SALES INVOICE

Lexington Manufacturing

37 Oswego Street ▪ Baldensville, NY 13027-3124

SOLD TO: Tyler Drug Store Supplies
1800 Northridge Dr.
Syracuse, NY
            13214-1717

VENDOR NUMBER: **64117**
TERMS: **N/30**
INVOICE NUMBER: **37318**
DATE: **02/12**

QTY	UPC NO.	DESCRIPTION	PRICE	EXTENDED AMOUNT
40	28500 83530	Multiple Vit./100	9.29	371.60
70	00347 11560	Rubbing Alc. 16 oz	1.09	76.30
24	50003 70793	Children's Vit./60	6.59	158.16
			GRAND TOTAL	606.06

MANIAN BROTHERS, INC.
411 POND ST. ✻ SYRACUSE, NY 13208-0649

SALES INVOICE

SOLD TO: Tyler Drug Store Supplies
1800 Northridge Dr.
Syracuse, NY
13214-1717

VENDOR NUMBER: 08917
TERMS: N/30
INVOICE NUMBER: 54263
DATE: 02/13

QTY	UPC NO.	DESCRIPTION	PRICE	EXTENDED AMOUNT
64	43000 10010	Breath Spray 2 oz	2.59	165.76
12	10450 47900	Mini Blow Dryer	13.95	167.40
60	51700 00810	Lip Balm	1.39	83.40
36	00750 15600	Plaque Rin. 20 oz	3.99	143.64
			GRAND TOTAL	560.20

ABELINE DISTRIBUTORS, LTD.
311 STOUTENGER ST. ▲ EAST SYRACUSE. NY 13057-2028

SALES INVOICE

SOLD TO: Tyler Drug Store Supplies
1800 Northridge Dr.
Syracuse, NY
13214-1717

VENDOR NUMBER: 62797
TERMS: N/30
INVOICE NUMBER: 92466
DATE: 02/13

QTY	UPC NO.	DESCRIPTION	PRICE	EXTENDED AMOUNT
24	30600 05900	Contact Sol. 1 oz	9.29	222.96
48	21400 64400	Flossing Swords/32	1.89	90.72
48	19990 00320	Face Scrub 2.6 oz	5.79	277.92
60	16999 10710	Shower Cap	1.49	89.40
			GRAND TOTAL	681.00

SALES INVOICE

Thompson Industries

1601 Burnet Ave.
Syracuse, NY 13206-7435

SOLD
TO:
Tyler Drug Store Supplies
1800 Northridge Dr.
Syracuse, NY
13214-1717

VENDOR NUMBER: **29888**
TERMS: **N/30**
INVOICE NUMBER: **95145**
DATE: **03/10**

QTY	UPC NO.	DESCRIPTION	PRICE	EXTENDED AMOUNT
40	16000 00017	Baby Powder 14 oz	1.79	71.60
40	30600 27550	Moist Wipes/84	3.79	151.60
50	43300 27500	Hair Gel 5.2 oz	3.69	184.50
50	17000 91747	Hair Mousse 5.2 oz	3.89	194.50
24	48100 27000	Shamp./Cond. 11 oz	3.34	80.16
			GRAND TOTAL	682.36

MJC Inc.

36 Canoga Street   Auburn, NY 13021-3838

SALES INVOICE

Sold
To:
Tyler Drug Store Supplies
1800 Northridge Dr.
Syracuse, NY
13214-1717

Vendor Number: **73577**
Terms: **2/15, N/30**
Invoice Number: **13198**
Date: **02/25**

QTY	UPC NO.	DESCRIPTION	PRICE	EXTENDED AMOUNT
32	00028 72536	Ath. Ft. Pwdr. 11 oz	4.19	134.08
32	00924 00413	Ath. Ft. Spr. 11 oz	5.29	169.28
40	13075 28500	Antacid Tablets/150	5.59	223.60
40	56100 00010	Antacid Tablets/75	2.39	95.60
			GRAND TOTAL	622.56

 **MED-TECH** I N C.   271 DeWITT STREET I SYRACUSE, NY 13203-1968

SALES INVOICE

SOLD TO:
Tyler Drug Store Supplies
1800 Northridge Dr.
Syracuse, NY
13214-1717

VENDOR NUMBER:	**27958**
TERMS:	**N/30**
INVOICE NUMBER:	**22342**
DATE:	**03/10**

QTY	UPC NO.	DESCRIPTION	PRICE	EXTENDED AMOUNT
40	48001 01000	Antacid Liquid 12 oz	3.19	127.60
35	24600 27074	Aspirin Caplets/50	3.79	132.65
35	24600 27075	Aspirin Caplets/30	2.79	97.65
24	43300 22808	Sunblock #15 4 oz	7.39	177.36
24	43000 22810	Sunblock #4 4 oz	5.39	129.36
			GRAND TOTAL	664.62

 *Perkins Pharmaceuticals* | 842 North Salina Street / Syracuse, NY 13208-1912

SALES INVOICE

SOLD TO:
Tyler Drug Store Supplies
1800 Northridge Dr.
Syracuse, NY
13214-1717

VENDOR NUMBER:	**11946**
TERMS:	**N/30**
INVOICE NUMBER:	**36923**
DATE:	**02/13**

QTY	UPC NO.	DESCRIPTION	PRICE	EXTENDED AMOUNT
30	40028 26106	Cotton Swabs/375	.88	26.40
			GRAND TOTAL	26.40

LIVERPOOL DISTRIBUTORS
4033 Wafer Ash Way   Liverpool, NY 13088-3160

SALES INVOICE

SOLD TO: Tyler Drug Store Supplies
1800 Northridge Dr.
Syracuse, NY
           13214-1717

VENDOR NUMBER:	90999
TERMS:	N/30
INVOICE NUMBER:	85151
DATE:	03/10

QTY	UPC NO.	DESCRIPTION	PRICE	EXTENDED AMOUNT
24	27000 48000	Liquid Aspirin 4 oz	4.99	119.76
30	03130 27782	Acne Pads/75	4.98	149.40
30	03130 27700	Acne Cream 3/4 oz	4.29	128.70
24	72770 01310	Cologne 1.1 oz	12.50	300.00
			GRAND TOTAL ▶	697.86

R.J. JONES SUPPLIERS
356 State Fair Blvd. ◆ Syracuse, NY 13204-3933

SALES INVOICE

SOLD TO: Tyler Drug Store Supplies
1800 Northridge Dr.
Syracuse, NY
           13214-1717

VENDOR NUMBER:	18845
TERMS:	N/30
INVOICE NUMBER:	83471
DATE:	03/13

QTY	UPC NO.	DESCRIPTION	PRICE	EXTENDED AMOUNT
36	41000 16820	Vitamin C/250	6.97	250.92
			GRAND TOTAL ▶	250.92

GATEWAY, INC.
121 Harrison St. / Syracuse, NY 13202-9128

SALES INVOICE

SOLD TO: Tyler Drug Store Supplies
1800 Northridge Dr.
Syracuse, NY
13214-1717

VENDOR NUMBER:	94824
TERMS:	N/30
INVOICE NUMBER:	39520
DATE:	02/25

QTY	UPC NO.	DESCRIPTION	PRICE	EXTENDED AMOUNT
40	41580 81004	Lime Aft. Shave 4 oz	5.39	215.60
40	41580 81010	Lem. Aft. Shave 4 oz	5.39	215.60
30	28500 11560	Allergy Tablets/24	4.99	149.70
30	11200 02100	Nose Spray 1/2 oz	5.29	158.70
		GRAND TOTAL		739.60

MICHELSON'S DISTRIBUTORS
301 SOUTH MANLIUS / FAYETTEVILLE, NY 13066-8860

SALES INVOICE

SOLD TO: Tyler Drug Store Supplies
1800 Northridge Dr.
Syracuse, NY
13214-1717

VENDOR NUMBER:	35605
TERMS:	1/15, N/30
INVOICE NUMBER:	75887
DATE:	03/10

QTY	UPC NO.	DESCRIPTION	PRICE	EXTENDED AMOUNT
24	44700 11569	First Aid Spray 4 oz	3.29	78.96
50	39000 52017	Bandages/70	2.79	139.50
12	02900 31010	Adhesive Tape 10 yds	3.29	39.48
12	00217 12537	Knee Brace	8.49	101.88
				359.82
		GRAND TOTAL		

Central Suppliers
1421 Lodi Street O Syracuse, NY 13208-5112

SALES INVOICE

SOLD TO: Tyler Drug Store Supplies
1800 Northridge Dr.
Syracuse, NY
13214-1717

VENDOR NUMBER: **42751**
TERMS: **N/30**
INVOICE NUMBER: **41012**
DATE: **03/13**

QTY	UPC NO.	DESCRIPTION	PRICE	EXTENDED AMOUNT
36	05251 13600	Mouthwash 32 oz	3.78	136.08
			GRAND TOTAL	136.08

Swartz & Sons, Inc.
213 South Salina Syracuse, NY 13202-2947

SALES INVOICE

SOLD TO: Tyler Drug Store Supplies
1800 Northridge Dr.
Syracuse, NY
13214-1717

VENDOR NUMBER: **33362**
TERMS: **N/30**
INVOICE NUMBER: **54704**
DATE: **02/03**

QTY	UPC NO.	DESCRIPTION	PRICE	EXTENDED AMOUNT
24	53900 15233	Lime Shav. Gel 11 oz	1.89	45.36
12	77600 03061	Hand Mirror	2.79	33.48
24	47605 21200	Hair Pump 6 oz	4.89	117.36
24	11771 00023	Shaving Gel 7 oz	1.89	45.36
		GRAND TOTAL ➤		241.56

Expressway Suppliers, Inc.   1120 Milton Ave. ● Syracuse, NY 13204-6710

SOLD TO: Tyler Drug Store Supplies
1800 Northridge Dr.
Syracuse, NY
　　　　　　13214-1717

VENDOR NUMBER: **18312**
TERMS: **N/30**
INVOICE NUMBER: **99221**
DATE: **03/10**

QTY	UPC NO.	DESCRIPTION	PRICE	EXTENDED AMOUNT
12	26000 38040	Lens Cln. Sol. 1 oz	3.59	43.08
24	46000 40510	Moist. Lotion 13 oz	6.37	152.88
SALES INVOICE			GRAND TOTAL	195.96

TOMLINSON MANUFACTURERS
213 SOUTH CENTRAL AVE. / MINOA, NY 13116-7765

SALES INVOICE

SOLD TO: Tyler Drug Store Supplies
1800 Northridge Dr.
Syracuse, NY
　　　　　　13214-1717

VENDOR NUMBER: **33360**
TERMS: **N/30**
INVOICE NUMBER: **54644**
DATE: **03/25**

QTY	UPC NO.	DESCRIPTION	PRICE	EXTENDED AMOUNT
18	28005 48867	Elbow Brace	10.29	185.22
18	62100 61531	Athletic Bandage	4.29	77.22
24	41060 86200	Pre-elec. Shv. 5 oz	4.59	110.16
30	76000 27500	Lime Shv. Crm. 11 oz	1.59	47.70
40	34500 40306	Coc. Shv. Crm. 11 oz	1.59	63.60
			GRAND TOTAL	483.90

Activity 6

PAYROLL RECORDS

LEARNING OBJECTIVES

Upon completion of this activity, you will be able to:

1 Define gross pay, deductions, net pay, pay period, and payroll.

2 Identify the different methods of calculating employees' pay.

3 Key-enter data for a payroll system.

DATA ENTRY APPLICATION AND JOB DESCRIPTION

*A*ll companies must pay their employees for the work they perform. The total amount an employee earns is known as gross pay or total earnings. **Gross pay** is the total amount of pay due to an individual employee before any deductions. **Deductions** are amounts withheld from an employee's wages for taxes, insurance, retirement plans, and/or charitable contributions. **Net pay**, also known as take-home pay, is the amount of money paid to an employee after all deductions have been subtracted from the gross pay. The length of time covered for this payment, normally one week, two weeks, one-half month, or one month, is termed a **pay period. Payroll** is the total gross amount paid to all the employees of a company for a pay period.

Businesses can calculate an employee's gross pay many ways, depending on the employee's pay type. Three common pay types are salary, hourly wage, and salary plus commission. A **salary** is a fixed amount paid to an employee for each pay period. The salary amount is paid regardless of the actual number of hours spent in the work place. Salaried employees usually work in professional, management, or supervisory capacities.

Employees classified as **hourly** are paid a certain rate for each hour worked. A regular work week consists of 40 hours. **Regular hours** are hours worked up to the normal 40-hour work week. **Overtime hours** are hours worked beyond the 40 regular hours in the work week. When an hourly employee works more than 40 hours in one week, financial consideration is normally given for the overtime hours. The overtime rate is the rate of pay given for overtime hours. Usually, the employee is paid one and one-half times the hourly rate of pay for each additional hour worked beyond the normal 40 hours. Thus, overtime pay is commonly called "time and a half."

Salespeople are frequently paid a salary plus a commission. The **commission** is calculated by multiplying the total sales by a percentage rate. This amount is then added to the salary. Employees with this pay type have a lower base salary than a straight salaried salesperson. A salary plus commission plan creates an incentive to produce greater sales.

Before the computer can process a payroll, a master file of information must be established. This master file contains general data, such as name, address, social security number, and pay type for each employee. An electronic database may be used to create the master file. The amount of taxes and other deductions withheld from an employee's wages are dependent upon marital status, number of dependents, and the amount employees want to contribute to their health insurance and pension funds. The computerized payroll system is prepared by key-entering and storing this data for each employee. In this activity you will be key-entering payroll data for Merrimac Industries, Inc., a successful locally owned and operated specialty shop for customized gifts. Figure 6.1 shows the payroll setup form for Merrimac Industries, Inc. Each payroll setup form contains data for one employee.

Merrimac Industries, Inc.   **Payroll Setup Form**

EMPLOYEE NUMBER: _____

NAME (LAST, FIRST): _____

STREET ADDRESS: _____

CITY: _____ STATE: _____ ZIP: _____

SSN: _____ MARITAL STATUS: _____ DEPENDENTS: _____

PAY TYPE: _____ HOURLY RATE: $ _____ SALARY: $ _____ COMMISSION: _____

HEALTH INSURANCE: $ _____ PENSION: $ _____

PAY TYPE CODE: HOURLY = 1   SALARY = 2   COMMISSION + SALARY = 3

FIGURE 6.1 Payroll Setup Form

From time to time some employee payroll data may change. These changes, or updates, may include an employee's name, marital status, address, or payroll deductions. The updates are first recorded on a source document, the payroll update form, and then key-entered into the computerized payroll system. The payroll update form for Merrimac Industries, Inc., is shown in Figure 6.2. A payroll update form may contain changes for several employees.

Merrimac Industries, Inc.
Payroll Update Form

EMP. NO.	LAST NAME	FIRST NAME	STREET ADDRESS	CITY	STATE	ZIP	SS #	MAR. STAT.	DEP.	PAY TYPE	HOUR RATE	SAL.	COMM.	HEALTH INSUR.	PENSION

FIGURE 6.2 Payroll Update Form

INPUT FIELDS

In this activity you will set up payroll records for 21 employees of Merrimac Industries, Inc. You will then update those payroll records by making changes to some of the employee payroll records.

Two types of source documents are used to enter data into Merrimac Industries, Inc., computerized payroll system—the payroll setup form and the payroll update form. Information from these forms is key-entered into fields on data entry screens. A description of each field is provided below.

Employee Number. This numeric field is five characters in length and contains the number assigned to each employee by the employer.

Last Name. This field is a maximum of 13 characters in length and contains an employee's surname.

First Name. This field is a maximum of eight characters in length and contains an employee's given name.

Street Address. This field is a maximum of 19 characters in length and contains an employee's address.

City. This field is a maximum of 11 characters in length and contains the name of the city in which an employee resides.

State. This field is two characters in length and contains the appropriate two-letter state abbreviation used by the postal authorities.

ZIP. This field is nine characters in length for an extended ZIP code. You should not key-enter the hyphen.

SSN (Social Security Number). This field is nine characters in length and contains the unique number assigned to each working person by the Social Security Administration. Because every worker's social security number is different, these numbers are used for identification purposes. The hyphens should not be key-entered.

Marital Status. This field is one character in length and contains the abbreviation of "S" or "M" representing an employee's marital status. The single classification is to be used for any status other than married.

Dependents. This field is a maximum of one character in length and contains the number of dependents that an employee claims.

Pay Type. This field is one character in length and contains a number identifying an employee as either hourly, salaried, or commissioned. Using Merrimac's payroll system, "1" indicates an hourly employee, "2" indicates a salary employee, and "3" indicates a salary plus commission employee.

Hourly. This field is a maximum of four characters in length and contains the rate of pay that an hourly Merrimac employee receives for each hour worked.

Salary. This field is a maximum of six characters in length and contains the gross pay that a salaried employee receives for a pay period.

Commission. This field is a maximum of one character in length and contains the percentage of sales that an employee receives as a commission. This employee will also have an entry in the salary field.

Health Insurance. This field is a maximum of five characters in length and contains the amount of money that is deducted from an employee's pay each pay period for family or dependent health insurance.

Pension. This field is a maximum of five characters in length and contains the amount of money an employee contributes each pay period toward a pension plan.

(OBJECTIVE 3)

GET READY

Follow the start-up procedures for your computer that are found in Appendix A.

COMPLETE ALPHA-NUMERIC DEXTERITY DRILL

```
43750  01136  80461  MO  968526  480063  33512
631211  CRESTON  320021  517942  05622  52506
304436  34634  16689  200058  ST  CHARLES  375
531607  63033  4675250  PENSION  16631  69226
37397  SALARY  L73438  462161  48969  7035442
```

STEP 1   From the *Activities* menu, select *Activity 6 Payroll Records*.

STEP 2   Select *Alpha-Numeric Dexterity Drill*.

STEP 3   Enter the data for each line. Press *enter* or *return* at the end of each line.

STEP 4   Select *OK* when you are finished key-entering. Review your score.

STEP 5   Select *Review* to review any errors that were made. After you have reviewed your performance, select *OK*.

Repeat the Alpha-Numeric Dexterity Drill as many times as instructed by your teacher.

COMPLETE KEYPAD DEXTERITY DRILL

```
78924  97825  89565  27369  51531  47574  3506
20749  62358  45132  30075  50371  30157  7204
90387  22901  50417  18830  18609  78501  7183
45893  02754  32685  13245  00357  71530  7013
79689  34677  89053  28219  30997  90224  9329
```

STEP 1   From the *Activities* menu, select *Activity 6 Payroll Records*.

STEP 2   Select *Keypad Dexterity Drill*.

STEP 3   Enter the data for each line. Press *enter* or *return* at the end of each line.

STEP 4   Select *OK* when you are finished key-entering. Review your score.

STEP 5   Select *Review* to review any errors that were made. After reviewing your performance, select *OK*.

Repeat the Keypad Dexterity Drill as many times as instructed by your teacher.

COMPLETE PAYROLL SETUP FORMS

STEP 1   Remove and separate all of the payroll setup forms for Merrimac Industries, Inc., that are located at the end of this activity.

STEP 2   From the *Activities* menu, select *Activity 6 Payroll Records*.

STEP 3   Select *Payroll Setup Form*. The display on your screen should be similar to that shown in Figure 6.3.

FIGURE 6.3

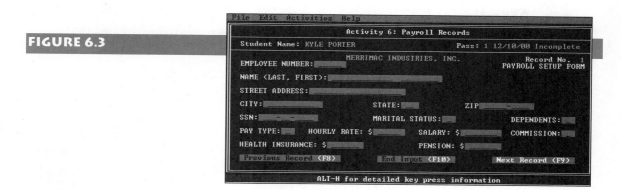

STEP 4   Key-enter the Employee Number, Name, Street Address, City, State, ZIP, Marital Status, Dependents, Social Security Number, and Pay Type data in the appropriate fields for your first record. Key the first five digits of the ZIP Code, then key-enter the remaining four digits. The hyphen is already displayed on the screen, so you do not need to key the hyphen. The hyphens used in the Social-Security field are also displayed on the screen and do not need to be keyed.

STEP 5   Key-enter the Hourly Rate, Salary, and Commission data in the appropriate fields for your first record. (Some of the fields will remain blank.)

STEP 6   Key-enter the Health Insurance and Pension data in the appropriate field for your first record. After key-entering the data for the first record, select *Next Record*.

STEP 7   Key-enter the remaining records.

✍ **Note: If you are interrupted before key-entering all of the records, follow the necessary procedures to end your input and to begin the next session. Refer to the detailed instructions for this procedure in Activity 4, if necessary.**

STEP 8   After key-entering the 21 payroll setup forms, select *End Input*. If you notice errors after you have selected End Input, select *Edit* and then move to the appropriate fields to key-enter the corrections. After making the corrections, select *End Input* again.

Print the payroll setup form that is on the screen if instructed by your teacher.

STEP 9   Select *Analyze*. Review the information presented.

STEP 10   Select *Review*. Any errors will be highlighted. Print the payroll setup form if instructed by your teacher.

STEP 11   Select *Done*.

STEP 12   You may generate a report of your performance in this activity. To do so,

- From the *File* menu, select *Open Report* and select *Activity 6 Payroll Records*.

- Select *Payroll Setup Form*.

- Select *Get Report*.

- From the *File* menu, select *Print*.

- Select *Print* again.

- Select *Done*.

✍ **Note: In a real work situation, you would strive for completely accurate records. Therefore, it is suggested that once you have completed all of the steps listed here, you should go back into the records and correct any errors. To do this:**

- From the *Activities* menu, select *Activity 6 Payroll Records*.

- Select *Payroll Setup Form*.

- Select *Open*.

- **Use the appropriate keys to locate the proper record and field and then key-enter the correction.**
- **Select *End Input*.**
- **Select *Analyze*.**
- **Select *Review*.**
- **Select *Done*.**
- **Print the payroll setup form if instructed by your teacher.**

COMPLETE PAYROLL UPDATE FORM

STEP 1   Remove the payroll update form for Merrimac Industries, Inc., that is located at the end of this activity.

STEP 2   From the *Activities* menu, select *Activity 6 Payroll Records*.

STEP 3   Select *Payroll Update Form*.

STEP 4   All of the correct data will appear on the screen. You must use the return, enter, or tab key to move to the first field that you wish to edit.

> ✍ **Note: The employee numbers will not be changed during this exercise. They are listed for your reference only.**

STEP 5   Key-enter the remaining records.

> ✍ **Note: If you are interrupted before key-entering all of the records, follow the necessary procedures to end your input and to begin the next session. Refer to the detailed instructions for this procedure in Activity 4, if necessary.**

STEP 6   After key-entering the ten payroll update records, select *End Input*. If you notice errors after you have selected End Input, select *Edit* and then move to the appropriate fields to key-enter the corrections. After making the corrections, select *End Input* again.

Print the update form that is on the screen if instructed by your teacher.

STEP 7   Select *Analyze*. Review the information presented.

STEP 8   Select *Review*. Any errors will be highlighted. Print the payroll setup form if instructed by your teacher.

STEP 9   Select *Done*.

→

STEP 11   You may generate a report of your performance in this activity. To do so,

- From the *File* menu, select *Open Report.*

- From the *Activities* menu, *Activity 6 Payroll Records.*

- Select *Payroll Update Form.*

- Select Get Report.

- From the File menu, select Print.

- Select Print again.

- Select Done.

Note: In a real work situation, you would strive for completely accurate records. Therefore, it is suggested that once you have completed all of the steps listed here, you should go back into the records and correct any errors. To do this:

- **From the Activities menu, select *Activity 6 Payroll Records.***

- **Select *Payroll Update Form.***

- **Select *Open.***

- **Use the appropriate keys to locate the proper record and field and then key-enter the correction.**

- **Select *End Input.***

- **Select *Analyze.***

- **Select *Review.***

- **Select *Done.***

- **Print the payroll update form that is on the screen if instructed by your teacher.**

VOCABULARY

commission
deductions
gross pay
hourly
net pay
overtime hours
pay period
payroll
regular hours
salary

Activity 6 Study Guide

PAYROLL RECORDS

PART 1

➥ **Match the vocabulary terms with the best definitions. Write the letter of the term in the space to the left of the definition. You will not use every vocabulary term.**

A. **commission**
B. **deductions**
C. **gross pay**

D. **hourly**
E. **net pay**
F. **overtime rate**

G. **payroll**
H. **regular hours**
I. **salary**

_____ 1. This pay type is a fixed amount paid to an employee each pay period.

_____ 2. Employees classified as this pay type are paid a certain rate for each hour worked.

_____ 3. The company pays this total amount to all of its employees in a pay period.

_____ 4. This pay rate is often called "time and a half."

_____ 5. This amount is paid to the employee after deductions are subtracted from gross pay.

_____ 6. This amount is calculated by multiplying total sales by a percentage.

_____ 7. These amounts are withheld from an employee's gross pay.

Each of the following statements is either true or false. Indicate your choice by circling T for a true statement or F for a false statement.

T   F   **1.** Net pay and gross pay mean the same thing.

T   F   **2.** Taxes are usually added to gross pay to calculate total earnings.

T   F   **3.** Payroll is the total amount of pay an employee receives in a year.

T   F   **4.** A pay period can be any one of several varying lengths of time.

T   F   **5.** The amount of pay after all deductions have been subtracted is called gross pay.

T   F   **6.** A social security number is used for identification purposes in the working world.

T   F   **7.** Salaried workers often receive overtime pay for the extra hours they work in a pay period.

T   F   **8.** The method used to compute an employee's total earning depends on the employee's pay type.

Briefly answer each of the following items. Write your answers on the lines provided.

1. Define gross pay.

_____

_____

2. Define hourly pay.

_____

_____

3. Define pay period.

_____

_____

4. Explain how overtime hours are usually calculated.

_____

_____

5. Explain how a commission is calculated.

_____

_____

_____

☞ **Remove the Activity 6 Study Guide from your text-workbook and hand it to your instructor for correcting.**

Total Points Possible	37
(Minus) Incorrect Points	_____
Total Points Earned	_____
Percent Correct	_____
Grade	_____

Merrimac Industries, Inc.   **Payroll Setup Form**

EMPLOYEE NUMBER: 16408

NAME (LAST, FIRST): Caldwell   Donald

STREET ADDRESS: 4854 Gibson Ave.

CITY: St. Louis   STATE: MO   ZIP: 63110-4800

SSN: 337-26-5864   MARITAL STATUS: M   DEPENDENTS: 3

PAY TYPE: 3   HOURLY RATE: $ _____   SALARY: $ 437.50   COMMISSION: 5

HEALTH INSURANCE: $ 49.63   PENSION: $ 35.00

PAY TYPE CODE: HOURLY = 1   SALARY = 2   COMMISSION + SALARY = 3

Merrimac Industries, Inc.   **Payroll Setup Form**

EMPLOYEE NUMBER: 18629

NAME (LAST, FIRST): Jasinski   Thomas

STREET ADDRESS: 1356 Creston Ave.

CITY: St. Louis   STATE: MO   ZIP: 63121-1350

SSN: 768-69-8462   MARITAL STATUS: S   DEPENDENTS: 1

PAY TYPE: 2   HOURLY RATE: $ _____   SALARY: $ 400.00   COMMISSION: _____

HEALTH INSURANCE: $ 21.27   PENSION: $ 32.00

PAY TYPE CODE: HOURLY = 1   SALARY = 2   COMMISSION + SALARY = 3

Merrimac Industries, Inc.   **Payroll Setup Form**

EMPLOYEE NUMBER: 73115

NAME (LAST, FIRST): Osborne   Susan

STREET ADDRESS: 3760 Fillmore Ave.

CITY: St. Louis   STATE: MO   ZIP: 63116-3610

SSN: 390-98-3608   MARITAL STATUS: S   DEPENDENTS: 2

PAY TYPE: 1   HOURLY RATE: $ 5.75   SALARY: $ _____   COMMISSION: _____

HEALTH INSURANCE: $ 49.63   PENSION: $ 18.40

PAY TYPE CODE: HOURLY = 1   SALARY = 2   COMMISSION + SALARY = 3

Merrimac Industries, Inc.

Payroll Setup Form

EMPLOYEE NUMBER: 57491

NAME (LAST, FIRST): Juarez   Maria

STREET ADDRESS: 650 Derhake Rd.

CITY: Florissant   STATE: MO   ZIP: 63033-1580

SSN: 725-05-9226   MARITAL STATUS: M   DEPENDENTS: 2

PAY TYPE: 2   HOURLY RATE: $ SALARY: $ 656.25   COMMISSION:

HEALTH INSURANCE: $ 49.63   PENSION: $ 52.50

PAY TYPE CODE: HOURLY = 1   SALARY = 2   COMMISSION + SALARY = 3

Merrimac Industries, Inc.

Payroll Setup Form

EMPLOYEE NUMBER: 30405

NAME (LAST, FIRST): Amato   Paul

STREET ADDRESS: 201 Robin Dr.

CITY: St. Charles   STATE: MO   ZIP: 63301-2100

SSN: 231-07-6027   MARITAL STATUS: M   DEPENDENTS: 4

PAY TYPE: 3   HOURLY RATE: $ SALARY: $ 468.75   COMMISSION: 6

HEALTH INSURANCE: $ 49.63   PENSION: $ 37.50

PAY TYPE CODE: HOURLY = 1   SALARY = 2   COMMISSION + SALARY = 3

Merrimac Industries, Inc.

Payroll Setup Form

EMPLOYEE NUMBER: 16631

NAME (LAST, FIRST): Stefanelli   Irene

STREET ADDRESS: 840 Kempton Dr.

CITY: St. Charles   STATE: MO   ZIP: 63301-2000

SSN: 058-22-4676   MARITAL STATUS: S   DEPENDENTS: 1

PAY TYPE: 2   HOURLY RATE: $ SALARY: $ 568.50   COMMISSION:

HEALTH INSURANCE: $ 21.27   PENSION: $ 30.00

PAY TYPE CODE: HOURLY = 1   SALARY = 2   COMMISSION + SALARY = 3

Merrimac Industries, Inc.

Payroll Setup Form

EMPLOYEE NUMBER: 96773

NAME (LAST, FIRST): Krislov   Anne

STREET ADDRESS: 842 Gerald Dr.

CITY: Sappington   STATE: MO   ZIP: 63426-8430

SSN: 442-94-0767   MARITAL STATUS: S   DEPENDENTS: 2

PAY TYPE: 1   HOURLY RATE: $ 6.25   SALARY: $ _____   COMMISSION: _____

HEALTH INSURANCE: $ 49.63   PENSION: $ 20.00

PAY TYPE CODE: HOURLY = 1   SALARY = 2   COMMISSION + SALARY = 3

Merrimac Industries, Inc.

Payroll Setup Form

EMPLOYEE NUMBER: 38935

NAME (LAST, FIRST): Ching   Charles

STREET ADDRESS: 1734 Potomac Ave.

CITY: St. Louis   STATE: MO   ZIP: 63123-6414

SSN: 397-37-4275   MARITAL STATUS: S   DEPENDENTS: 1

PAY TYPE: 1   HOURLY RATE: $ 5.95   SALARY: $ _____   COMMISSION: _____

HEALTH INSURANCE: $ 21.27   PENSION: $ 19.04

PAY TYPE CODE: HOURLY = 1   SALARY = 2   COMMISSION + SALARY = 3

Merrimac Industries, Inc.

Payroll Setup Form

EMPLOYEE NUMBER: 31624

NAME (LAST, FIRST): Hollingsworth   Martin

STREET ADDRESS: 4621 Rosa Ave.

CITY: St. Louis   STATE: MO   ZIP: 63116-2700

SSN: 489-68-7053   MARITAL STATUS: M   DEPENDENTS: 2

PAY TYPE: 2   HOURLY RATE: $ _____   SALARY: $ 487.50   COMMISSION: _____

HEALTH INSURANCE: $ 49.63   PENSION: $ 39.00

PAY TYPE CODE: HOURLY = 1   SALARY = 2   COMMISSION + SALARY = 3

Merrimac Industries, Inc.   Payroll Setup Form

EMPLOYEE NUMBER: 78919

NAME (LAST, FIRST): Mitchell   Yolanda

STREET ADDRESS: 5465 Vernon Ave.

CITY: St. Louis   STATE: MO   ZIP: 63112-7630

SSN: 848-64-6495   MARITAL STATUS: M   DEPENDENTS: 4

PAY TYPE: 1   HOURLY RATE: $ 7.00   SALARY: $ _____   COMMISSION: _____

HEALTH INSURANCE: $ 49.63   PENSION: $ 22.40

PAY TYPE CODE: HOURLY = 1   SALARY = 2   COMMISSION + SALARY = 3

Merrimac Industries, Inc.   Payroll Setup Form

EMPLOYEE NUMBER: 03931

NAME (LAST, FIRST): Stein   Charlene

STREET ADDRESS: 1274 Kettridge Ct.

CITY: Manchester   STATE: MO   ZIP: 63511-1420

SSN: 384-04-9431   MARITAL STATUS: M   DEPENDENTS: 3

PAY TYPE: 3   HOURLY RATE: $ _____   SALARY: $ 487.50   COMMISSION: 6

HEALTH INSURANCE: $ 49.65   PENSION: $ 31.00

PAY TYPE CODE: HOURLY = 1   SALARY = 2   COMMISSION + SALARY = 3

Merrimac Industries, Inc.   Payroll Setup Form

EMPLOYEE NUMBER: 74426

NAME (LAST, FIRST): Vickers   Gary

STREET ADDRESS: 7550 Winfield Ter.

CITY: Overland   STATE: MO   ZIP: 63614-3714

SSN: 654-02-1658   MARITAL STATUS: M   DEPENDENTS: 4

PAY TYPE: 2   HOURLY RATE: $ _____   SALARY: $ 537.50   COMMISSION: _____

HEALTH INSURANCE: $ 49.63   PENSION: $ 43.00

PAY TYPE CODE: HOURLY = 1   SALARY = 2   COMMISSION + SALARY = 3

Merrimac Industries, Inc.   **Payroll Setup Form**

EMPLOYEE NUMBER: 09033

NAME (LAST, FIRST): Ibarra   David

STREET ADDRESS: 716 Geyer Ave.

CITY: St. Louis   STATE: MO   ZIP: 63104-0716

SSN: 0105-57-904   MARITAL STATUS: S   DEPENDENTS: 1

PAY TYPE: 1   HOURLY RATE: $ 6.95   SALARY: $ COMMISSION:

HEALTH INSURANCE: $ 21.27   PENSION: $ 22.24

PAY TYPE CODE: HOURLY = 1   SALARY = 2   COMMISSION + SALARY = 3

Merrimac Industries, Inc.   **Payroll Setup Form**

EMPLOYEE NUMBER: 16153

NAME (LAST, FIRST): Newman   William

STREET ADDRESS: 1470 Ashby Rd.

CITY: Overland   STATE: MO   ZIP: 63614-7040

SSN: 970-25-6649   MARITAL STATUS: M   DEPENDENTS: 3

PAY TYPE: 2   HOURLY RATE: $ SALARY: $ 475.00   COMMISSION:

HEALTH INSURANCE: $ 49.63   PENSION: $ 38.00

PAY TYPE CODE: HOURLY = 1   SALARY = 2   COMMISSION + SALARY = 3

Merrimac Industries, Inc.   **Payroll Setup Form**

EMPLOYEE NUMBER: 21457

NAME (LAST, FIRST): Tomlinson   Michael

STREET ADDRESS: 76 Brittany Cir.

CITY: Hazelwood   STATE: MO   ZIP: 63744-0076

SSN: 5617-70-404   MARITAL STATUS: S   DEPENDENTS: 1

PAY TYPE: 1   HOURLY RATE: $ 5.25   SALARY: $ COMMISSION:

HEALTH INSURANCE: $ 21.27   PENSION: $ 16.80

PAY TYPE CODE: HOURLY = 1   SALARY = 2   COMMISSION + SALARY = 3

Merrimac Industries, Inc.   Payroll Setup Form

EMPLOYEE NUMBER: 21581

NAME (LAST, FIRST): Eagleman   James

STREET ADDRESS: 1016 Bissell St.

CITY: St. Louis   STATE: MO   ZIP: 63107-1070

SSN: 803-12-4802   MARITAL STATUS: M   DEPENDENTS: 2

PAY TYPE: 1   HOURLY RATE: $ 6.15   SALARY: $ _____   COMMISSION: _____

HEALTH INSURANCE: $ 49.63   PENSION: $ 19.68

PAY TYPE CODE: HOURLY = 1   SALARY = 2   COMMISSION + SALARY = 3

Merrimac Industries, Inc.   Payroll Setup Form

EMPLOYEE NUMBER: 55612

NAME (LAST, FIRST): Ballentie   Leslie

STREET ADDRESS: 613 Bromfield Ter.

CITY: Manchester   STATE: MO   ZIP: 63511-6013

SSN: 264-08-4359   MARITAL STATUS: M   DEPENDENTS: 3

PAY TYPE: 3   HOURLY RATE: $ _____   SALARY: $ 456.05   COMMISSION: 5

HEALTH INSURANCE: $ 49.63   PENSION: $ 36.50

PAY TYPE CODE: HOURLY = 1   SALARY = 2   COMMISSION + SALARY = 3

Merrimac Industries, Inc.   Payroll Setup Form

EMPLOYEE NUMBER: 44657

NAME (LAST, FIRST): Levine   Debra

STREET ADDRESS: 1215 Osage St.

CITY: St. Louis   STATE: MO   ZIP: 63118-1200

SSN: 435-91-7552   MARITAL STATUS: S   DEPENDENTS: 1

PAY TYPE: 2   HOURLY RATE: $ _____   SALARY: $ 375.00   COMMISSION: _____

HEALTH INSURANCE: $ 21.27   PENSION: $ 30.00

PAY TYPE CODE: HOURLY = 1   SALARY = 2   COMMISSION + SALARY = 3

Merrimac Industries, Inc.

Payroll Setup Form

EMPLOYEE NUMBER: 91340

NAME (LAST, FIRST): Johnson   Barbara

STREET ADDRESS: 3470 Rowles Ave.

CITY: Ferguson   STATE: MO   ZIP: 63835-3040

SSN: 653-41-4904   MARITAL STATUS: S   DEPENDENTS: 1

PAY TYPE: 1   HOURLY RATE: $ 6.95   SALARY: $ _____   COMMISSION: _____

HEALTH INSURANCE: $ 21.27   PENSION: $ 22.24

PAY TYPE CODE: HOURLY = 1   SALARY = 2   COMMISSION + SALARY = 3

Merrimac Industries, Inc.

Payroll Setup Form

EMPLOYEE NUMBER: 91227

NAME (LAST, FIRST): Gunderson   Keith

STREET ADDRESS: 716 Ridgewood Rd.

CITY: Kirkwood   STATE: MO   ZIP: 63922-7071

SSN: 964-95-8125   MARITAL STATUS: S   DEPENDENTS: 1

PAY TYPE: 1   HOURLY RATE: $ 5.65   SALARY: $ _____   COMMISSION: _____

HEALTH INSURANCE: $ 21.27   PENSION: $ 18.08

PAY TYPE CODE: HOURLY = 1   SALARY = 2   COMMISSION + SALARY = 3

Merrimac Industries, Inc.

Payroll Setup Form

EMPLOYEE NUMBER: 42238

NAME (LAST, FIRST): Brown   Donna

STREET ADDRESS: 156 Foxcrest Dr.

CITY: Hazelwood   STATE: MO   ZIP: 63742-1560

SSN: 193-08-8362   MARITAL STATUS: M   DEPENDENTS: 2

PAY TYPE: 1   HOURLY RATE: $ 7.15   SALARY: $ _____   COMMISSION: _____

HEALTH INSURANCE: $ 49.63   PENSION: $ 22.88

PAY TYPE CODE: HOURLY = 1   SALARY = 2   COMMISSION + SALARY = 3

Merrimac Industries, Inc.
Payroll Update Form

EMP. NO.	LAST NAME	FIRST NAME	STREET ADDRESS	CITY	STATE	ZIP	SS #	MAR. STAT.	DEP.	PAY TYPE	HOUR RATE	SAL.	COMM.	HEALTH INSUR.	PENSION
91340	Mulligan		8630 Derby Pl.	Florissant		63033-6030		M							
74426												580.00			46.40
21457										2	0	375.22			30.00
18629			68 Leisurewood Dr.	Florissant		63033-0068		M							
30405									5						
38935											6.35				20.32
09053								M	2		9.95			49.63	31.84
44657												400.00			32.00
31624			440 Deandell Ave.			63135-1440		S							
73115											7.00				22.40

Quiz 2

PART 1

(2 POINTS EACH)

Match the vocabulary terms with the best definitions. Write the letter of the term in the space to the left of the definition. You will not use every vocabulary term.

A. **accounts payable ledger**
B. **accounts receivable ledger**
C. **commission**
D. **deductions**
E. **gross pay**
F. **hourly pay**
G. **invoice number**
H. **net pay**
I. **overtime rate**
J. **pay period**
K. **payroll**
L. **statement**
M. **vendors**

_____ **1.** The company pays this total amount to all of its employees in a pay period.

_____ **2.** This pay rate is often called "time and a half."

_____ **3.** This amount is paid to the employees after deductions are subtracted.

_____ **4.** An alphabetic listing of a company's creditors and the amount owed to each creditor.

_____ **5.** These companies sell merchandise that is often purchased on account.

_____ **6.** This unique identifying number distinguishes one invoice from another.

_____ **7.** This form shows all items purchased, the amount of all payments, and the total amount due.

_____ **8.** The length of time covered for the payment of wages.

_____ **9.** A certain rate paid to an employee for each hour worked.

_____ **10.** The total amount of pay due to an individual employee before any deductions are subtracted.

_____ **11.** This record of all customers and the amount they owe is arranged alphabetically.

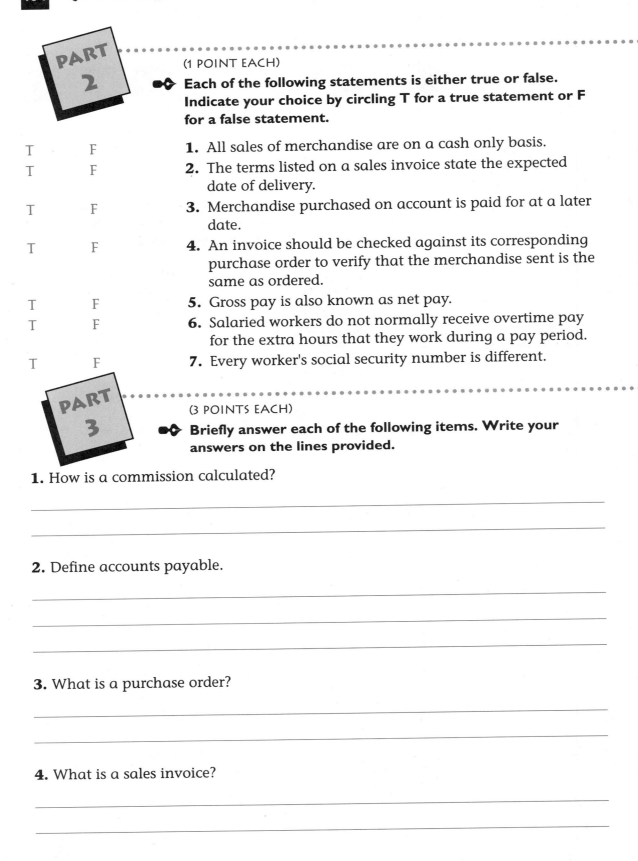

PART 2

(1 POINT EACH)

➥ **Each of the following statements is either true or false. Indicate your choice by circling T for a true statement or F for a false statement.**

T   F   **1.** All sales of merchandise are on a cash only basis.

T   F   **2.** The terms listed on a sales invoice state the expected date of delivery.

T   F   **3.** Merchandise purchased on account is paid for at a later date.

T   F   **4.** An invoice should be checked against its corresponding purchase order to verify that the merchandise sent is the same as ordered.

T   F   **5.** Gross pay is also known as net pay.

T   F   **6.** Salaried workers do not normally receive overtime pay for the extra hours that they work during a pay period.

T   F   **7.** Every worker's social security number is different.

PART 3

(3 POINTS EACH)

➥ **Briefly answer each of the following items. Write your answers on the lines provided.**

1. How is a commission calculated?

_____

_____

2. Define accounts payable.

_____

_____

_____

3. What is a purchase order?

_____

_____

4. What is a sales invoice?

_____

_____

5. What is a cash sale?

_____

_____

6. Define deductions.

_____

_____

7. Define sale on account.

_____

_____

☞ **Remove Quiz 2 from your text-workbook and hand it to your instructor for correcting.**

Total Points Possible	50
(Minus) Incorrect Points	_____
Total Points Earned	_____
Percent Correct	_____
Grade	_____

Activity 7

CENSUS SURVEY

1 Show how often a complete U.S. census is taken.
2 Define the term census.
3 Identify the primary reason for taking a census.
4 Name the title of the government department that administers the census.
5 List four pieces of data collected by the census survey.
6 Describe the general activities involved in gathering and tallying census information.
7 List three different types of jobs available through the Bureau of the Census.
8 Key-enter data for a census survey.

DATA ENTRY APPLICATION AND JOB DESCRIPTION

*T*he Constitution of the United States calls for a population census to be taken every ten years. The first census in the United States was conducted in 1790. In 1902 the U.S. Bureau of the Census was established. A census of the U.S. population attempts to count everyone in the country at a specific time. This self-portrait is one of our nation's most vital documents. A **census** is a population survey that is conducted by the government. This survey attempts to contact every household in the country and to gather information on every individual in that household. The original purpose of the census was to divide the seats in the United States House of Representatives fairly among the states, based on the population. This purpose remains as one of the major reasons the census is taken today. In addition, the census provides other valuable information concerning the people of the United States.

The population census is not the only census taken. In fact, every five years, economic, agriculture, and government censuses are conducted. These censuses provide additional data pertaining to each of these areas. In order to update the large amount of data between censuses, the government also conducts sample **surveys**—questionnaires given to only a portion of the entire population. These surveys help government officials detect any major changes in the general population. This data collection is monitored by the **Bureau of the Census**, which is an agency of the federal government under the control of the **U.S. Department of Commerce.**

HOW CENSUS DATA IS COLLECTED AND TALLIED

Questionnaires containing questions about age, birthplace, sex, race, income, education, and occupation are used to collect the census data. A census questionnaire is shown in Figure 7.1. These questionnaires are carefully designed so that they are complete and easy to understand. Census workers collect the majority of the data by mail. Questionnaires are mailed to all households or businesses and the recipients are asked to complete and return them. Data can also be collected by phone. Some households are asked for additional information as a sample of the total population. To supplement the questionnaire, trained census workers are sent out to interview people directly. Records must be kept on each household or business completing the questionnaire so that the Bureau of the Census can ensure that data is collected on everyone.

The Census Bureau must compile a mailing list of the 110 million housing units in America. The Bureau did this job with the help of the Postal Service and mailing lists from magazines and other private organizations. In rural areas, the bureau had to create its own. Nearly 30,000 bureau employees will walk or drive to every household to double-check each address. If all else fails and if census workers have clear evidence that someone lives at an address, the bureau will estimate how many people on average live in a housing unit. Nine months later (from Census Day) the Census Bureau must deliver the final figures to the President to be used in reapportioning congressional representation to reflect population shifts. The bureau must deliver the figures—divided by block and street—to every state so they can begin redrawing the legislative districts.

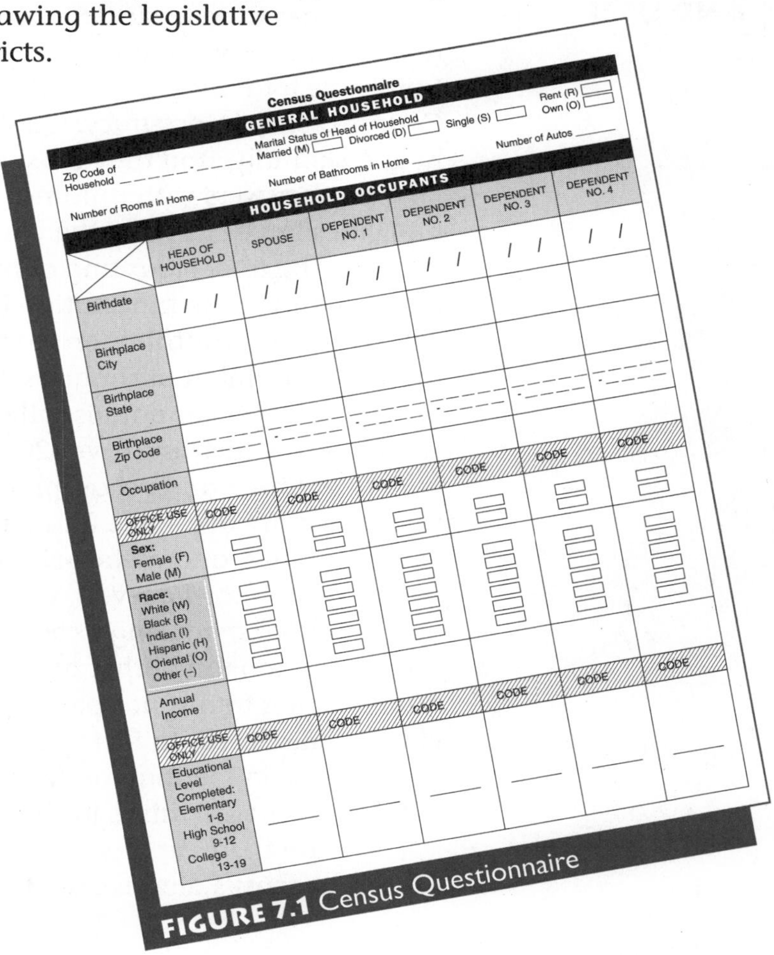

FIGURE 7.1 Census Questionnaire

As the completed questionnaires are returned, the data is tallied. This process involves recording millions of pieces of information. During the 1890 census, a punchcard system and other mechanical tabulating equipment were first used. This equipment greatly increased the speed with which the census results could be published. Today, electronic equipment, such as computers, are a major component of the data processing system operated by the Bureau of the Census. Computers are not only used to tally the data, but are also used to keep lists of addresses of each household or business. By using the computer, the Bureau of the Census can keep track of which households and businesses have responded to the census and thus control the quality of the data collected.

HOW CENSUS DATA IS PUBLISHED AND USED

Census data is used in several ways by the government, its agencies, and by business firms. The data is used in market research, forecasting trends in employment, labor resources, educational requirements, and demands for public services. Data ranges from basic data on the growth, age, and location of a country's population to the composition of the family, its total income, and the standard of living. Censuses vary in accuracy. Questions must be asked tactfully and skillfully, and they must be worded in order to elicit objective answers with minimal room for error. Many states and cities have criticized the U.S. for **undercounting,** particularly the undercounting of minorities and illegal/legal aliens living in the inner cities. Undercounting affects the level of federal contributions to welfare programs as well as the apportionment of congressional representation.

Once the census data is tallied, the Bureau of the Census combines the facts into over 200 reports covering a wide variety of topics and geographic areas. For example, housing reports are available for regions of the country, states, counties, cities, and metropolitan areas. Similar reports are available for income levels, types of occupations, occupational outlooks, housing expenses, unemployment, age of the population, and other areas. Census reports only list numbers and totals; no specific information about an individual is disclosed. In fact, information about each individual is kept confidential for 72 years and is then given only to the National Archives for historical use.

How are these reports used? There are thousands of ways that census data is used by businesses and government agencies. The following examples have been provided by the Bureau of the Census.

- During a heat wave, public health officials in St. Louis used census data to locate neighborhoods with large numbers of the elderly. City workers saved lives by going door-to-door convincing many of the elderly to go to "cooling centers."
- Census data in a midwest city revealed a high number of working mothers with small children in a low-income neighborhood. This information helped community leaders organize a day care center there.
- In San Francisco, transportation planners used census information to select bus routes, subway stops, and highways that needed widening.

JOB OPPOR- TUNITIES WITH THE BUREAU OF THE CENSUS	Gathering data about every individual and every business in the United States requires thousands of workers. Jobs are available in many different areas and at many different levels. Employees are needed to design questionnaires, collect the data, key-enter the data into the computer system, compile the data into reports, and publish the reports. Computer specialists play an important role in all of these activities.

- -

INPUT FIELDS

*I*n this activity you will enter the data from the source document (census questionnaires) for five families. Information from census questionnaires is key-entered into input fields on the data entry screen. The input fields for this activity can be grouped into two categories: fields relating to the household and fields relating to individuals within each household. These two categories, along with their corresponding input fields, are described below and on the following page.

HOUSEHOLD FIELDS	**ZIP Code.** This field is nine characters in length and contains sufficient space for the extended ZIP code for each household. Do not enter the hyphen between the two groups of digits.

Marital Status. This field is one character in length. Key-enter only one letter in this field, M for married, D for divorced, or S for single.

Rent or Own Home. This field is one character in length. Key-enter the letter R if the family rents or the letter O if the family owns a home. This information is used to determine what percentage of Americans own homes and what percentage rent their living quarters.

Number Of Rooms In Home. This field is a maximum of two characters in length and contains the number of rooms in the home.

Number Of Bathrooms. This field is a maximum of two characters in length and contains the number of bathrooms in the home.

Number Of Autos. This field is one character in length and contains the total number of autos for a household.

Birthdate. This field is six characters in length and contains the month, the day, and the year of birth for each individual.

Birthplace City. This field is a maximum of ten characters in length and contains the name of the city of birth for each individual.

Birthplace State. This field is two characters in length and contains the two-letter abbreviation of the state of birth for each individual.

Birthplace ZIP Code. This field is nine characters in length and contains the extended ZIP code (no hyphen) of the city of birth for each individual.

Occupation. This field is two characters in length and contains the code that represents a specific occupation. A list of occupations and corresponding codes is provided in the next section. You must determine the proper occupational code for each individual and key-enter it into the computer.

Sex. This field is one character in length and contains either an F or an M to indicate female or male.

Race. This field is one character in length and contains the appropriate abbreviation for the racial origin of each individual.

Income Range. This field is two characters in length and contains the code that represents the income range for each individual. The income ranges and corresponding codes are provided in the next section. You must determine the proper income code for each individual and key-enter it into the computer.

Education. This field is two characters in length and contains the number of years of education each individual has had. For example, if a person has completed four years of college, you would key-enter a 16 (12 years of high school plus four years of college).

Step-by-Step Instructions

GET READY

Follow the start-up procedures for your computer that are found in Appendix A.

COMPLETE ALPHA-NUMERIC DEXTERITY DRILL

```
80451 7287 DENVER 80204 3949 CO 58000 15
06001 834 061441 STANFORD CT 2281 687736
12 CONSTRUCTION 06783 14 09 61 38000 438
WILMINGTON 9 1628 061146 198050996 19958
050442 ATLANTA 30320 GA 14240 SAVANNAH 2
```

STEP 1   From the *Activities* menu, select *Activity 7 Census Questionnaire.*

STEP 2   Select *Alpha-Numeric Dexterity Drill.*

STEP 3   Enter the data for each line. Press *enter* or *return* at the end of each line.

STEP 4   Select *OK* when you are finished key-entering. Review your score.

STEP 5   Select *Review* to review any errors that were made. After reviewing your performance, select *OK.*

Repeat the Alpha-Numeric Dexterity Drill as many times as instructed by your teacher.

COMPLETE KEYPAD DEXTERITY DRILL

```
63813  90114  30379  41137  77501  17549  2117
28382  69200  16498  01560  25250  04475  8266
92817  32736  98000  15432  00646  28962  1959
01777  49175  11512  60021  69256  54569  5661
94412  82238  96001  91648  20759  01838  2094
```

STEP 1   From the *Activities* menu, select *Activity 7 Census Questionnaire.*

STEP 2   Select *Keypad Dexterity Drill.*

STEP 3   Enter the data for each line. Press *enter* or *return* at the end of each line.

STEP 4   Select *OK* when you are finished key-entering. Review your score.

STEP 5   Select *Review* to review any errors that were made. After reviewing your performance, select *OK.*

Repeat the Keypad Dexterity Drill as many times as instructed by your teacher.

COMPLETE CENSUS QUESTIONNAIRE FORMS

STEP 1   Remove the Census Questionnaires that are located at the end of this activity.

STEP 2   From the *Activities* menu, select *Activity 7 Census Questionnaire.*

STEP 3   Select *Census Form.* The display on the screen will be similar to that shown in figure 7.2.

FIGURE 7.2

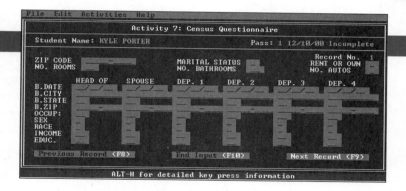

STEP 4 Key-enter the data that is relevant to everyone on the form, including the ZIP Code of Household, Marital Status of Head of Household, Rent or Own, Number of Rooms, Number of Bathrooms, and Number of Autos.

STEP 5 Key-enter the data for each individual in the household. You will need to determine the proper occupation and income codes for each person in the household based on the following tables.

OCCUPATION CODES

Occupation	Code	Occupation	Code
Accountant	16	Homemaker	30
Artist	14	Janitor	38
Bus driver	91	Laborer	37
Clerk typist	20	Maid	32
Construction	86	Nurse	06
Cosmetologist	33	Sales clerk	29
Dental	07	Secretary	20
Engineer	03	Teacher	09
Food service	52	Truck driver	90
Gas station	93	Unemployed	99

INCOME CODES

At least	But not more than	Code
0	4,999	01
5,000	9,999	02
10,000	14,999	03
15,000	19,999	04
20,000	29,999	05
30,000	39,999	06
40,000	49,999	07
50,000	74,999	08
75,000	99,999	09
	Over 100,000	99

STEP 6   Once you have finished entering all of the data on a form, select *Next Record* to key-enter the remaining records of the activity.

✍ **Note: If you are interrupted before key-entering all of the records, follow the necessary procedure to end your input and to begin the next session. Refer to the detailed instructions for this procedure in Activity 4, if necessary.**

STEP 7   After key-entering all of the Census Questionnaire forms, select *End Input*. If you notice errors after you have selected End Input, select *Edit* and then move to the appropriate fields to key-enter the corrections. After making the corrections, select *End Input*.

STEP 8   Print the census questionnaires if instructed by your teacher. To do this, from the *File* menu, select *Print*.

STEP 9   Select *Analyze* and review the information presented.

STEP 10   Select *Review*. Any errors will be highlighted.

STEP 11   Select *Done*.

STEP 12   You may generate a report of your performance in this activity. You may refer to the directions in Activity 6 if necessary.

✍ **Note: In a real work situation, you would strive for completely accurate records. Therefore, it is suggested that once you have completed all of the steps listed here, you should go back into the records and correct any errors.**

To do this:

- **From the *Activities* menu, select *Activity 7 Census Questionnaire*.**
- **Select *Census Form*.**
- **Select *Open*.**
- **Use the appropriate keys to locate the proper record and field and then key-enter the correction.**
- **Select *End Input*.**
- **Select *Analyze*.**
- **Select *Review*.**
- **Select *Done*.**
- **Print the census questionnaire forms if instructed by your teacher.**

VOCABULARY

Bureau of the Census
census
surveys
undercounting
U.S. Department of Commerce

Activity 7 Study Guide

CENSUS SURVEY

PART 1

OBJECTIVES 1, 3, AND 4 (2 POINTS EACH)

Match the vocabulary terms with the best definitions. Write the letter of the term in the space to the left of the definition.

A. **census**
B. **sample survey**
C. **undercounting**

D. **U.S. Department of Commerce**

E. **U.S. House of Representatives**

_____ 1. May cause the level of federal contributions to welfare programs as well as the apportionment of congressional representation to decrease.

_____ 2. The Bureau of Census is an agency of the federal government under the control of this government body.

_____ 3. Used to update the large amount of data between censuses.

_____ 4. The population survey of the United States that must be taken every ten years.

_____ 5. The original purpose of the census was to divide the seats in this government body.

PART 2

OBJECTIVES 2, 5, AND 6 (1 POINT EACH)

Each of the following statements is either true or false. Indicate your choice by circling **T** for a true statement or **F** for a false statement.

T   F   1. A complete census is taken every five years.

T   F   2. Every household is not contacted during the taking of the census.

T   F   3. To update the data, the government usually takes or conducts sample surveys.

T   F   4. The Department of Commerce is the agency having control over the Bureau of the Census.

T	F	**5.** The primary reason for taking a census is to see where people are living for the purpose of assigning seats in the House of Representatives.
T	F	**6.** Someone must take the responsibility to fill out the questionnaire.
T	F	**7.** The Bureau of Census cannot determine the number of people in a household from a complete questionnaire.
T	F	**8.** Some of the ways the data from the census is helpful is by using the information in such a way that allows community leaders to organize and select transportation routes.
T	F	**9.** The U. S. Department of Commerce is responsible for gathering census data.
T	F	**10.** Census reports only list numbers and totals, not specific information about an individual is disclosed.

PART 3

OBJECTIVES 2, 5, 6, AND 7 (3 POINTS EACH)

●◆ **Briefly answer each of the following items. Write your answers on the lines provided.**

1. Define the term undercounting.

_____

_____

2. There are many statistics collected by the Census Bureau. List five.

_____

_____

_____

_____

3. Explain the close workmanship between the postal service and the Census Bureau.

_____

_____

4. List three types of jobs related to the Bureau of the Census.

_____

_____

_____

5. List at least two censuses other than the population census that are completed by the Bureau of the Census.

_____

_____

☞ **Remove the Activity 7 Study Guide from your text-workbook and hand it to your instructor for correcting.**

Total Points Possible	35
(Minus) Incorrect Points	_____
Total Points Earned	_____
Percent Correct	_____
Grade	_____

Census Questionnaire

GENERAL HOUSEHOLD

Zip Code of Household __0 6 0 0 1__ - __3 0 5 4__

Marital Status of Head of Household — Married (M) [X]   Divorced (D) [ ]   Single (S) [ ]

Rent (R) [ ]   Own (O) [X]

Number of Rooms in Home __08__   Number of Bathrooms in Home __02__   Number of Autos __4__

HOUSEHOLD OCCUPANTS

	HEAD OF HOUSEHOLD	SPOUSE	DEPENDENT NO. 1	DEPENDENT NO. 2	DEPENDENT NO. 3	DEPENDENT NO. 4
Birthdate	06/14/41	08/20/44	12/09/61	07/05/66	01/03/71	/ /
Birthplace City	Avon	Stanford	New Haven	Waterbury	Hartford	
Birthplace State	CT	CT	CT	CT	CT	
Birthplace Zip Code	06001 -7438	06877 -2281	06467 -3675	06783 -1070	06248 -4877	-
Occupation	Construction	Cosmetologist	Laborer	Truck Driver	Sales Clerk	
OFFICE USE ONLY	CODE	CODE	CODE	CODE	CODE	CODE
Sex: Female (F)		X	X	X	X	
Male (M)	X					
Race: White (W)						
Black (B)	X	X	X	X	X	
Indian (I)						
Hispanic (H)						
Oriental (O)						
Other (–)						
Annual Income	80,000	22,000	38,000	35,000	21,000	
OFFICE USE ONLY	CODE	CODE	CODE	CODE	CODE	CODE
Educational Level Completed: Elementary 1-8 High School 9-12 College 13-19	12	12	19	14	12	

Census Questionnaire

GENERAL HOUSEHOLD

Zip Code of Household **1 9 8 0 5 - 0 9 0 6**

Marital Status of Head of Household
Married (M) **X** Divorced (D) [ ] Single (S) [ ]

Rent (R) **X**
Own (O) [ ]

Number of Rooms in Home **09** Number of Bathrooms in Home **02** Number of Autos **1**

HOUSEHOLD OCCUPANTS

	HEAD OF HOUSEHOLD	SPOUSE	DEPENDENT NO. 1	DEPENDENT NO. 2	DEPENDENT NO. 3	DEPENDENT NO. 4
Birthdate	09/14/53	06/11/56	07/29/74	03/18/77	/ /	/ /
Birthplace City	Wilmington	Dover	Wilmington	Wilmington		
Birthplace State	DE	DE	DE	DE		
Birthplace Zip Code	19805-1628	19958-6136	19804-0828	19804-0070	-_____	-_____
Occupation	Engineer	Unemployed	Food Service	Gas Station		
OFFICE USE ONLY	CODE	CODE	CODE	CODE	CODE	CODE
Sex: Female (F)	X	[ ]	[ ]	[ ]	[ ]	[ ]
Male (M)	[ ]	X	X	X	[ ]	[ ]
Race: White (W)	X	X	X	X	[ ]	[ ]
Black (B)	[ ]	[ ]	[ ]	[ ]	[ ]	[ ]
Indian (I)	[ ]	[ ]	[ ]	[ ]	[ ]	[ ]
Hispanic (H)	[ ]	[ ]	[ ]	[ ]	[ ]	[ ]
Oriental (O)	[ ]	[ ]	[ ]	[ ]	[ ]	[ ]
Other (–)	[ ]	[ ]	[ ]	[ ]	[ ]	[ ]
Annual Income	81,000	1,500	8,000	3,000		
OFFICE USE ONLY	CODE	CODE	CODE	CODE	CODE	CODE
Educational Level Completed: Elementary 1-8 High School 9-12 College 13-19	16	12	13	11		

Census Questionnaire

GENERAL HOUSEHOLD

Zip Code of Household 3 0 3 2 0 - 2 1 8 1

Marital Status of Head of Household
Married (M) [ ] Divorced (D) [X] Single (S) [ ]

Rent (R) [ ]
Own (O) [X]

Number of Rooms in Home __06__   Number of Bathrooms in Home __02__   Number of Autos __2__

HOUSEHOLD OCCUPANTS

	HEAD OF HOUSEHOLD	SPOUSE	DEPENDENT NO. 1	DEPENDENT NO. 2	DEPENDENT NO. 3	DEPENDENT NO. 4
Birthdate	05 /04 /47	/ /	07 /02 /73	05 /03 /76	10 /16 /78	/ /
Birthplace City	Atlanta		Buffalo	Savannah	Columbus	
Birthplace State	GA		NY	GA	GA	
Birthplace Zip Code	3 0 3 2 0 -3 9 6 1	-	1 4 2 4 0 -0 3 1 0	3 1 4 1 8 -0 2 8 3	3 1 8 2 9 -0 4 1 1	-
Occupation	Dentist		Unemployed	Gas Station	Cosmetologist	
OFFICE USE ONLY	CODE	CODE	CODE	CODE	CODE	CODE
Sex: Female (F)	[X]	[ ]	[X]	[ ]	[X]	[ ]
Male (M)	[ ]	[ ]	[ ]	[X]	[ ]	[ ]
Race: White (W)	[ ]	[ ]	[ ]	[ ]	[ ]	[ ]
Black (B)	[ ]	[ ]	[ ]	[ ]	[ ]	[ ]
Indian (I)	[X]	[ ]	[X]	[X]	[X]	[ ]
Hispanic (H)	[ ]	[ ]	[ ]	[ ]	[ ]	[ ]
Oriental (O)	[ ]	[ ]	[ ]	[ ]	[ ]	[ ]
Other (–)	[ ]	[ ]	[ ]	[ ]	[ ]	[ ]
Annual Income	35,000		15,000	6,000	18,000	
OFFICE USE ONLY	CODE	CODE	CODE	CODE	CODE	CODE
Educational Level Completed: Elementary 1-8 High School 9-12 College 13-19	16		15	12	09	

Census Questionnaire

GENERAL HOUSEHOLD

Zip Code of Household __1 9 6 0 6__ - __6 8 2 5__

Marital Status of Head of Household
Married (M) [ ] Divorced (D) [ ] Single (S) [X]

Rent (R) [X]
Own (O) [ ]

Number of Rooms in Home ___04___   Number of Bathrooms in Home ___01___   Number of Autos __2__

HOUSEHOLD OCCUPANTS

	HEAD OF HOUSEHOLD	SPOUSE	DEPENDENT NO. 1	DEPENDENT NO. 2	DEPENDENT NO. 3	DEPENDENT NO. 4
Birthdate	02/ 31 /66	/ /	/ /	/ /	/ /	/ /
Birthplace City	Reading					
Birthplace State	PA					
Birthplace Zip Code	1 9 6 0 6 -5 1 2 2	- _ _ _ _ _	- _ _ _ _ _	- _ _ _ _ _	- _ _ _ _ _	- _ _ _ _ _
Occupation	Accountant					
OFFICE USE ONLY	CODE	CODE	CODE	CODE	CODE	CODE
Sex: Female (F) Male (M)	[ ] [X]	[ ] [ ]	[ ] [ ]	[ ] [ ]	[ ] [ ]	[ ] [ ]
Race: White (W) Black (B) Indian (I) Hispanic (H) Oriental (O) Other (–)	[ ] [ ] [ ] [X] [ ] [ ]	[ ] [ ] [ ] [ ] [ ] [ ]	[ ] [ ] [ ] [ ] [ ] [ ]	[ ] [ ] [ ] [ ] [ ] [ ]	[ ] [ ] [ ] [ ] [ ] [ ]	[ ] [ ] [ ] [ ] [ ] [ ]
Annual Income	73,000					
OFFICE USE ONLY	CODE	CODE	CODE	CODE	CODE	CODE
Educational Level Completed: Elementary 1-8 High School 9-12 College 13-19	16					

Census Questionnaire

GENERAL HOUSEHOLD

Zip Code of Household 0 2 0 5 6 - 9 2 6 4

Marital Status of Head of Household
Married (M) [X]   Divorced (D) [ ]   Single (S) [ ]

Rent (R) [ ]
Own (O) [X]

Number of Rooms in Home __10__   Number of Bathrooms in Home __02__   Number of Autos __2__

HOUSEHOLD OCCUPANTS

	HEAD OF HOUSEHOLD	SPOUSE	DEPENDENT NO. 1	DEPENDENT NO. 2	DEPENDENT NO. 3	DEPENDENT NO. 4
Birthdate	12 / 08 / 51	03 / 04 / 57	07 / 17 / 81	01 / 26 / 84	05 / 25 / 89	08 / 14 / 93
Birthplace City	Boston	Warwick	Lowell	Lynn	Butler	Butler
Birthplace State	MA	RI	MA	MA	PA	PA
Birthplace Zip Code	0 2 0 5 6 -7 7 7 4	0 3 8 8 6 -3 3 1 0	0 1 8 5 0 -8 1 2 0	0 1 9 0 5 -0 0 1 1	1 6 0 0 1 -1 1 5 0	1 6 0 0 1 -1 1 5 0
Occupation	Nurse	Food Service	Unemployed	Unemp.	Unemp.	Unemp.
OFFICE USE ONLY	CODE	CODE	CODE	CODE	CODE	CODE
Sex: Female (F)	[ ]	[X]	[ ]	[ ]	[X]	[ ]
Male (M)	[X]	[ ]	[X]	[X]	[ ]	[X]
Race: White (W)	[X]	[X]	[X]	[X]	[X]	[X]
Black (B)	[ ]	[ ]	[ ]	[ ]	[ ]	[ ]
Indian (I)	[ ]	[ ]	[ ]	[ ]	[ ]	[ ]
Hispanic (H)	[ ]	[ ]	[ ]	[ ]	[ ]	[ ]
Oriental (O)	[ ]	[ ]	[ ]	[ ]	[ ]	[ ]
Other (–)	[ ]	[ ]	[ ]	[ ]	[ ]	[ ]
Annual Income	46,000	22,000	750.00	200.00	0	0
OFFICE USE ONLY	CODE	CODE	CODE	CODE	CODE	CODE
Educational Level Completed: Elementary 1-8 High School 9-12 College 13-19	17	13	07	04	01	00

Activity 8

Auto Insurance Application

193

LEARNING OBJECTIVES

Upon completion of this activity, you will be able to:

→ 1 Define automobile insurance, policyholder, premium, coverage, actuary, deductible, discount, and agent.

2 Explain how insurance works.

3 Explain how and why insurance companies establish actuarial tables.

4 Identify at least three items that affect the premium amount the policyholder pays for auto insurance.

5 Explain the system used to determine the premium.

6 Explain how to obtain auto insurance.

7 List three ways insurance companies use information.

8 Explain how the insurance industry uses data processing.

9 Key-enter data for insurance applications.

● ●

DATA ENTRY APPLICATION AND JOB DESCRIPTION

*M*ost people have formed opinions about automobile insurance. Some look upon automobile insurance as a necessary evil, only tolerated because of the benefits of driving. Others believe that insurance companies offer a real service that is well worth the required payments.

Automobile insurance is protection against financial loss due to some accidental event connected with an automobile. The written agreement between the purchaser and the insurance company is called the **policy.** The person who purchases the insurance policy is called the **policyholder.** When policyholders purchase automobile insurance, they agree to pay a specific amount to the insurance company for this protection. This amount is known as the **premium. Coverage** is the amount and types of protection purchased by the policyholder. Each type of insurance coverage may be purchased at various levels of protection. If you suffer a financial loss that is covered by the policy, the insurance company will pay for the loss up to the level of protection purchased. The insurance company receives money from the premium payments and pays money to policyholders when they suffer a covered loss. The insurance company also increases its revenue by investing the money it receives from the premium payments.

Automobile insurance coverage is required in many states. If people want the privilege of driving an automobile, they must purchase automobile insurance protection. However, many people choose to purchase automobile insurance even when it is not required by state law. These policyholders believe that it is better to pay small amounts over a period of time than to pay a large amount if an accident occurs.

DIFFERENT TYPES OF AUTOMOBILE INSURANCE COVERAGE	Many different types of automobile insurance coverage are available for automobiles. Policyholders may purchase any or all of the various types of automobile insurance. Different levels may be purchased for each type of insurance.

Collision insurance is coverage for an automobile involved in an accident. If policyholders purchase collision insurance and are involved in an accident, their insurance companies will either pay to have the car repaired or will give them the fair market value of the car. Most often collision insurance includes a deductible. A **deductible** is a certain amount that the insurance company will deduct before paying to have the car repaired. The policyholder must pay this deductible. For example, if a policy includes collision insurance with a $250 deductible, the policyholder will pay the first $250 of any damage caused by a collision. If the damage is more than $250, the insurance company will pay for all repairs over $250.

Another type of automobile insurance is comprehensive insurance. **Comprehensive insurance** is coverage for an automobile when it has been damaged, but not as a result of a collision. Some events covered under comprehensive insurance include: a tree falling on a car during a storm, a windshield cracking after being hit by a stone, or hailstones damaging a car. Comprehensive insurance often includes a deductible.

Liability insurance may also be purchased by a policyholder. **Liability insurance** is coverage for policyholders when they are at fault for injuring another person or for damaging another person's property. Bodily injury liability covers those in other cars, those riding in the policyholder's car, and pedestrians. Property damage liability covers damage to the property of others such as cars, light poles, and buildings.

Uninsured motorist insurance covers the policyholder's losses if injured by a driver who does not have insurance coverage. There is also automobile insurance available that covers a policyholder's losses due to injuries when the person is involved in any type of an automobile accident.

HOW RATES ARE ESTABLISHED

How do insurance companies determine how much to charge for insurance coverage? The insurance company must set the premium amount so that more money is received from the premium payments of all policyholders than is paid out to all policyholders who suffer a loss. If the insurance company charges too much, automobile owners will purchase insurance from other companies. If the company charges too little, it may have to pay out more than it collects. Obviously, if this continued for a long period of time, the company would go out of business.

To make sure that the premiums fall somewhere between the two extremes, insurance companies keep accurate records of past losses. An **actuary** is a person who studies an insurance company's past payments to determine what premiums to charge in the future. By studying payment records and statistical data, the actuary can determine how likely it is that certain groups of individuals will have an accident or suffer a loss covered by insurance. For instance, it has been found that smokers have more accidents than non-smokers. Therefore, the insurance company can expect to pay more in losses to policyholders who smoke. Statistics show that young male drivers incur more losses than either females or older male drivers. Actuaries also look at data from individual drivers. The actuary studies the number of traffic tickets received by the policyholder, the number of miles the policyholder drives each day, the type of car that is to be insured, the grade-point average of young drivers, and whether the policyholder has taken a driver's education course.

All of these statistics are combined into what is referred to as actuarial tables. An **actuarial table** shows how likely it is that certain people will suffer an insurance loss. It is based on actual records of accidents. By using these tables, insurance companies can determine how much the premium payment should be for an individual wishing to purchase insurance coverage.

WHY RATES VARY

If policyholders compare their insurance premiums with other insurance premiums, they probably will find a difference. In fact, sometimes the difference can be quite large. For instance, the six-month premium for the same type of automobile coverage for one vehicle can vary from $238.00 (for an adult male driver) to $655.00 (for a male under the age of 25). This discrepancy is due to the method used by insurance companies in deciding how much a person will pay for insurance.

Premiums may vary even when the policyholders are very similar. There are several reasons for this. First, the premium depends on what types of automobile insurance coverage a person chooses to purchase. The premium increases as the amount of coverage increases. In addition, if a policyholder chooses a low deductible, the premium will increase. A second factor that determines the premium is the type of car insured. If the car is an expensive, newer model, the policyholder will pay more for insurance protection. Actuarial tables take into account the size of the engine and the expense involved in repairing collision damage for that particular make of car. A third factor is the people who will be driving the automobile. Again, actuarial tables are used to estimate the likelihood of those people suffering a loss. This is where the driving records, the miles driven each day, and the age and sex of each driver are considered.

A **discount** is a decrease in the premium amount and is available from some insurance companies. A company may give a discount because a policyholder insures more than one automobile with that company, has a particularly good driving record, or does not use the automobile often. Other discounts include passive restraint systems (either a type of belt which automatically fastens without any action by the driver or front seat passenger), passive anti-theft devices (systems installed which are activated automatically when the driver turns the ignition key to the off position (but does not include an ignition interlock provided as a standard feature by the manufacturer), and drivers who are 55 and older who have successfully completed a driver improvement course.

All of this sounds quite complicated, and it is. When determining the amount of a premium, some insurance companies assign a number value to each factor. Factors that involve a higher risk, such as higher levels of protection, newer or more expensive cars, and young male drivers, are assigned higher point values. All the point values are added together to determine the amount of premium. Numeric tables are then established to equate the point values for all the risk factors with the appropriate premium amount. The higher the number, the more the policyholder will pay in premiums. This system of assigning numeric values to risk factors for determining the premium amount is sometimes called a **point system**.

HOW TO OBTAIN INSURANCE

When you wish to purchase insurance, you must first contact an agent. An **agent** is a person who is licensed to sell insurance. If this is the first time you are purchasing insurance, you will probably want to meet the agent in person to discuss your insurance needs. The agent should be able to advise you on what types and how much coverage is right for you. Once the proper coverage has been determined, you must fill out an automobile insurance application, similar to the one shown in Figure 8.1. If you only need to change the amount of the insurance you already have or add another vehicle to the policy, you can usually contact your agent by phone. These simple changes can be made without your having to meet with the agent in person.

AUTOMOBILE INSURANCE APPLICATION

APPLICANT NAME:

| LAST | FIRST | M.I. |

MAILING ADDRESS:

| STREET | CITY |

| STATE | ZIP CODE |

	AUTO 1	AUTO 2	AUTO 3
YEAR			
MAKE			
MODEL			
FUEL TYPE:			
REGULAR (R)	☐	☐	☐
UNLEADED (U)	☐	☐	☐
DIESEL (D)	☐	☐	☐
VIN			
LIABILITY	YES ☐ NO ☐	YES ☐ NO ☐	YES ☐ NO ☐
COLLISION	YES ☐ NO ☐	YES ☐ NO ☐	YES ☐ NO ☐
COMPREHENSIVE	YES ☐ NO ☐	YES ☐ NO ☐	YES ☐ NO ☐
UNINSURED MOTOR	YES ☐ NO ☐	YES ☐ NO ☐	YES ☐ NO ☐

	DRIVER 1	DRIVER 2	DRIVER 3
FIRST NAME			
MIDDLE INITIAL			
BIRTHDATE			
SEX	F ☐ M ☐	F ☐ M ☐	F ☐ M ☐
MILES TO WORK			
NO. TICKETS			
DRIVERS ED.	YES ☐ NO ☐	YES ☐ NO ☐	YES ☐ NO ☐
NO. ACCIDENTS			

FIGURE 8.1 Auto Insurance Application

HOW INSURANCE APPLICATIONS ARE PROCESSED

If the agent comes to your home to discuss your insurance application, that agent will usually write the information on the application. The application may be sent to a central processing center for entry into a computer or the agent may do the key-entering upon returning to the local office. If you go to your agent's office, the agent will either complete the application by hand and send it to a central processing center or have the data key-entered into a computer immediately. If the processing is done at a central location, it may take a few weeks for the application to be processed.

In either case, however, the agent should be able to tell you the amount of your premium immediately.

Computers have helped make processing applications much easier. The agent can key-enter different information about the prospective policyholder and the type of insurance coverage desired into the computer. The computer can quickly determine the premium amount for that coverage. If the insurance applicant would like to consider several different insurance packages, the different premium amounts can be easily calculated.

HOW STORED DATA IS USED

Once the data is key-entered into the computer system, that data can be used in various ways. For example, the expiration date of a policy is kept on record so that the insurance company can send a reminder to the policyholders to renew their insurance. Renewal bills can also be printed by most computer systems.

Sometimes changes in the law require the insurance company to make changes to a policy. If this occurs, the insurance company may need to contact the policyholder. By recording the types of coverage each policyholder has purchased, it is quite simple for the company to notify, for example, only those policyholders who have collision insurance. If you do suffer a loss due to a collision, the insurance company needs to verify that you have purchased collision insurance and check to see if you have a deductible amount. The insurance company can make these checks on the computer.

Your agent may use this stored data in other ways. For example, your agent may contact you as your automobile insurance needs change, suggesting that you obtain more insurance, change the amount of coverage, or change the deductible amounts. In addition, an agent may suggest other types of insurance such as life, homeowner's, or hospitalization.

Finally, as the insurance company receives premiums and pays for losses, this data is used to update the statistics that are studied by the actuary when determining future premium amounts. In this way, premium amounts remain current.

RELATED JOBS

Since computers play such an important role in the insurance industry, there are many data entry jobs available. These jobs range from those requiring only a small amount of key-entering skills to those requiring excellent skills.

For example, the local agent may need to enter smaller amounts of data directly into a computer. It would be beneficial for that agent to have some previous data entry skills. If the data entry is done at a central location, much higher level skills would be required. It takes many people to keep insurance records current and accurate. Each time a policy is changed, the data must be updated in the computer. If a policyholder gets a traffic ticket, is involved in an accident, or changes addresses, that policyholder's record must be changed. Insurance companies offer many job opportunities for people who have data entry skills.

INPUT FIELDS

*I*n this activity you will key-enter data into the computer from insurance applications. Information from the automobile insurance applications is key-entered into input fields on the data entry screen. The input fields for this activity can be grouped into three categories: fields relating to the applicant, fields relating to the vehicle(s) being insured, and fields relating to all the family members who will be driving the vehicle(s). These three categories, along with their corresponding input fields, are described below and on the next page.

FIELDS RELATING TO THE APPLICANT

Name (Last, First, M.I.). This entry is three separate fields, key-entered separately. The last name field can contain up to 12 characters, the first name field can contain six characters, and the middle initial can contain one character.

Street Address. This field contains both the house number and the street name of each applicant.

City. This field identifies the city of the applicant.

State. This field identifies the two-letter abbreviation for the state of the applicant.

ZIP. This field contains the nine-character ZIP code of the applicant.

FIELDS RELATING TO THE VEHICLE(S) BEING INSURED

Year. This field contains the last two digits of the year the vehicle was made.

Make. This field identifies the make of the vehicle, such as Ford, Chevrolet, Toyota, etc.

Model. This field identifies the model of the vehicle, such as Escort, Cavalier, Supra, etc.

Type Of Fuel. This field is designed to accept an abbreviation standing for the type of fuel the car requires. Key-enter only the one-letter abbreviation that appears in parentheses on the application.

Vehicle Identification Number (VIN). This field represents the serial number assigned by the manufacturer to each vehicle. This number is a combination of letters and digits.

Liability. This field indicates whether the applicant would like liability insurance. You must key-enter Y for yes (the applicant wishes to have this liability coverage) or N for no (the applicant does not wish to have this coverage).

Collision, Comprehensive, and Uninsured Motorist. Your treatment of each of these three fields should follow the same procedure as the liability field above. Each field indicates whether the applicant wishes to have the vehicle covered by that type of insurance.

FIELDS RELATING TO ALL DRIVERS

First Name, Initial. It is assumed that the last name of all drivers will be the same as the last name of the applicant. Therefore, it is only necessary to key-enter each driver's first name and middle initial. These are treated as two separate alphabetic fields; the first name field can contain nine letters and the middle initial field can contain one letter.

Birthdate. This field contains the month, the day, and the year of birth for each driver.

Sex. This field contains the appropriate abbreviation for the sex of an individual, either F for female, or M for male.

Miles To Work. This field indicates the number of miles the driver must travel each way to work.

No. Tickets. This field represents the number of previous traffic tickets shown on the driver's record.

Driver's Ed. This field indicates whether the driver has had a driver's education course. Key-enter Y for yes or N for no.

No. Accidents. This field contains the number of accidents each driver has on the driving records.

GET READY

Follow the start-up procedures for your computer that are found in Appendix A.

COMPLETE ALPHA-NUMERIC DEXTERITY DRILL

```
402 89063874 CARSON CITY 061341 10 00 53
HONDA GD222XJ 577160 04 0 08 53 RAYMONDX
25 10 24 48 RONALD 86 7554 DIPLOMAT 8950
8958101 NV 01 15 50 JK2TN5 68JB3228 1210
LEXINGTON 900S 0316 36 LIABILITY 8943140
```

STEP 1 From the *Activities* menu, select *Activity 8 Auto Insurance Application.*

STEP 2 Select *Alpha-Numeric Dexterity Drill.*

STEP 3 Enter the data for each line. Press *enter* or *return* at the end of each line.

STEP 4 Select *OK* when you are finished key-entering. Review your score.

STEP 5 Select *Review* to review any errors that were made. After you have reviewed your performance, select *OK.*

Repeat the Alpha-Numeric Dexterity Drill as many times as instructed by your teacher.

COMPLETE KEYPAD DEXTERITY DRILL

```
45748  62674  85682  38282  93606  70513  8258
99319  59347  39948  89375  21715  80626  6545
29651  29256  28529  48111  74431  75414  4428
15531  47575  86241  20067  97588  95063  9148
85403  20594  23568  53214  17003  37510  8213
```

STEP 1   From the *Activities* menu, select *Activity 8 Auto Insurance Application.*

STEP 2   Select *Keypad Dexterity Drill.*

STEP 3   Enter the data for each line. Press enter or return at the end of each line.

STEP 4   Select *OK* when you are finished key-entering. Review your score.

STEP 5   Select *Review* to review any errors that were made. After you have reviewed your performance, select *OK.*

Repeat the Keypad Dexterity Drill as many times as instructed by your teacher.

COMPLETE AUTOMOBILE INSURANCE APPLICATION FORMS

STEP 1   Remove the Automobile Insurance Application forms that are located at the end of this activity.

STEP 2   From the *Activities* menu, select *Activity 8 Auto Insurance Application.*

STEP 3   Select *Application Form.* Your screen will be similar to that shown in Figure 8.2.

FIGURE 8.2

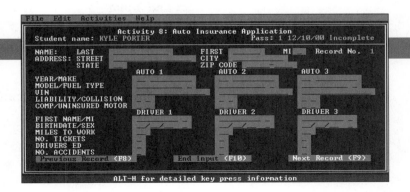

STEP 4   Key-enter the Applicant Name: Last, First, Middle Initial and Applicant Mailing Address: Street, City, State and ZIP Code.

STEP 5   Key-enter the data for auto one, driver one, auto two, driver two, and so on. Once you have finished entering all of the data on a form, select *Next Record*.

STEP 6   Key-enter the remaining records.

> **Note: If you are interrupted before key-entering all of the records, follow the necessary procedures to end your input and to begin the next session. Refer to the detailed instructions for this procedure in Activity 4, if necessary.**

STEP 7   After key-entering all of the Auto Insurance Application forms, select *End Input*. If you notice errors after you have selected End Input, select *Edit* and then move to the appropriate fields to key-enter the corrections.

STEP 8   Print the auto insurance application forms if instructed by your teacher. To do this, from the *File* menu, select *Print*.

STEP 9   Select *Analyze*. Review the information presented.

STEP 10   Select *Review*. Any errors will be highlighted.

STEP 11   Select *Done*.

STEP 12   You may generate a report of your performance.

> **Note: In a real work situation, you would strive for completely accurate records. Therefore, it is suggested that once you have completed all of the steps listed here, you should go back into the records and correct any errors. To do this:**
>
> - **From the *Activities* menu, select *Activity 8 Auto Insurance Application*.**
> - **Select *Application Form*.**
> - **Select *Open*.**
> - **Use the appropriate keys to locate the proper record and field and then key-enter the correction.**
> - **Select *End Input*.**
> - **Select *Analyze*.**
> - **Select *Review*.**
> - **Select *Done*.**
> - **Print the auto insurance application forms if instructed by your teacher.**

➡

VOCABULARY

actuarial table
actuary
agent
automobile insurance
collision insurance
comprehensive insurance
coverage
deductible
discount
liability insurance
point system
policy
policyholder
premium
uninsured motorist insurance

Activity 8 Study Guide

AUTO INSURANCE APPLICATION

PART 1

OBJECTIVES 1, 3, AND 6 (2 POINTS EACH)

Match the vocabulary terms with the best definitions. Write the letter of the term in the space to the left of the definition.

A. **actuarial table**
B. **actuary**
C. **agent**
D. **automobile insurance**
E. **collision insurance**

F. **comprehensive insurance**
G. **coverage**
H. **deductible**
I. **discount**
J. **liability insurance**

K. **policy**
L. **policyholder**
M. **premium**
N. **uninsured motorist insurance**

_____ 1. A way to protect against financial loss due to an accidental event connected with an automobile.

_____ 2. A written agreement between a buyer of insurance and an insurance company.

_____ 3. The person who purchases an insurance policy.

_____ 4. Policyholders pay this amount to be covered for insurance protection.

_____ 5. The amount and type of insurance protection purchased.

_____ 6. Studies of past payment practices to determine future payment rates.

_____ 7. A statistical table showing the likelihood that certain people will suffer an insurance loss.

_____ 8. Coverage for an automobile involved in an accident.

_____ 9. The amount deducted by the insurance company before they pay for the repair.

_____ 10. You are protected by this when your automobile is damaged other than by a collision.

_____ 11. You are protected by this when you are injured while riding in a car whose driver does not have insurance coverage.

_____ 12. This coverage protects policyholders who are injured because of an accident with someone who doesn't have insurance.

207

_____ **13.** A decrease in the premium amount because of seat belts, passive anti-theft devices, and taking a driving improvement course.

_____ **14.** A person who is licensed to sell insurance.

OBJECTIVES 2, 3, AND 4 (1 POINT EACH)

➭ **Each of the following statements is either true or false. Indicate your choice by circling T for a true statement or F for a false statement.**

T   F   **1.** The insurance company will pay for the loss up to the level of protection purchased.

T   F   **2.** The insurance company may elect to give customer's the fair market value for their damaged car.

T   F   **3.** Insurance is available that covers a policyholder's losses due to injuries when the person is involved in any type of automobile accident.

T   F   **4.** All young drivers will pay the same for insurance coverage.

T   F   **5.** Insurance companies can expect to pay more in losses to policyholders who smoke.

T   F   **6.** An agent is licensed to sell insurance.

T   F   **7.** When policyholders purchase auto insurance, they agree to pay a specific amount called a premium.

T   F   **8.** Auto insurance is not required in all states.

T   F   **9.** The insurance company may subtract the deductible from the payment.

T   F   **10.** Older male drivers are charged more for insurance because they receive more traffic tickets.

PART 3

OBJECTIVES 2, 3, 4, 5, 6, 7, AND 8 (3 POINTS EACH)

➨ **Briefly answer each of the following items. Write your answers on the lines provided.**

1. Explain how actuarial tables are established by insurance companies.

_____

_____

_____

2. Explain the four different types of insurance.

_____

_____

_____

_____

3. Premium amounts paid for insurance are based on a policyholder's desire for different coverages. List three items one should take into consideration.

_____

_____

_____

4. Explain how a person would purchase car insurance.

_____

_____

☞ **Remove the Activity 8 Study Guide from your text-workbook and hand it to your instructor for correcting.**

Total Points Possible	55
(Minus) Incorrect Points	_____
Total Points Earned	_____
Percent Correct	_____
Grade	_____

AUTOMOBILE INSURANCE APPLICATION

APPLICANT NAME: Genthner (LAST) Robert (FIRST) R (M.I.)

MAILING ADDRESS: 402 Agate Drive (STREET) Carson City (CITY)
NV (STATE) 89706-3874 (ZIP CODE)

	AUTO 1	AUTO 2	AUTO 3
YEAR	85	81	
MAKE	Mazda	Honda	
MODEL	LX	Accord	
FUEL TYPE:	D		
REGULAR (R)	☐	☐	☐
UNLEADED (U)	☐	X	☐
DIESEL (D)	X	☐	☐
VIN	GD222XJ1577I60	1HG5Z5442XDA017	
LIABILITY	YES X NO ☐	YES X NO ☐	YES ☐ NO ☐
COLLISION	YES X NO ☐	YES X NO ☐	YES ☐ NO ☐
COMPREHENSIVE	YES X NO ☐	YES ☐ NO X	YES ☐ NO ☐
UNINSURED MOTOR	YES X NO ☐	YES ☐ NO X	YES ☐ NO ☐

	DRIVER 1	DRIVER 2	DRIVER 3
FIRST NAME	Robert	Maria	
MIDDLE INITIAL	R	M	
BIRTHDATE	06/23/41	04/18/53	
SEX	F ☐ M X	F X M ☐	F ☐ M ☐
MILES TO WORK	10	22	
NO. TICKETS	1	0	
DRIVERS ED.	YES ☐ NO X	YES X NO ☐	YES ☐ NO ☐
NO. ACCIDENTS	1	0	

AUTOMOBILE INSURANCE APPLICATION

APPLICANT NAME: Vaillancourt (LAST) Ronald (FIRST) S (M.I.)

MAILING ADDRESS: 76 Ambrose Circle (STREET) Reno (CITY)
NV (STATE) 89511-8101 (ZIP CODE)

	AUTO 1	AUTO 2	AUTO 3
YEAR	86	84	
MAKE	Dodge	Pontiac	
MODEL	Diplomat	Lemans	
FUEL TYPE:			
REGULAR (R)	☐	☐	☐
UNLEADED (U)	X	X	☐
DIESEL (D)	☐	☐	☐
VIN	CPJIGAGI75532	KL2TN5168JB3222	
LIABILITY	YES X NO ☐	YES X NO ☐	YES ☐ NO ☐
COLLISION	YES X NO ☐	YES X NO ☐	YES ☐ NO ☐
COMPREHENSIVE	YES X NO ☐	YES ☐ NO X	YES ☐ NO ☐
UNINSURED MOTOR	YES ☐ NO X	YES ☐ NO X	YES ☐ NO ☐

	DRIVER 1	DRIVER 2	DRIVER 3
FIRST NAME	Ronald	Angela	Grace
MIDDLE INITIAL	S	L	T
BIRTHDATE	10/24/53	01/15/55	08/10/75
SEX	F ☐ M X	F X M ☐	F X M ☐
MILES TO WORK	25	12	05
NO. TICKETS	1	0	0
DRIVERS ED.	YES ☐ NO X	YES ☐ NO X	YES X NO ☐
NO. ACCIDENTS	1	1	1

AUTOMOBILE INSURANCE APPLICATION

APPLICANT NAME: Garcia (LAST) Jesus (FIRST) P (M.I.)

MAILING ADDRESS: 914 Lexington Way (STREET) Sparks (CITY) NV (STATE) 89423-4190 (ZIP CODE)

	AUTO 1	AUTO 2	AUTO 3
YEAR	85	84	79
MAKE	Chrysler	Saab	Buick
MODEL	Fifth Ave	9005	Century
FUEL TYPE:			
REGULAR (R)			X
UNLEADED (U)		X	
DIESEL (D)	X		
VIN	1C3BF66R5JW1372	V53A54528H20240	7G4A15IW9HJ407O
LIABILITY	YES X NO	YES X NO	YES X NO
COLLISION	YES X NO	YES X NO	YES NO X
COMPREHENSIVE	YES X NO	YES NO X	YES NO X
UNINSURED MOTOR	YES X NO	YES X NO	YES NO X

	DRIVER 1	DRIVER 2	DRIVER 3
FIRST NAME	Jesus	Maria	Maria
MIDDLE INITIAL	P	D	H
BIRTHDATE	03/16/36	06/30/33	06/01/71
SEX	F M X	F X M	F X M
MILES TO WORK	10	00	10
NO. TICKETS	0	2	0
DRIVERS ED.	YES NO X	YES NO X	YES X NO
NO. ACCIDENTS	1	0	0

AUTOMOBILE INSURANCE APPLICATION

APPLICANT NAME: Eng (LAST) Brian (FIRST) T (M.I.)

MAILING ADDRESS: 736 Wells Street (STREET) Elko (CITY) NV (STATE) 89833-7045 (ZIP CODE)

	AUTO 1	AUTO 2	AUTO 3
YEAR	86		
MAKE	Chevrolet		
MODEL	Nova		
FUEL TYPE:			
REGULAR (R)	X		
UNLEADED (U)			
DIESEL (D)			
VIN	1Y1SR5749HZ0109		
LIABILITY	YES X NO	YES NO	YES NO
COLLISION	YES X NO	YES NO	YES NO
COMPREHENSIVE	YES X NO	YES NO	YES NO
UNINSURED MOTOR	YES X NO	YES NO	YES NO

	DRIVER 1	DRIVER 2	DRIVER 3
FIRST NAME	Brian		
MIDDLE INITIAL	T		
BIRTHDATE	08/12/64		
SEX	F M X	F M	F M
MILES TO WORK	35		
NO. TICKETS	1		
DRIVERS ED.	YES X NO	YES NO	YES NO
NO. ACCIDENTS	1		

AUTOMOBILE INSURANCE APPLICATION

APPLICANT NAME: _____ LAST _____ FIRST _____ M.I.

MAILING ADDRESS: _____ STREET _____ CITY

_____ STATE _____ ZIP CODE

	AUTO 1	AUTO 2	AUTO 3
YEAR			
MAKE			
MODEL			
FUEL TYPE:			
REGULAR (R)	[ ]	[ ]	[ ]
UNLEADED (U)	[ ]	[ ]	[ ]
DIESEL (D)	[ ]	[ ]	[ ]
VIN			
LIABILITY	YES[ ] NO[ ]	YES[ ] NO[ ]	YES[ ] NO[ ]
COLLISION	YES[ ] NO[ ]	YES[ ] NO[ ]	YES[ ] NO[ ]
COMPREHENSIVE	YES[ ] NO[ ]	YES[ ] NO[ ]	YES[ ] NO[ ]
UNINSURED MOTOR	YES[ ] NO[ ]	YES[ ] NO[ ]	YES[ ] NO[ ]

	DRIVER 1	DRIVER 2	DRIVER 3
FIRST NAME			
MIDDLE INITIAL			
BIRTHDATE			
SEX	F[ ] M[ ]	F[ ] M[ ]	F[ ] M[ ]
MILES TO WORK			
NO. TICKETS			
DRIVERS ED.	YES[ ] NO[ ]	YES[ ] NO[ ]	YES[ ] NO[ ]
NO. ACCIDENTS			

AUTOMOBILE INSURANCE APPLICATION

APPLICANT NAME: _Chewonki_ LAST _Melody_ FIRST _R_ M.I.

MAILING ADDRESS: _924 Apawana Lane_ STREET _Las Vegas_ CITY

_NV_ STATE _89144-7245_ ZIP CODE

	AUTO 1	AUTO 2	AUTO 3
YEAR	82		
MAKE	Pontiac		
MODEL	Grand Prix		
FUEL TYPE:			
REGULAR (R)	[ ]	[ ]	[ ]
UNLEADED (U)	[X]	[ ]	[ ]
DIESEL (D)	[ ]	[ ]	[ ]
VIN	1GT2WJ14WJ7F241		
LIABILITY	YES[X] NO[ ]	YES[ ] NO[ ]	YES[ ] NO[ ]
COLLISION	YES[ ] NO[X]	YES[ ] NO[ ]	YES[ ] NO[ ]
COMPREHENSIVE	YES[ ] NO[X]	YES[ ] NO[ ]	YES[ ] NO[ ]
UNINSURED MOTOR	YES[ ] NO[X]	YES[ ] NO[ ]	YES[ ] NO[ ]

	DRIVER 1	DRIVER 2	DRIVER 3
FIRST NAME	Melody	Elizabeth	
MIDDLE INITIAL	R	S	
BIRTHDATE	11/16/46	03/22/70	
SEX	F[X] M[ ]	F[X] M[ ]	F[ ] M[ ]
MILES TO WORK	08	20	
NO. TICKETS	0	1	
DRIVERS ED.	YES[ ] NO[X]	YES[X] NO[ ]	YES[ ] NO[ ]
NO. ACCIDENTS	0	0	

Activity 9

DRIVER'S LICENSE APPLICATION

LEARNING OBJECTIVES

Upon completion of this activity, you will be able to:

1 Define the following terms: endorsements, restrictions and organ donor.

2 Explain why states restrict and control the right to drive a motor vehicle.

3 Explain how states control the right to drive.

4 List five types of data included in a driver's license application.

5 Explain the procedure followed when applying for a driver's license.

6 Key-enter data for driver's license applications.

● ●

DATA ENTRY APPLICATION AND JOB DESCRIPTION

*T*he ability to drive a car is one activity that many young people look forward to for many years. In fact, this ability often gives young people a chance to become less dependent on their parents. No longer will they have to arrange for rides to and from social outings, school events, and community activities. Along with the benefits of driving come the responsibilities of knowing how to operate the vehicle safely. To ensure that this responsibility is not ignored, state governments, usually the **Department of Transportation**, will control the right to drive.

WHY STATES CONTROL THE RIGHT TO DRIVE

There are several reasons why states control the right to drive. The major reason is the safety of the citizens. Without restrictions on drivers, there would be no assurance that drivers know the rules of the road, and have the ability to handle and control the vehicle. State governments usually dictate the physical requirements deemed necessary to be considered a safe driver. Physical handicaps such as poor vision, poor hearing, or lack of coordination may be seen as a safety hazard to other drivers and to pedestrians.

By requiring all drivers to register with the state before being able to drive, the state compiles records on each driver. If a person is stopped for a traffic violation, the law enforcement officer will usually check that individual's driving record to ensure that there are no outstanding tickets, warrants, or accidents. On a broader scope, these records can be used to track people who have been involved in illegal activities.

Some states have a special license, issued to 16/17 year-olds, called a Junior Driver's License. This license is issued to those people who have had their parents or guardian sign for them to take the driving test. However, there are area restrictions placed on the driving usage of the license. No person may hold more than one valid license at any time.

HOW STATES CONTROL THE RIGHT TO DRIVE

A driver's license application must be completed before a person can drive legally. A driver's license application contains questions about the name, address, birthdate, height, weight, and sex of the applicant. A driver's license application is shown in Figure 9.1. Each state determines what requirements must be met for a license to be issued to a driver. Usually road, written, and vision tests are required the first time a driver is issued a license. Once these three provisions are met and a fee paid, the driver will usually be issued a driver's license. This license would generally allow the person to drive a personal-use vehicle. In most states, a parent or guardian must verify that a minor is able to control the vehicle and then give permission to the minor to obtain a driver's license. The application data may be entered into a computer at the local licensing center or it may be sent to a central processing center to be entered. In either case, the applicant is usually issued a temporary license. The actual driver's license is then mailed to the driver.

DRIVER'S LICENSE APPLICATION

LAST NAME _____

FIRST NAME _____ MIDDLE INITIAL _____

STREET ADDRESS _____

CITY _____ STATE _____

ZIP CODE _____ BIRTHDATE _____ EXPIRATION DATE _____

HEIGHT _____ WEIGHT _____ EYE COLOR _____

SEX ☐ MALE
    ☐ FEMALE

ORGAN DONOR ☐ YES
            ☐ NO

RESTRICTIONS _____

ENDORSEMENTS _____

☐ (FOR OFFICE USE ONLY)

FIGURE 9.1 Driver's License Application

If applicants want to drive a special kind of vehicle, such as a school bus, taxicab, motorcycle, or a delivery vehicle, they must apply for an endorsement. An **endorsement** is an additional right to drive specialized vehicles. Endorsements may require additional training or testing to determine if the applicant can handle the added responsibilities. For instance, the applicant may have to take a physical exam and pay additional fees for an endorsement.

Another way for the state to control the ability to drive is to put specific restrictions on a driver's license. A **restriction** is a condition that must be met in order for the driver's license to be valid. A common restriction is "corrective lenses," which means that a driver must be wearing contacts or glasses when operating a motor vehicle. Other common restrictions include "hand controls" for some physical disabilities, "brake and gas pedal extensions" for people whose legs do not reach the normal pedals, or "daylight driving only" for those drivers who have trouble seeing at night. These restrictions are typically listed on the individual's driver's license.

Because the state does control the issuing of driver's licenses, the driver's license has become an accepted form of identification and proof of age. It is against the law to drive without having your driver's license with you. A licensed driver should never loan his/her license to another person for any reason. In many states, drivers can indicate on their licenses that they wish to be organ donors. An **organ donor** is a person who wishes to donate internal organs in the event of death in a car accident or some other fatal tragedy. Since people carry a driver's license with them most of the time, it is an appropriate place to indicate organ donor information. All licenses expire periodically. To renew the license, the driver may have to take additional tests such as a vision or driving test. Records of the expiration dates for licenses are kept by the state and are used to notify drivers when their licenses need to be renewed.

PHOTO IDENTIFICATION CARD

Almost all retailers ask for a form of identification when they are presented with a check with which to pay a bill. This can be taken care of by a **Photo Identification Card**. It is the size of a credit card and includes the person's name, address, date of birth, signature, and picture. This card may be obtained from the Bureau of Transportation. A fee is collected for obtaining the card. The qualifications could be any of the following:

1. Do not have a valid driver's license.
2. Surrendered the valid driver's license because of age.
3. Failed to pass the physical exam for license.
4. Suspended license for one year or longer.

HOW STORED DATA IS USED

A record of each driver is kept in a computer data bank and can be used in various ways. In some states, this record is considered public information, meaning anyone can have access to it. In other states, laws have been enacted to make a driver's record private information, meaning only authorized personnel (such as law enforcement officers) have access to it. In many states, any traffic violations a driver receives are reported to that driver's insurance company.

JOBS AVAILABLE IN RELATED AREAS

In addition to key-entering data for new applications and renewals, computer operators are required to retrieve drivers' records when requested by insurance companies, law enforcement officers, or other individuals. When data entry is done in a local licensing center, all clerks would need training in key-entering data. In those instances where the applications are sent to a central processing center, the employees at the center would be required to have good data entry skills.

INPUT FIELDS

*I*n this activity you will enter data from the source documents, license applications, for 20 individuals. Information from license applications is key-entered into input fields on the data entry screen. A brief description of each field is provided below.

Name (Last, First, M.I.). This entry is three separate fields, key-entered separately. The last name field can contain up to ten characters, the first name field can contain eight characters, and the middle initial can contain one character.

Street Address. This field contains both the house number and the street name of each applicant.

City. This field identifies the city of the applicant.

State. This field identifies the two-letter abbreviation for the state of the applicant.

ZIP. This field contains the nine-character ZIP code of the applicant.

Birthdate. This field contains the month, the day, and the year of birth for each applicant.

Expiration Date. This field contains the month, the day, and the year in which the license must be renewed.

Height. This field indicates the applicant's height. You do not need to key-enter the tick marks (5'10") representing feet and inches. The software program will insert them in the appropriate places. You must enter leading zeros where appropriate (007) for the computer to correctly insert the tick marks.

Weight. This field indicates the applicant's weight. Key-enter the data exactly as it appears on the applications.

Eyes. This field contains the abbreviation for the applicant's eye color.

Sex. This field contains the appropriate abbreviation for the sex of an individual, either F for female, or M for male.

Organ Donor. This field indicates whether a person wants to be an organ donor. Key-enter either Y if the applicant does wish to be an organ donor or N if the applicant does not want to be an organ donor.

Restrictions. This field contains restrictions placed on an applicant's driver's license. You will need to determine the codes for applicants and enter them into the computer. A list of codes is provided in the following section.

Endorsements. This field contains any endorsements this driver would have. You will need to determine the codes for applicants and enter them into the computer. A list of codes is provided in the following section.

GET READY

Follow the start-up procedures for your computer.

COMPLETE ALPHA-NUMERIC DEXTERITY DRILL

```
223089726 511 160 NONE 022092 150170 602
FAIRFAX 26040442 29901 AUTOMATIC 0402924
20543992 STONEHEDGE 132 046 VA 510231025
MOPED 734402332 ABBES 155001 040421 2651
9600 L 510BL MOTORCYCLE 1180148 5753 022
```

STEP 1   From *Activities* menu, select *Activity 9 Driver's License Application.*

STEP 2   Select *Alpha-Numeric Dexterity Drill.*

STEP 3   Enter the data for each line. Press *enter* or *return* at the end of each line.

STEP 4   Select *OK* when you are finished key-entering. Review your score.

STEP 5   Select *Review* to review any errors that were made. After you have reviewed your performance, select *OK.*

Repeat the Alpha-Numeric Dexterity Drill as many times as instructed by your teacher.

```
56775 56199 74644 51332 50025 42625 3759
28033 11967 68319 56039 05967 94933 5456
48599 36375 18749 88532 88725 10872 2793
47051 83081 09167 69207 85017 31738 4883
54596 63851 11409 30739 13714 77107 5617
```

STEP 1   From the *Activities* menu, select *Activity 9 Driver's License Application.*

STEP 2   Select *Keypad Dexterity Drill.*

STEP 3   Enter the data for each line. Press *enter* or *return* at the end of each line.

STEP 4   Select *OK* when you are finished key-entering. Review your score.

STEP 5   Select *Review* to review any errors that were made. After reviewing your performance, select *OK.*

Repeat the Keypad Dexterity Drill as many times as instructed by your teacher.

COMPLETE DRIVER'S LICENSE APPLICATION FORMS

STEP 1   Remove the Driver's License Application forms that are located at the end of this activity.

STEP 2   From the *Activities* menu, select *Activity 9 Driver's License Application.*

STEP 3   Select *Application Form.* Your screen will be similar to that shown in Figure 9.2.

FIGURE 9.2

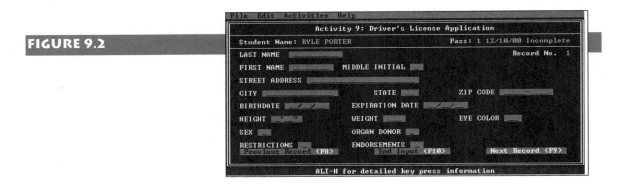

STEP 4   Key-enter the Last Name, First Name, Middle Initial, Street, City, State, ZIP Code, and so on, until the record is completely keyed. The restrictions and endorsement codes are shown in the following table. You must determine the proper restriction and endorsement code for each applicant and enter the code into the computer.

RESTRICTIONS

Restriction	Code
Automatic Transmission	A
Corrective Lenses	B
Complete Hand Controls	C
Daylight Driving Only	D
No Restrictions	N

ENDORSEMENTS

Endorsement	Code
No Endorsements	N
Motorcycle	A
Moped	B
School Bus	C
Any Two-Axle Truck	D

STEP 5   Select *Next Record.*

STEP 6   Key-enter the remaining records.

✎ **Note: If you are interrupted before key-entering all of the records, follow the necessary procedures to end your input.**

STEP 7   After key-entering all of the driver's license applications forms, select *End Input.* If you notice errors after you have selected End Input, select *Edit* and then move to the appropriate fields to key-enter the corrections.

STEP 8   Print the driver's license applications forms if instructed by your teacher.

STEP 9   Select *Analyze.* Review the information presented.

STEP 10   Select *Review.* Any errors will be highlighted.

STEP 11   Select *Done.*

STEP 12   You may generate a report of your performance.

✎ **Note: In a real work situation, you would strive for completely accurate records. Therefore, it is suggested that once you have completed all the steps listed here, you should go back into the records and correct all errors.**

To do this:

> - **From *Activities* menu, select *Activity 9 Driver's License Application.***
> - **Select *Driver's License Form.***

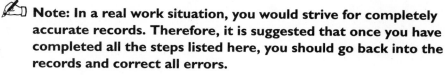

- Select *Open*.
- Use the appropriate keys to locate the proper record and field and then key-enter the correction.
- Select *End Input*.
- Select *Analyze*.
- Select *Review*.
- Select *Done*.
- Print the driver's license application forms if instructed by your teacher.

VOCABULARY

Department of Transportation
endorsement
organ donor
photo identification card
restriction

Activity 9 Study Guide

PART 1

OBJECTIVES 1, 4, 5, AND 6 (2 POINTS EACH)

☛ **Match the vocabulary terms with the best definitions. Write the letter of the term in the space to the left of the definition.**

A. **Department of Transportation**
B. **endorsement**

C. **photo identification card**

D. **restriction**
E. **state government**

_____ 1. The agency that controls the right to drive.

_____ 2. Dictates the physical requirements deemed necessary to be a safe driver.

_____ 3. Way to control the ability to drive specialized vehicles.

_____ 4. The wearing of glasses whenever you drive.

_____ 5. Used by people who do not have a driver's license.

PART 2

OBJECTIVES 2 AND 3 (1 POINT EACH)

☛ **Each of the following statements is either true or false. Indicate your choice by circling T for a true statement or F for a false statement.**

T   F   **1.** No person may hold more than one valid license at any one time in a state.

T   F   **2.** Restrictions are not listed on a driver's license.

T   F   **3.** The applicant may have to take a physical exam and pay additional fees for an endorsement.

T   F   **4.** A driver's license is an appropriate place to indicate organ donor information.

T   F   **5.** Because of privacy loss, a person's birthdate may not be listed on their driver's license

T   F   **6.** The ability and the right to drive additional types of motor vehicles is permitted by the proper endorsement.

T	F	**7.** An identification card with a picture the size of a credit card is obtainable.
T	F	**8.** All driver's licenses are issued for life.
T	F	**9.** It is against the law to lend your license to anyone else.
T	F	**10.** There is no age requirement to obtain a driver's license.

PART 3

OBJECTIVES 3 AND 4 (3 POINTS EACH)

➥ **Briefly answer each of the following items. Write your answers on the lines provided.**

1. Explain the four basic requirements for applying for a driver's license the first time.

_____

_____

_____

_____

2. An endorsement will usually allow you to drive many different kinds of vehicles; list four of them.

_____

_____

_____

_____

3. Explain what it means to be an organ donor.

_____

_____

_____

4. List five individual types of data that can be obtained from a driver's license application.

_____

_____

_____

_____

_____

5. List the four qualifications that one could use in obtaining an identification card.

_____

_____

☞ **Remove the Activity 9 Study Guide from your text-workbook and hand it to your instructor for correcting.**

Total Points Possible	35
(Minus) Incorrect Points	_____
Total Points Earned	_____
Percent Correct	_____
Grade	_____

DRIVER'S LICENSE APPLICATION

LAST NAME __Hutchinson__

FIRST NAME __Euray__   MIDDLE INITIAL __C__

STREET ADDRESS __62 Clarendon Blvd__

CITY __Alexandria__   STATE __VA__

ZIP CODE __22308-9726__   BIRTHDATE __04/14/66__   EXPIRATION DATE __02/20/94__

HEIGHT __5'09"__   WEIGHT __160__   EYE COLOR __BL__

SEX [X] MALE

[ ] FEMALE

ORGAN DONOR [X] YES

[ ] NO

RESTRICTIONS __None__

ENDORSEMENTS __None__

_____ [ ] (FOR OFFICE USE ONLY)

DRIVER'S LICENSE APPLICATION

LAST NAME __Illemann__

FIRST NAME __Adeline__   MIDDLE INITIAL __E__

STREET ADDRESS __302 Frederick Street__

CITY __Fairfax__   STATE __VA__

ZIP CODE __22203-2649__   BIRTHDATE __12/25/67__   EXPIRATION DATE __10/28/94__

HEIGHT __6'00"__   WEIGHT __150__   EYE COLOR __BR__

SEX [ ] MALE

[X] FEMALE

ORGAN DONOR [X] YES

[ ] NO

RESTRICTIONS __None__

ENDORSEMENTS __None__

_____ [ ] (FOR OFFICE USE ONLY)

DRIVER'S LICENSE APPLICATION

LAST NAME __Mendez__

FIRST NAME __Jose__   MIDDLE INITIAL __T__

STREET ADDRESS __26 Briarcliff Ave__

CITY __Arlington__   STATE __VA__

ZIP CODE __22901-1087__   BIRTHDATE __04/24/42__   EXPIRATION DATE __04/12/94__

HEIGHT __5'06"__   WEIGHT __214__   EYE COLOR __BR__

SEX   [X] MALE   RESTRICTIONS __Automatic Transmission__

      [ ] FEMALE   ENDORSEMENTS __None__

ORGAN DONOR [X] YES

      [ ] NO   [ ] (FOR OFFICE USE ONLY)

DRIVER'S LICENSE APPLICATION

LAST NAME __Ledfordton__

FIRST NAME __Reta__   MIDDLE INITIAL __C__

STREET ADDRESS __146 Stonehenge Ave__

CITY __Charlottesville__   STATE __VA__

ZIP CODE __23003-4502__   BIRTHDATE __04/25/54__   EXPIRATION DATE __04/25/95__

HEIGHT __5'10"__   WEIGHT __132__   EYE COLOR __BL__

SEX   [ ] MALE   RESTRICTIONS __Daylight Driving Only__

      [X] FEMALE   ENDORSEMENTS __Motorcycle__

ORGAN DONOR [X] YES

      [ ] NO   [ ] (FOR OFFICE USE ONLY)

DRIVER'S LICENSE APPLICATION

LAST NAME __Maazaoui__

FIRST NAME __Abbes__ MIDDLE INITIAL __J__

STREET ADDRESS __799 Amick Road__

CITY __Chesapeake__ STATE __VA__

ZIP CODE __23320-4437__ BIRTHDATE __10/05/51__ EXPIRATION DATE __09/30/95__

HEIGHT __5'08"__ WEIGHT __140__ EYE COLOR __BR__

SEX __X__ MALE

☐ FEMALE

ORGAN DONOR ☐ YES

__X__ NO

RESTRICTIONS __None__

ENDORSEMENTS __Moped__

☐ (FOR OFFICE USE ONLY)

DRIVER'S LICENSE APPLICATION

LAST NAME __Stevenson__

FIRST NAME __Warren__ MIDDLE INITIAL __L__

STREET ADDRESS __9600 Yakima Road__

CITY __Danville__ STATE __VA__

ZIP CODE __22524-1961__ BIRTHDATE __10/20/71__ EXPIRATION DATE __04/24/95__

HEIGHT __5'10"__ WEIGHT __180__ EYE COLOR __BL__

SEX __X__ MALE

☐ FEMALE

ORGAN DONOR ☐ YES

__X__ NO

RESTRICTIONS __Complete Hand Controls__

ENDORSEMENTS __Motorcycle__

☐ (FOR OFFICE USE ONLY)

DRIVER'S LICENSE APPLICATION

LAST NAME __Trafton__

FIRST NAME __Roberta__   MIDDLE INITIAL __A__

STREET ADDRESS __1180 Main Street__

CITY __Fairfax__   STATE __VA__

ZIP CODE __22249-3575__   BIRTHDATE __08/05/71__ EXPIRATION DATE __09/18/95__

HEIGHT __6'00"__   WEIGHT __148__   EYE COLOR __BL__

SEX [ ] MALE

[X] FEMALE

ORGAN DONOR [ ] YES

[X] NO

RESTRICTIONS __Automatic Transmission__

ENDORSEMENTS __None__

_____ [ ] (FOR OFFICE USE ONLY)

DRIVER'S LICENSE APPLICATION

LAST NAME __Wellman__

FIRST NAME __Marrine__   MIDDLE INITIAL __L__

STREET ADDRESS __5611 Gervais Drive__

CITY __Falls Church__   STATE __VA__

ZIP CODE __22046-5992__   BIRTHDATE __09/12/61__ EXPIRATION DATE __05/30/95__

HEIGHT __5'09"__   WEIGHT __160__   EYE COLOR __GR__

SEX [ ] MALE

[X] FEMALE

ORGAN DONOR [ ] YES

[X] NO

RESTRICTIONS __Corrective Lenses__

ENDORSEMENTS __None__

_____ [ ] (FOR OFFICE USE ONLY)

DRIVER'S LICENSE APPLICATION

LAST NAME __Favereau__

FIRST NAME __Maryjane__ MIDDLE INITIAL __M__

STREET ADDRESS __1207 Commonwealth Place__

CITY __Fredericksburg__ STATE __VA__

ZIP CODE __22404-8442__ BIRTHDATE __12/12/65__ EXPIRATION DATE __07/13/94__

HEIGHT __5'06"__ WEIGHT __162__ EYE COLOR __BL__

SEX [ ] MALE

[X] FEMALE

ORGAN DONOR [ ] YES

[X] NO

RESTRICTIONS __Corrective Lenses__

ENDORSEMENTS __None__

_____ [ ] (FOR OFFICE USE ONLY)

DRIVER'S LICENSE APPLICATION

LAST NAME __Fishette__

FIRST NAME __Ethel__ MIDDLE INITIAL __G__

STREET ADDRESS __1215 Darby Ave__

CITY __Hampton__ STATE __VA__

ZIP CODE __23669-9028__ BIRTHDATE __08/17/76__ EXPIRATION DATE __05/10/95__

HEIGHT __5'04"__ WEIGHT __110__ EYE COLOR __BL__

SEX [ ] MALE

[X] FEMALE

ORGAN DONOR [ ] YES

[X] NO

RESTRICTIONS __Corrective Lenses__

ENDORSEMENTS __None__

_____ [ ] (FOR OFFICE USE ONLY)

DRIVER'S LICENSE APPLICATION

LAST NAME __Townsend__

FIRST NAME __Maynard__ MIDDLE INITIAL __A__

STREET ADDRESS __1599 Bramblebush Court__

CITY __Herndon__ STATE __VA__

ZIP CODE __22670-6106__ BIRTHDATE __04/16/36__ EXPIRATION DATE __02/12/94__

HEIGHT __5'08"__ WEIGHT __162__ EYE COLOR __BL__

SEX [X] MALE

[ ] FEMALE

ORGAN DONOR [X] YES

[ ] NO

RESTRICTIONS __None__

ENDORSEMENTS __None__

_____ [ ] (FOR OFFICE USE ONLY)

DRIVER'S LICENSE APPLICATION

LAST NAME __Gallagher__

FIRST NAME __Karen__ MIDDLE INITIAL __D__

STREET ADDRESS __330 Eastwood Lane__

CITY __Lynchburg__ STATE __VA__

ZIP CODE __24506-2648__ BIRTHDATE __08/01/74__ EXPIRATION DATE __09/25/95__

HEIGHT __5'02"__ WEIGHT __120__ EYE COLOR __GR__

SEX [ ] MALE

[X] FEMALE

ORGAN DONOR [ ] YES

[X] NO

RESTRICTIONS __Corrective Lenses__

ENDORSEMENTS __Motorcycle__

_____ [ ] (FOR OFFICE USE ONLY)

DRIVER'S LICENSE APPLICATION

LAST NAME __Loveitt__

FIRST NAME __Herman__   MIDDLE INITIAL __H__

STREET ADDRESS __556 River Edge Road__

CITY __Manassas__   STATE __VA__

ZIP CODE __24604-8700__   BIRTHDATE __08/12/54__   EXPIRATION DATE __07/20/94__

HEIGHT __6'00"__   WEIGHT __150__   EYE COLOR __BL__

SEX   [X] MALE   RESTRICTIONS __Complete Hand Controls__

      [ ] FEMALE   ENDORSEMENTS __Motorcycle__

ORGAN DONOR [X] YES

      [ ] NO   _____ [ ] (FOR OFFICE USE ONLY)

DRIVER'S LICENSE APPLICATION

LAST NAME __Wakui__

FIRST NAME __Richard__   MIDDLE INITIAL __W__

STREET ADDRESS __1170 Rosemont Drive__

CITY __Norfolk__   STATE __VA__

ZIP CODE __23501-4287__   BIRTHDATE __06/03/56__   EXPIRATION DATE __07/15/94__

HEIGHT __5'04"__   WEIGHT __150__   EYE COLOR __BR__

SEX   [X] MALE   RESTRICTIONS __Daylight Driving Only__

      [ ] FEMALE   ENDORSEMENTS __Two-Axle Truck__

ORGAN DONOR [X] YES

      [ ] NO   _____ [ ] (FOR OFFICE USE ONLY)

DRIVER'S LICENSE APPLICATION

LAST NAME __Shepherd__

FIRST NAME __Eugenia__   MIDDLE INITIAL __A__

STREET ADDRESS __2940 Samson Place__

CITY __Petersburg__   STATE __VA__

ZIP CODE __23801-6580__   BIRTHDATE __03/13/72__   EXPIRATION DATE __01/12/94__

HEIGHT __4'11"__   WEIGHT __98__   EYE COLOR __BL__

SEX   [ ] MALE

[X] FEMALE

ORGAN DONOR [X] YES

[ ] NO

RESTRICTIONS __Corrective Lenses__

ENDORSEMENTS __Motorcycle__

_____ [ ] (FOR OFFICE USE ONLY)

DRIVER'S LICENSE APPLICATION

LAST NAME __Tinksword__

FIRST NAME __Jennifer__   MIDDLE INITIAL __P__

STREET ADDRESS __700 Courthouse Rd N__

CITY __Richmond__   STATE __VA__

ZIP CODE __23201-2239__   BIRTHDATE __09/15/62__   EXPIRATION DATE __06/14/95__

HEIGHT __5'08"__   WEIGHT __155__   EYE COLOR __BL__

SEX   [ ] MALE

[X] FEMALE

ORGAN DONOR [X] YES

[ ] NO

RESTRICTIONS __None__

ENDORSEMENTS __Moped__

_____ [ ] (FOR OFFICE USE ONLY)

DRIVER'S LICENSE APPLICATION

LAST NAME __Walker__

FIRST NAME __Reuben__   MIDDLE INITIAL __M__

STREET ADDRESS __459 Berring Street__

CITY __Arlington__   STATE __VA__

ZIP CODE __22916-1947__   BIRTHDATE __05/15/48__   EXPIRATION DATE __10/11/95__

HEIGHT __6'02"__   WEIGHT __190__   EYE COLOR __BR__

SEX __X__ MALE   __☐__ FEMALE

ORGAN DONOR __☐__ YES   __X__ NO

RESTRICTIONS __None__

ENDORSEMENTS __Two-Axle Truck__

__☐__ (FOR OFFICE USE ONLY)

DRIVER'S LICENSE APPLICATION

LAST NAME __Zollinger__

FIRST NAME __Michael__   MIDDLE INITIAL __J__

STREET ADDRESS __3095 Indian Rock Street__

CITY __Roanoke__   STATE __VA__

ZIP CODE __24022-6365__   BIRTHDATE __12/16/33__   EXPIRATION DATE __08/10/95__

HEIGHT __5'08"__   WEIGHT __180__   EYE COLOR __BL__

SEX __X__ MALE   __☐__ FEMALE

ORGAN DONOR __☐__ YES   __X__ NO

RESTRICTIONS __Automatic Transmission__

ENDORSEMENTS __School Bus__

__☐__ (FOR OFFICE USE ONLY)

DRIVER'S LICENSE APPLICATION

LAST NAME __Sherwood__

FIRST NAME __Stephen__ MIDDLE INITIAL __H__

STREET ADDRESS __5499 Accomac Street__

CITY __Springfield__ STATE __VA__

ZIP CODE __22151-2705__ BIRTHDATE __04/16/70__ EXPIRATION DATE __09/15/95__

HEIGHT __6'06"__ WEIGHT __193__ EYE COLOR __BR__

SEX [X] MALE
[ ] FEMALE

ORGAN DONOR [ ] YES
[X] NO

RESTRICTIONS __Corrective Lenses__

ENDORSEMENTS __None__

_____ [ ] (FOR OFFICE USE ONLY)

DRIVER'S LICENSE APPLICATION

LAST NAME __Piechowski__

FIRST NAME __Jerry__ MIDDLE INITIAL __F__

STREET ADDRESS __4916 Godwin Street__

CITY __Suffolk__ STATE __VA__

ZIP CODE __23434-0260__ BIRTHDATE __07/03/66__ EXPIRATION DATE __07/13/94__

HEIGHT __5'11"__ WEIGHT __192__ EYE COLOR __BL__

SEX [X] MALE
[ ] FEMALE

ORGAN DONOR [ ] YES
[X] NO

RESTRICTIONS __None__

ENDORSEMENTS __None__

_____ [ ] (FOR OFFICE USE ONLY)

Quiz 3

PART 1

(2 POINTS EACH)

➤ **Match the vocabulary terms with the best definitions. Write the letter of the term in the space to the left of the definition. You will not use every vocabulary term.**

A. **agent**
B. **actuarial table**
C. **actuary**
D. **coverage**
E. **census**

F. **deductible**
G. **discount**
H. **endorsement**
I. **point system**
J. **photo identification card**

K. **policyholder**
L. **premium**
M. **restriction**
N. **survey**

_____ 1. The U.S. Government is responsible to count the population every ten years.

_____ 2. The collection of data by the government to perform statistical analysis.

_____ 3. Policyholders pay this amount for insurance protection.

_____ 4. This term identifies the person who purchases insurance.

_____ 5. On this table, statistics are combined to show how likely it is that certain people will suffer an insurance loss.

_____ 6. The insurance company deducts this amount from the repair bill before paying for the repairs.

_____ 7. This term identifies a decrease in the premium amount due to good grades, low miles driven daily, or good driving records of the policyholder.

_____ 8. Used by people who do not have a driver's license.

_____ 9. This term identifies a person who is licensed to sell insurance.

_____ 10. This term identifies the amount and type of insurance protection purchased.

_____ 11. An additional right to drive specialized vehicles.

_____ 12. A condition that must be met in order for the driver's license to be valid.

251

PART 2

(1 POINT EACH)

✏ **Each of the following statements is either true or false. Indicate your choice by circling T for a true statement or F for a false statement.**

T F **1.** A driver's license is an appropriate place to indicate organ donor information.

T F **2.** To update the data, the government usually takes or conducts sample surveys.

T F **3.** The Bureau of Census cannot determine the number of people in a household from a completed census questionnaire.

T F **4.** The U.S. Department of Commerce is responsible for gathering census data.

T F **5.** The insurance company may elect to give the customer the fair market value for their damaged car.

T F **6.** Insurance companies can expect to pay more in losses to policyholders who smoke.

T F **7.** When determining the amount of the premium, an insurance company sometimes considers the engine size of the insured automobile.

T F **8.** It is illegal for insurance companies to discriminate against teenagers by charging them more for the same insurance protection than they charge a 30-year old adult.

PART 3

(3 POINTS EACH)

✏ **Briefly answer each of the following items. Write your answers on the lines provided.**

1. Define the term undercounting.

_____

_____

2. There are at least five types of data collected when a census is taken. List them.

_____

_____

_____

3. Premium amounts paid for insurance are based on policyholders' desires for different coverages. List three items agents should take into consideration.

_____

_____

_____

4. State why insurance companies give discounts.

_____

_____

5. Explain the three requirements for applying for a driver's license the first time.

_____

_____

_____

6. List five individual types of data that can be obtained from a driver's license application.

_____

_____

_____

_____

_____

☞ **Remove Quiz 3 from your text-workbook and hand it to your instructor for correcting.**

Total Points Possible	50
(Minus) Incorrect Points	_____
Total Points Earned	_____
Percent Correct	_____
Grade	_____

Activity 10

AUTOMOBILE REGISTRATION

→ **1** Define automobile registration, certificate of title, mandatory insurance, odometer and lien holder.

2 State the major reason why states monitor the ownership of vehicles.

3 Explain how vehicle registration can assist in law enforcement.

4 Explain why it is important for the seller to ensure that a vehicle's title is transferred to the buyer.

5 Explain the process of vehicle registration.

6 Key-enter data for a computerized automobile registration system.

DATA ENTRY APPLICATION AND JOB DESCRIPTION

When automobiles were first invented, it was quite easy to match a car with its owner because very few were on the road. There was no need for the owners to register their automobiles with any governmental agency. However, time has drastically changed this picture. In most towns and cities today it is virtually impossible, due to the increased number of vehicles on the roadways, to match drivers with their automobiles. Therefore, states have found it necessary to monitor vehicle ownership. **Automobile registration** is the method used to follow automobile ownership. You must own a vehicle before you can register it. When a vehicle is registered, the Department of Motor Vehicles gives the owner a certificate of registration and license plates or tags. The certificate identifies both the car and the owner, and it must be in the vehicle any time the vehicle is in use. The license plates allow the police and others to identify the car. Automobile owners must complete an automobile registration application, shown in Figure 10.1, to establish a record of ownership for a particular vehicle. During this process, the owner receives a **certificate of title**, a document that verifies the true ownership of the vehicle, and a license plate for the automobile. The bureau will create a new title in the name of the new buyer and mail it, unless money was borrowed to buy the car. If this is the case, the title will be sent to the bank or finance company. After the loan is paid in full, the lender is required to send the title to the vehicle owner.

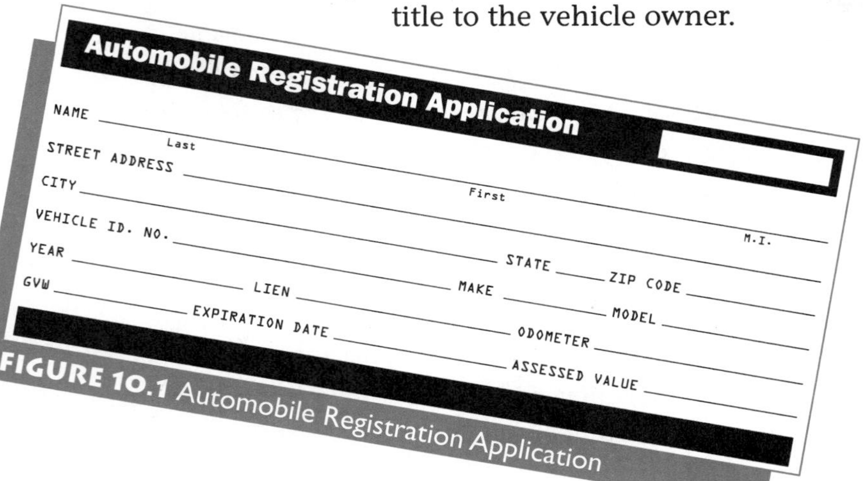

Automobile Registration Application

NAME _____
                Last
STREET ADDRESS _____
CITY _____   First
VEHICLE ID. NO. _____   M.I. _____
YEAR _____ STATE _____ ZIP CODE _____
GVW _____ LIEN _____ MAKE _____
        EXPIRATION DATE _____ MODEL _____
                        ODOMETER _____
                        ASSESSED VALUE _____

FIGURE 10.1 Automobile Registration Application

When you register your vehicle, you record its serial number, the make, the model, and the year of the auto, the reading on the odometer, and the name of the lien holder. The **odometer** is the dial on a car's dashboard that keeps track of the total number of miles the car has been driven. The seller must indicate the mileage of the car when the title changes hands. This is done by copying the odometer reading. In addition to establishing vehicle ownership by transferring the title, you must register it to get a license plate. The **lien holder** is the name of the person (or financial institution) to whom money is owed for financing the purchase of the car.

WHY STATES MONITOR THE OWNERSHIP OF VEHICLES

There are several reasons why states require automobile registration. The major reason is to hold owners responsible for their automobiles. For instance, if you illegally park your car, a law enforcement officer will issue a ticket and record the vehicle's license plate number. The officer will then use this license plate number to identify the owner and hold that person accountable for the ticket. The same procedure can be followed if a vehicle is involved in a "hit and run" accident. If someone is able to obtain the license plate number of the vehicle involved, it is possible to identify the vehicle and its owner. You are responsible for a vehicle registered in your name. When you sell a vehicle, you must make sure the title is transferred to the new owner. If not, you could be held responsible for the the new owner's actions.

Automobile registration also helps deter automobile theft. Because the serial number, make, model, and year of the auto are on record with the state, it is easier for a vehicle to be traced and identified. It also makes it more difficult to transfer the title illegally if the car is stolen.

Another reason states monitor vehicle ownership is for tax purposes. Each state imposes a yearly tax on motor vehicles. In most cases, the amount of the tax is based on the value and weight of the vehicle. Part of the monies collected is used for improvement and maintenance of the roads.

Many states have **mandatory insurance** laws dictating that all vehicle owners must have a minimum amount of insurance coverage. This law guarantees that if you are in an accident and the other driver is at fault, some or all of your expenses will be paid by the other driver's insurance coverage. In states where mandatory insurance is in effect, motor vehicle registration helps the state enforce this law. When registering your vehicle, you must report the name of your insurance company and the policy number. This gives the state a formal record of every driver's insurance coverage.

Finally, registration of motor vehicles assists law enforcement officers. When a driver is stopped for a traffic violation, it is common for the enforcement officer to check on both the driver's record and the vehicle registration. The officer may use a two-way radio to give the vehicle's license plate number and the driver's license number to a data processing operator at a central location. Some police cars are equipped with a computer terminal that is connected to a large computerized database. Whichever technique is used, the use of computers makes it is possible to get a record of both the driver and the vehicle to see if there are any outstanding traffic tickets or criminal warrants on the driver.

HOW STATES MONITOR VEHICLE REGISTRATION

With so many vehicles on the roads today, it may seem difficult for states to enforce the vehicle registration law. However, this is not the case. In fact, it is relatively easy to identify vehicles that are not registered. When registering a new vehicle, the owner is issued a license plate that must be legible, lighted, and displayed on the vehicle. When the owner renews the registration and pays the tax for the year, either a new license plate or a sticker tab for the original plate is issued. The expiration date of the registration is stated on the license plate (or **sticker tab**) so that it is visible at all times. In addition, the state keeps track of the expiration date of each registration and renewal notices are usually sent to the owner as a reminder.

HOW TO REGISTER A VEHICLE

The method for vehicle registration varies from state to state. However, most states allow the owner to either register the vehicle in person or mail in the registration form. The typical process followed to transfer the title from one person to another is to pay a fee and complete a title transfer form signed by both the seller and buyer. If the state has a mandatory insurance law, the buyer would have to give the required insurance information. In most states the title transfer form will be processed and the new owner will receive the certificate of title in the mail. Renewal of a vehicle registration is completed in much the same manner. The renewal can be done in person or through the mail. A renewal form must be completed and a fee paid. In many states, the owner will receive the renewed title immediately.

HOW STORED DATA IS USED

Since computers are generally used to store and process all of this information, it is possible to use the data in various ways. Vehicle registration data is considered public information in many states. This means that anyone has access to the data, although sometimes a fee is charged for this information. Some states have laws that protect the owner by classifying this information as private. This means that only authorized personnel (such as law enforcement officers) can have access to it.

JOBS AVAILABLE IN RELATED AREAS

The computer has made the registration process more efficient. In many cases, the information is key-entered at each local office. Some states send the application or renewal forms to a central data processing location to be key-entered. Data entry jobs related to motor vehicle registration vary from location to location. In smaller towns and cities, the data may not be key-entered at the local site. Instead, it may be sent to a central location. In many larger cities, the data is key-entered at local offices. Central processing centers require trained key-entry operators to input new registrations, renewals, and title transfers. In addition, operators are needed to respond to law enforcement officers' requests for information.

INPUT FIELDS

*I*n this activity you will key-enter data from 20 automobile registration applications. Information from driver's license applications is key-entered into input fields on the data entry screen. The input fields for this activity are described below and on the next page.

Name (Last, First, M.I.). This entry is three separate fields, key-entered separately. The last name field can contain up to twelve characters, the first name field can contain six characters, and the middle initial can contain one character.

Street Address. This 21-character field contains both the applicant's house number and the street name. If an address is longer than the field, you should key-enter as much of the address as there is space and drop the rest of the letters.

City. This field identifies the applicant's city.

State. This field identifies the applicant's two-letter state abbreviation.

ZIP. This field contains the applicant's nine-character ZIP code.

Vehicle Identification Number (VIN). This field represents the serial number assigned to each vehicle by the manufacturer. This number is a combination of letters and digits.

Make. This field identifies the make of the vehicle, such as Ford, Chevrolet, Toyota, etc.

Model. This field identifies the model of the vehicle, such as Escort, Cavalier, Supra, etc.

Year. This two-character field identifies the year the car was made.

Lien. This 15-character field contains the name of the person (or financial institution) to whom money is owed for financing the purchase of the car. Key-enter the lien holder's name as it appears on the application form.

Odometer. In this six-character field you will key-enter the odometer reading as it appears on the application form. The odometer reading indicates the total number of miles the car has been driven.

GVW (Gross Vehicle Weight). One of two factors that is used to determine the registration fee is the weight of the vehicle. This five-character field contains the weight of the applicant's vehicle.

Expiration Date. This six-character field contains the month, day, and the year the registration must be renewed.

Assessed Value. The second factor used to determine the registration fee is the value of the automobile. This five-character field contains the assessed value of the applicant's vehicle.

Step-by-Step Instructions (OBJECTIVE 7)

GET READY

Follow the start-up procedures for your computer.

COMPLETE ALPHA-NUMERIC DEXTERITY DRILL

```
15623  63021  653890  CHEVROLET  GU602337872
437453  2800  L986  3076525050261  CAPRICE  E
13799  630318166  88  93  70995  J71134VU6519
HAZELWOOD  GC438  83181788945  63042  439086
JT1126391  35  893076  CHEROKEE  101  0387731
```

STEP 1   From the *Activities* menu, select *Activity 10 Automobile Registration Application.*

STEP 2   Select *Alpha-Numeric Dexterity Drill.*

STEP 3   Enter the data for each line. Press *enter* or *return* at the end of each line.

STEP 4   Select *OK* when you are finished key-entering. Review your score.

STEP 5   Select *Review* to review any errors that were made. After you have reviewed your performance, select *OK*.

Repeat the Alpha-Numeric Dexterity Drill as many times as instructed by your teacher.

COMPLETE KEYPAD DEXTERITY DRILL

```
20155  94633  49542  38428  89889  27850  8210
56698  53488  69213  01255  34325  39176  2080
90736  24251  08352  12643  90370  89603  8513
52466  53455  25448  45863  25489  65723  2366
45465  45987  56354  37169  15080  60437  0589
```

STEP 1 From the *Activities* menu, select *Activity 10 Automobile Registration Application.*

STEP 2 Select *Keypad Dexterity Drill.*

STEP 3 Enter the data for each line. Press *enter* or *return* at the end of each line.

STEP 4 Select *OK* when you are finished key-entering. Review your score.

STEP 5 Select *Review* to review any errors that were made. After you have reviewed your performance, select *OK.*

Repeat the Keypad Dexterity Drill as many times as instructed by your teacher.

COMPLETE AUTOMOBILE REGISTRATION APPLICATION FORMS

STEP 1 Remove all of the Automobile Registration Application forms that are located at the end of this activity.

STEP 2 From the *Activities* menu, select *Activity 10 Automobile Registration Application.*

STEP 3 Select *Registration Application.* Your screen will be similar to that shown in Figure 10.2.

FIGURE 10.2

```
 File  Edit  Activities  Help
┌──────────────────────────────────────────────────────────────┐
│              Activity 10: Automobile Registration              │
│  Student Name: KYLE PORTER         Pass: 1 12/10/00 Incomplete │
│                                                 Record No.  1  │
│                                                                │
│  NAME:  LAST [        ]     FIRST [      ]    M.I. [ ]         │
│  STREET ADDRESS [               ]                              │
│  CITY [          ]        STATE [  ]      ZIP CODE [    - ]    │
│  VIN [          ]         MAKE [      ]   MODEL [       ]      │
│  YEAR [    ]              LIEN [      ]   ODOMETER [    ]      │
│  GVW [   ]       EXPIRATION DATE [  /  / ]  ASSESSED VALUE $[  ]│
│                                                                │
│  [Previous Record <F8>]   [End Input <F10>]  [Next Record <F9>]│
│              ALT-H for detailed key press information          │
└──────────────────────────────────────────────────────────────┘
```

STEP 4 Key-enter the Name: Last, First, M.I., Street Address, City, State, ZIP, VIN, Make, Model, Year, Lien, Odometer, GVW, Expiration Date and Assessed Value in the appropriate fields for your first record.

STEP 5 Select *Next Record.*

STEP 6 Key-enter the remaining records.

✍ **Note: If you are interrupted before key-entering all of the records, follow the necessary procedures to end input.**

STEP 7 After key-entering all of the Automobile Registration Application forms, select *End Input*. If you notice errors after you have selected End Input, select *Edit* and then move to the appropriate fields to key-enter the corrections.

STEP 8 Print the automobile registration application forms if instructed by your teacher.

STEP 9 Select *Analyze*. Review the information presented.

STEP 10 Select *Review*. Any errors will be highlighted.

STEP 11 Select *Done*.

STEP 12 You may generate a report of your performance.

Note: In a real work situation, you would strive for completely accurate records. Therefore, it is suggested that once you have completed all of the steps listed here, you should go back into the records and correct any errors. To do this:

- From the *Activities* menu, select *Activity 10 Automobile Registration Application*.

- Select *Registration Application*.

- Select *Open*.

- Use the appropriate keys to locate the proper record and field and then key-enter the correction.

- Select *End Input*.

- Select *Analyze*.

- Select *Review*.

- Select *Done*.

- Print the automobile registration application forms if instructed by your teacher.

VOCABULARY

automobile registration
certificate of title
lien holder
mandatory insurance
odometer
sticker tab

Activity 10 Study Guide

AUTOMOBILE REGISTRATION

PART 1

OBJECTIVES 1, 2, 3, AND 4 (1 POINT EACH)

➥ **Match the vocabulary terms with the best definitions. Write the letter of the term in the space to the left of the definition.**

A. **automobile registration**
B. **certificate of title**
C. **computer terminal**
D. **lien holder**
E. **mandatory insurance**
F. **odometer**
G. **sticker tab**

_____ 1. A minimum amount of insurance coverage for all vehicles is required in some states.

_____ 2. The true ownership of an automobile is verifiable by this document.

_____ 3. The most common method used by each state to monitor automobile ownership.

_____ 4. Found in many police cars to get current information on drivers and the vehicle when they are stopped.

_____ 5. A method that a state uses to tell police that a vehicle is registered for the current year.

_____ 6. The instrument that measures the distance traveled.

_____ 7. The person from whom the money has been borrowed to purchase an automobile.

PART 2

OBJECTIVES 2, 3, AND 5 (1 POINT EACH)

➥ **Each of the following statements is either true or false. Indicate your choice by circling T for a true statement or F for a false statement.**

T   F   1. The seller of an automobile does not have to indicate the mileage when the title changes to another person.

T   F   2. The certificate of registration identifies both the automobile and owner.

T   F   3. The certificate of registration must be in the vehicle any time it is in use.

T   F   4. A vehicle does not have an identifying serial number.

T   F   **5.** Vehicle registration data is considered public information in many states.

T   F   **6.** The bureau will create a new title in the name of the buyer (unless there is a lien holder) and mail it.

PART 3

OBJECTIVES 2, 3, AND 4 (3 POINTS EACH)

👉 **Briefly answer each of the following items. Write your answers on the lines provided.**

1. Explain the difference, if any, between the speedometer and the odometer.

_____

_____

2. Give several reasons why states require automobile registration.

_____

_____

3. Why is it important to the seller of an automobile to see that the vehicle's title is properly and quickly transferred to the buyer?

_____

_____

4. Explain the renewal registration process.

_____

_____

5. List five pieces of data found on the Registration Application.

_____

_____

👉 **Remove the Activity 10 Study Guide from your text-workbook and hand it to your instructor for correcting.**

Total Points Possible	28
(Minus) Incorrect Points	_____
Total Points Earned	_____
Percent Correct	_____
Grade	_____

Automobile Registration Application   No. 001

NAME Romero   Monica   C
       Last   First   M.I.
STREET ADDRESS 15623 Richway Dr

CITY Balwin   STATE MO   ZIP CODE 63242-6538

VEHICLE ID. NO. MZ0055434948752   MAKE Chevrolet   MODEL Blazer

YEAR 94   LIEN Union State Bnk   ODOMETER 041260

GVW 04200   EXPIRATION DATE 12/09/96   ASSESSED VALUE 16000

Automobile Registration Application   No. 002

NAME Fisher   James   E
       Last   First   M.I.
STREET ADDRESS 307 Bristol Ct

CITY Columbia   STATE MO   ZIP CODE 65205-0261

VEHICLE ID. NO. GU6023378722147   MAKE Cadillac   MODEL Eldorado

YEAR 91   LIEN N/A   ODOMETER 043753

GVW 4100   EXPIRATION DATE 03/24/93   ASSESSED VALUE 10700

Automobile Registration Application   No. 003

NAME Guerra   Susanna   E
       Last   First   M.I.
STREET ADDRESS 31799 Taylor Way

CITY Florissant   STATE MO   ZIP CODE 63029-8166

VEHICLE ID. NO. J71134270418519   MAKE Chevrolet   MODEL Cavalier

YEAR 90   LIEN Midstate Saving   ODOMETER 026000

GVW 03600   EXPIRATION DATE 06/12/93   ASSESSED VALUE 05000

Automobile Registration Application

NAME _Gustafson_ _Timothy_ _A_
Last   First   M.I.

STREET ADDRESS _2550 Beverly Dr_

CITY _Hazelwood_   STATE _MO_   ZIP CODE _63742-4390_

VEHICLE ID. NO. _GC4383181788945_   MAKE _Jaguar_   MODEL _XJE_

YEAR _94_   LIEN _Capital Corp_   ODOMETER _055212_

GVW _3600_   EXPIRATION DATE _07/02/96_   ASSESSED VALUE _26675_

Automobile Registration Application

NAME _Pollack_ _John_ _G_
Last   First   M.I.

STREET ADDRESS _8800 Glenwood Street_

CITY _Independence_   STATE _MO_   ZIP CODE _64050-5307_

VEHICLE ID. NO. _G22470321445429_   MAKE _Pontiac_   MODEL _Grand Prix_

YEAR _90_   LIEN _GMAC Finance_   ODOMETER _042000_

GVW _34000_   EXPIRATION DATE _08/14/91_   ASSESSED VALUE _05375_

Automobile Registration Application

NAME _Belanger_ _Raoul_ _G_
Last   First   M.I.

STREET ADDRESS _101 Comingo Ave_

CITY _Joplin_   STATE _MO_   ZIP CODE _64802-5431_

VEHICLE ID. NO. _JT1263914809153_   MAKE _Jeep_   MODEL _Cherokee_

YEAR _93_   LIEN _1st California_   ODOMETER _038773_

GVW _03076_   EXPIRATION DATE _04/17/95_   ASSESSED VALUE _14995_

Automobile Registration Application — No. 007

NAME Aporte (Last)   Aria (First)   L (M.I.)
STREET ADDRESS 4326 Fairmont Ave
CITY Kansas City   STATE MO   ZIP CODE 64142-1934
VEHICLE ID. NO. JL7356461110686   MAKE Hyundai   MODEL Scoupe
YEAR 90   LIEN N/A   ODOMETER 036021
GVW 02475   EXPIRATION DATE 07/27/93   ASSESSED VALUE 09865

Automobile Registration Application — No. 008

NAME Pontau (Last)   Richelle (First)   R (M.I.)
STREET ADDRESS 530 Saratoga Hts
CITY Saint Charles   STATE MO   ZIP CODE 63302-5950
VEHICLE ID. NO. LY7028276767368   MAKE Ford   MODEL Explorer
YEAR 90   LIEN N/A   ODOMETER 012281
GVW 03500   EXPIRATION DATE 02/23/93   ASSESSED VALUE 18000

Automobile Registration Application — No. 009

NAME Pooters (Last)   Stephen (First)   C (M.I.)
STREET ADDRESS 153 Woodbine Rd
CITY Saint Joseph   STATE MO   ZIP CODE 64505-7544
VEHICLE ID. NO. MS6001923747115   MAKE Buick   MODEL Century
YEAR 90   LIEN Western Life   ODOMETER 042012
GVW 03265   EXPIRATION DATE 06/06/93   ASSESSED VALUE 08600

Automobile Registration Application — No. 010

NAME: Speranza (Last) — Richard (First) — J (M.I.)
STREET ADDRESS: 1133 Washington Ave
CITY: Saint Louis — STATE: MO — ZIP CODE: 63129-9082
VEHICLE ID. NO.: H11490898166435 — MAKE: Chevrolet — MODEL: Camaro
YEAR: 92 — LIEN: Union State Bnk — ODOMETER: 057555
GVW: 2575 — EXPIRATION DATE: 08/14/94 — ASSESSED VALUE: 06300

Automobile Registration Application — No. 011

NAME: Southport (Last) — William (First) — M (M.I.)
STREET ADDRESS: 4600 Harvard Ave
CITY: Springfield — STATE: MO — ZIP CODE: 65808-5365
VEHICLE ID. NO.: GWE406126206415 — MAKE: Oldsmobile — MODEL: Delta 88
YEAR: 90 — LIEN: Southwest Bank — ODOMETER: 045222
GVW: 03300 — EXPIRATION DATE: 07/14/92 — ASSESSED VALUE: 06300

Automobile Registration Application — No. 012

NAME: Diaz (Last) — Lisa (First) — M (M.I.)
STREET ADDRESS: 417 Aaron Dr
CITY: Columbia — STATE: MO — ZIP CODE: 65216-9238
VEHICLE ID. NO.: J12AE94R3L33883 — MAKE: Toyota — MODEL: Corolla
YEAR: 91 — LIEN: N/A — ODOMETER: 015625
GVW: 03100 — EXPIRATION DATE: 06/24/93 — ASSESSED VALUE: 06750

Automobile Registration Application

NAME Vendervoort   Howard   K
      _____   _____   _____
           Last   First   M.I.

STREET ADDRESS 129 Village Meadow Drive
                _____

CITY Balwin   STATE MO   ZIP CODE 63211-6762
      _____   _____   _____

VEHICLE ID. NO. YV1AX4941C17316   MAKE Volvo   MODEL DL
                 _____   _____   _____

YEAR 89   LIEN City Bank Corp   ODOMETER 026435
      _____   _____   _____

GVW 03475   EXPIRATION DATE 02/15/93   ASSESSED VALUE 08125
     _____   _____   _____

Automobile Registration Application

NAME Trueworthy   Ivan   M
      _____   _____   _____
           Last   First   M.I.

STREET ADDRESS 8737 Independence Ctr
                _____

CITY Independence   STATE MO   ZIP CODE 64045-4914
      _____   _____   _____

VEHICLE ID. NO. 1HGCA5642JA1747   MAKE Honda   MODEL Accord
                 _____   _____   _____

YEAR 91   LIEN 1st California   ODOMETER 057229
      _____   _____   _____

GVW 2600   EXPIRATION DATE 06/17/93   ASSESSED VALUE 07500
     _____   _____   _____

Automobile Registration Application

NAME Younker   Michelle   H
      _____   _____   _____
           Last   First   M.I.

STREET ADDRESS 101 McIntosh Circle
                _____

CITY Joplin   STATE MO   ZIP CODE 64826-7158
      _____   _____   _____

VEHICLE ID. NO. 1HGCA5646JA0384   MAKE Honda   MODEL Accord
                 _____   _____   _____

YEAR 96   LIEN 1st National   ODOMETER 040156
      _____   _____   _____

GVW 02600   EXPIRATION DATE 07/10/97   ASSESSED VALUE 06500
     _____   _____   _____

Automobile Registration Application — No. 016

NAME Zeamer Barbara D
      Last First M.I.

STREET ADDRESS 52 Baltimore Dr

CITY Kansas City STATE MO ZIP CODE 64128-1427

VEHICLE ID. NO. 3J57F7159521093 MAKE Oldsmobile MODEL Cutlass Su

YEAR 89 LIEN First State Bnk ODOMETER 011639

GVW 03625 EXPIRATION DATE 12/13/93 ASSESSED VALUE 05150

Automobile Registration Application — No. 017

NAME Zimmerman Bruce T
      Last First M.I.

STREET ADDRESS 1425 Hawthorne Ave

CITY Saint Charles STATE MO ZIP CODE 63302-2444

VEHICLE ID. NO. 2MEB75F1KX61571 MAKE Mercury MODEL Grand Marq

YEAR 87 LIEN Federal Credit ODOMETER 142125

GVW 03480 EXPIRATION DATE 03/17/91 ASSESSED VALUE 06200

Automobile Registration Application — No. 018

NAME Albonegon Peter K
      Last First M.I.

STREET ADDRESS 73 Sierra Madre Ave

CITY Columbia STATE MO ZIP CODE 65266-1577

VEHICLE ID. NO. IC33F66PYEX5340 MAKE Chrysler MODEL Fifth Ave

YEAR 90 LIEN N/A ODOMETER 092725

GVW 03475 EXPIRATION DATE 08/15/93 ASSESSED VALUE 22500

Automobile Registration Application

No. 019

NAME _Cantwell_ _Thomas_ _R_
Last   First   M.I.

STREET ADDRESS _208 Spring Valley Dr_

CITY _Saint Charles_ STATE _MO_ ZIP CODE _63326-0328_

VEHICLE ID. NO. _JF2AN5386GF4010_ MAKE _Subaru_ MODEL _GL_

YEAR _89_ LIEN _American Saving_ ODOMETER _066923_

GVW _03700_ EXPIRATION DATE _10/15/91_ ASSESSED VALUE _07350_

Automobile Registration Application

No. 020

NAME _Daugherty_ _Linda_ _M_
Last   First   M.I.

STREET ADDRESS _5321 Concordia Ave_

CITY _Saint Louis_ STATE _MO_ ZIP CODE _63100-5812_

VEHICLE ID. NO. _1G1AW35X1FG1229_ MAKE _Chevrolet_ MODEL _Camaro_

YEAR _90_ LIEN _Western Life_ ODOMETER _043715_

GVW _03600_ EXPIRATION DATE _11/15/93_ ASSESSED VALUE _11500_

Activity 11

STUDENT CLASS REGISTRATION

1 Define closed class, required course and elective course.

2 Explain the two major methods for scheduling.

3 Explain why career goal setting is important.

4 Identify the roles of computers in scheduling courses.

5 Key-enter data for class registration forms.

DATA ENTRY APPLICATION AND JOB DESCRIPTION

*W*hen you were in elementary school, you had little choice of what subjects you studied. Parents and teachers decided what and how much of each subject would be taught. When you reach the college level, you are expected to make the decisions for yourself. Of course, you may seek the advice of parents and professors, but in the end, you are responsible for choosing which courses you take.

Every school's administration does much planning and work to determine an effective class registration process for its school. In order to do this process properly, the administration has to build a master schedule. A **master schedule** is the matrix that connects a school's curricular offerings, available staff, and student enrollment. In short, it is the complete statement of the students who are enrolled in specific courses including information regarding teachers, meeting days, and classrooms. Information available on a master schedule includes: what will be the required subjects per grade or student; how many sections of a particular subject there will be; what will be the number of students to be allowed in a class (maximum); and what will be the minimum of students to allow a course to run. These and many other questions are evaluated by the administration before the master schedule is put together. In this activity, you will learn how Grant Johnson State College sets up a course schedule and assigns students to these courses. In addition, you will learn the role that computers play in this process.

HOW COLLEGES DETERMINE COURSE OFFERINGS

Most colleges use one of two methods to determine their course offerings. Under the first method, school administrators decide what courses will be offered and how many sections of each will be available. The administrators must also take into consideration the number of professors who can teach the course and their availability at that time on the scheduled day. When placing professors in a master schedule, administrators must be certain that the schedules are reasonable for the staff as to the number of periods they are teaching, the number of preparations they have, and the level of experience in the subject matter. Once this has been done, the students will examine the entire schedule, choose which classes they would like to take, determine if these courses are offered at times that fit into their schedules, and register for classes. Under this method, a maximum number of students are permitted to register for each class. A **closed class** means that the maximum number of students allowed has registered and no more students will be permitted to register for that class. If other sections of that course are offered, a student may have to make a schedule change to accommodate the new time period. When this method is used, students have a great deal of control over which courses they take and at what time of the day classes are taken. The administration has a great deal of control over which courses and how many sections are offered.

There is an alternative method of scheduling courses. Under this second method, the administration determines the general courses that are to be offered, but does not limit the number of sections of each that may be taught. At registration time, the students choose only the courses they wish to take. There is no opportunity for the student to indicate the class period desired for each course. After every student has registered, the school administrators will tally the results and determine the number of sections of each course that will be taught. The administration will then arbitrarily assign the students to sections of the courses they chose. In this system, there is little problem with **closed sections** because enough sections are allowed to accommodate the total number of students registered in each course. However, another problem does arise. Often a course on the original list does not attract enough student interest. This course may then be **canceled**, and the few students who registered for it will be forced to choose another course. Even so, when this method is used, the students have more control over which courses will be taught. If enough students register for a course, it will be available.

REQUIRED AND ELECTIVE COURSES

Most people feel that college students should have a choice as to what courses they take, yet at the same time there should be certain basic education courses that should be taken by all students. These basic education courses are sometimes called **required courses**. Required courses are typically in the areas of language arts, mathematics, science, and social science. In addition, some other areas, such as business education, physical education, home economics, industrial arts, and fine arts may be addressed. Many colleges identify specific courses in these areas that are required for everyone. Students are allowed to choose courses within each area, but the schools dictate how many courses must be taken in each department.

To complete a class schedule, students must choose other courses, known as elective courses. **Elective courses** are not required by the administration, but are chosen, or "elected," by the students. These courses give students a chance to explore different areas. Some examples of elective courses include accounting, computer science, word processing, child development, woodworking, and keyboarding. With so many courses available, it is very difficult for students to decide which courses to take. Many students intentionally sample a wide variety of courses to gain general knowledge in all areas. This method may help students determine the careers and hobbies that are of interest to them. After taking a few elective courses, a student may want to concentrate on courses that will help in preparing for a specific career. For example, a sophomore named Michelle chose general business and industrial arts as her electives. During the general business course, Michelle realized that she found business very interesting and she decided to take accounting as one of her electives. The next year, Michelle did well in the accounting course and is now thinking about accounting as a career. In addition to her elective business courses, Michelle also took the courses required by her department. By the time she graduates, Michelle may be ready to decide if she wants to continue with accounting as a career.

HOW REGISTRATION IS COMPLETED

The procedure for class registration is similar from college to college. Students must make course decisions and communicate these choices to school administrators. This can be accomplished by having the students write the names of the courses they want on a sheet of paper. Usually a standardized class registration form is filled out by each student. A sample class registration form is shown in Figure 11.1. In many schools, students will use computerized forms to indicate their choices. These forms can be scanned directly by the computer to be tallied.

TALLYING THE RESULTS

Computers play a very important role in tallying class registration data and assigning students to specific sections of each course. If the students registered on non-computerized forms, all of the data would have to be key-entered into the computer. As with all data-entry activities, key-entering student registration data must be done very accurately because a student could end up in a different course than the one originally chosen. College administrators can use the computer to develop a master schedule, listing all the classes to be offered and all the students in each class. In some cases, the computer can assign rooms for each class, double check to ensure that a student is not enrolled in two classes meeting at the same time and print a class schedule for each student. Finally, some computer programs will print grade sheets for the instructors and course grades for students.

INPUT FIELDS

*I*n this activity, you will key-enter data from class registration forms for 20 students from Grant Johnson State College. A sample registration form is shown in Figure 11.1. The input fields are described on the next page.

GRANT JOHNSON STATE COLLEGE
REGISTRATION

Student Number _____

Name _____
          Last   First   M.I.

Sex: Male ☐   Female ☐   Class _____

Language Arts:		Mathematics:	
____ 91004	World Lit.	____ 30011	Pre-Algebra
____ 91009	Am. Lit. (1)	____ 30113	Applied Math
____ 91010	Am. Lit. (2)	____ 30015	Statistics
____ 91023	Communications	____ 30018	Algebra 1
____ 91024	Adv. Comm.	____ 30030	Geometry
____ 91026	Drama	____ 30053	Trig.
____ 91029	Mass Media	____ 30272	Pre-Calculus
____ 91031	Short Stories	____ 30230	Calculus
____ 91035	Develop. Studies	____ 30250	Computer Sci.

Science:		Social Science:	
____ 02001	Biology	____ 11007	Sociology
____ 02101	Chemistry	____ 11017	Psychology 1
____ 02102	Chem. Lab.	____ 11018	Psychology 2
____ 02201	Psysics	____ 11021	Economics
____ 02213	Geology	____ 11083	World History
____ 02401	Research	____ 11206	Family Studies
		____ 11207	Social Research

Electives:

_____   _____   _____
Elective 1   Elective 2   Elective 3

_____   _____   _____
For Office Use   For Office Use   For Office Use

FIGURE 11.1

Student Number. For identification purposes, each student's social security number is used as the student number. When key-entering this number, do not key the hyphens.

Name (Last, First, M.I.). This entry is three separate fields, key-entered separately. The last name field can contain up to ten characters, the first name field can contain ten characters, and the middle initial can contain one character. If a name is longer than the field, you should key-enter as much of the name as there is space and drop the rest of the letters.

Sex. This one-character field contains the appropriate abbreviation for the sex of the student, either F for female, or M for male.

Class. This two-character field indicates the grade level of the student.

Course Number. This five-character field contains the course number corresponding to the student's course choice. You will key-enter a course number for each course a student has selected. To complete the data entry for the elective courses, you will have to determine the appropriate codes, which are listed in the following section.

(OBJECTIVE 5)

GET READY

Follow the start-up procedures for your computer.

COMPLETE ALPHA-NUMERIC DEXTERITY DRILL

```
818339344 02001 WOODWORKING 30018 910244
ANDERSON 01026 0221311 57791 9462 MARTHA
11021 302230 GENERAL BUSINESS 91026 0466
07211 91035 SMALL ENGINES 91009 BUSINESS
910123 02101 30053 DRAFTING 277268216 CA
```

STEP 1 From the *Activities* menu, select *Activity 11 Student Course Registration*.

STEP 2 Select *Alpha-Numeric Dexterity Drill.*

STEP 3 Enter the data for each line. Press *enter* or *return* at the end of each line.

STEP 4 Select *OK* when you are finished key-entering. Review your score.

STEP 5 Select *Review* to review any errors that were made. After you have reviewed your performance, select *OK*.

Repeat the Alpha-Numeric Dexterity Drill as many times as instructed by your teacher.

COMPLETE KEYPAD DEXTERITY DRILL

```
87445  76246  98526  83822  06369  13750  1097
12157  97835  39984  93745  91939  25139  2919
57575  02651  29825  14811  17510  17514  5012
79020  77596  86518  24724  51323  00256  5078
88789  33280  69117  31698  23656  90563  2986
```

STEP 1 From the *Activities* menu, select *Activity 11 Student Course Registration*.

STEP 2 Select *Keypad Dexterity Drill.*

STEP 3 Enter the data for each line. Press *enter* or *return* at the end of each line.

STEP 4 Select *OK* when you are finished key-entering. Review your score.

STEP 5 Select *Review* to review any errors that were made. After you have reviewed your performance, select *OK*.

Repeat the Keypad Dexterity Drill as many times as instructed by your teacher.

COMPLETE STUDENT COURSE REGISTRATION FORMS

STEP 1 Remove all of the Student Registration Application Forms that are located at the end of this activity.

STEP 2 From the From the *Activities* menu, select *Activity 11 Student Course Registration.*

STEP 3 Select *Registration Form.* Your screen will be similar to that shown in Figure 11.2.

FIGURE 11.2

```
 File  Edit  Activities  Help
┌──────────────────────────────────────────────────────────┐
│           Activity 11: Student Course Registration        │
│  Student name: KYLE PORTER          Pass: 1 12/10/00 Incomplete │
│              GRANT JOHNSON STATE COLLEGE       Record No.  1 │
│                     REGISTRATION                          │
│                                  STUDENT NUMBER [        ] │
│   Name:  LAST [        ]      FIRST [        ]      M.I. [ ] │
│   SEX [ ]    CLASS [ ]                                     │
│   LANGUAGE ARTS [     ]     MATHEMATICS   [     ]         │
│   SCIENCE       [     ]     SOCIAL SCIENCE [     ]         │
│   ELECTIVE 1    [     ]     ELECTIVE 2  [     ]   ELECTIVE 3 [    ] │
│                                                           │
│   [ Previous Record <F8> ]   [ End Input <F10> ]   [ Next Record <F9> ] │
├──────────────────────────────────────────────────────────┤
│          ALT-H for detailed key press information          │
└──────────────────────────────────────────────────────────┘
```

STEP 4 Key-enter the Student Number; Name: Last, First, M.I.; Sex; Class; Language Arts; Mathematics; Science; Social Science; Elective 1; Elective 2; and Elective 3. To complete the codes for the elective courses, you will need to refer to the following table.

ELECTIVE COURSE CODES

Course	Code	Course	Code
Accounting	05205	Drawing	08010
Advanced Physical Ed.	04606	General Business	05005
Auto Repair	08325	Graphics	08350
Business Machines	05301	Health	04103
Business Management	06020	Interior Design	07211
Child Development	07011	Intermediate Physical Ed.	04605
Clothing	07251	Keyboarding	06017
Construction	08525	Notetaking	05109
Drafting	08003	Small Engines	08313
Foods	07511	Woodworking	08012
		Word Processing	06002

STEP 5 Select *Next Record.*

STEP 6 Key-enter the remaining records.

Note: **If you are interrupted before key-entering all of the records, follow the necessary procedures to end input.**

STEP 7   After key-entering all of the Student Registration Application forms, select *End Input*. If you notice errors after you have selected End Input, select *Edit* and then move to the appropriate fields to key-enter the corrections.

STEP 8   Print the student course registration forms if instructed by your teacher.

STEP 9   Select *Analyze*. Review the information presented.

STEP 10   Select *Review*. Any errors will be highlighted.

STEP 11   Select *Done*.

STEP 12   You may generate a report of your performance.

Note: In a real work situation, you would strive for completely accurate records. Therefore, it is suggested that once you have completed all the steps listed here, you should go back into the records and correct all errors. To do this:

- **From the *Activities* menu, select *Activity 11 Student Course Registration*.**
- **Select *Registration Form*.**
- **Select *Open*.**
- **Use the appropriate keys to locate the proper record and field and then key-enter the correction.**
- **Select *End Input*.**
- **Select *Analyze*.**
- **Select *Review*.**
- **Select *Done*.**
- **Print the student course registration forms if instructed by your teacher.**

VOCABULARY

canceled course
closed class
closed section
elective course
master schedule
required course

Activity 11 Study Guide

STUDENT CLASS REGISTRATION

OBJECTIVES 2, 3, AND 4 (2 POINTS EACH)

➡◆ **Match the vocabulary terms with the best definitions. Write the letter of the term in the space to the left of the definition.**

A. **canceled**   C. **required courses**   E. **master schedule**
B. **closed**   D. **elective courses**

_____ **1.** A matrix that connects curricular offerings to available staff and student enrollment.

_____ **2.** A maximum number of students have enrolled or registered in a class.

_____ **3.** What may happen to a course that does not attract enough student interest.

_____ **4.** Courses such as English, Language, or Science.

_____ **5.** Courses that give a student a chance to explore different areas.

OBJECTIVES 2 AND 3 (1 POINT EACH)

➡◆ **Each of the following statements is either true or false. Indicate your choice by circling T for a true statement or F for a false statement.**

T   F   **1.** Every administration does much planning to determine an effective class registration.

T   F   **2.** Most colleges use three methods to determine their course offerings.

T   F   **3.** The number of teachers need not be taken into consideration when scheduling.

T   F   **4.** An administration usually requires no limit (maximum or minimum) for class sizes.

T   F   **5.** A closed class is one for which students may still register.

T   F   **6.** Courses that are not required by the administration are called elective courses.

| T | F | **7.** Students make their class choices on registration forms. |

T   F   **7.** Students make their class choices on registration forms.

T   F   **8.** Many students sample courses in a wide variety to gain insight and a general knowledge into all areas.

T   F   **9.** Administrators have a great deal of control over what is offered and when it is offered.

T   F   **10.** The course number is a random number assigned to each student.

PART 3

OBJECTIVES 1, 2, 3, AND 4 (3 POINTS EACH)

❧ **Briefly answer each of the following items. Write your answers on the lines provided.**

1. Define master schedule.

_____

_____

2. Explain the two major methods of scheduling.

_____

_____

3. Explain closed class.

_____

_____

4. Explain required course.

_____

_____

5. Explain an elective course.

_____

_____

☛ **Remove the Activity 11 Study Guide from your text-workbook and hand it to your instructor for correcting.**

Total Points Possible	35
(Minus) Incorrect Points	_____
Total Points Earned	_____
Percent Correct	_____
Grade	_____

GRANT JOHNSON STATE COLLEGE
REGISTRATION

Student Number 947-82-9873

Name: Quinlan (Last) / Gary (First) / N (M.I.)

Class: Fr

Sex: Male [X] Female [ ]

Mathematics:
- ___ 30011 Pre-Algebra
- [X] 30013 Applied Math
- ___ 30015 Statistics
- ___ 30018 Algebra 1
- ___ 30030 Geometry
- ___ 30053 Trig.
- ___ 30272 Pre-Calculus
- ___ 30230 Calculus
- ___ 30250 Computer Sci.

Language Arts:
- ___ 91004 World Lit.
- ___ 91009 Am. Lit. (1)
- [X] 91010 Am. Lit. (2)
- ___ 91023 Communications
- ___ 91024 Adv. Comm.
- ___ 91026 Drama
- ___ 91029 Mass Media
- ___ 91031 Short Stories
- ___ 91035 Develop. Studies

Social Science:
- ___ 11007 Sociology
- ___ 11017 Psychology 1
- [X] 11018 Psychology 2
- ___ 11021 Economics
- ___ 11083 World History
- ___ 11206 Family Studies
- ___ 11207 Social Research

Science:
- ___ 02001 Biology
- ___ 02101 Chemistry
- [X] 02102 Chem. Lab.
- ___ 02201 **Physics**
- ___ 02213 Geology
- ___ 02401 Research

Electives:

Clothing — Elective 1 _____ For Office Use

Accounting — Elective 2 _____ For Office Use

Business Machines — Elective 3 _____ For Office Use

GRANT JOHNSON STATE COLLEGE
REGISTRATION

Student Number 931-43-8241

Name: Collamore (Last) / Susan (First) / J (M.I.)

Class: So

Sex: Male [ ] Female [X]

Mathematics:
- ___ 30011 Pre-Algebra
- [X] 30013 Applied Math
- ___ 30015 Statistics
- ___ 30018 Algebra 1
- ___ 30030 Geometry
- ___ 30053 Trig.
- ___ 30272 Pre-Calculus
- ___ 30230 Calculus
- ___ 30250 Computer Sci.

Language Arts:
- ___ 91004 World Lit.
- ___ 91009 Am. Lit. (1)
- ___ 91010 Am. Lit. (2)
- ___ 91023 Communications
- ___ 91024 Adv. Comm.
- ___ 91026 Drama
- ___ 91029 Mass Media
- ___ 91031 Short Stories
- [X] 91035 Develop. Studies

Social Science:
- ___ 11007 Sociology
- ___ 11017 Psychology 1
- ___ 11018 Psychology 2
- ___ 11021 Economics
- [X] 11083 World History
- ___ 11206 Family Studies
- ___ 11207 Social Research

Science:
- ___ 02001 Biology
- ___ 02101 Chemistry
- ___ 02102 Chem. Lab.
- ___ 02201 **Physics**
- [X] 02213 Geology
- ___ 02401 Research

Electives:

Health — Elective 1 _____ For Office Use

Child Development — Elective 2 _____ For Office Use

Elective 3 _____ For Office Use

GRANT JOHNSON STATE COLLEGE
REGISTRATION

Name __Zwaam__ __Nicholas__ __L__
Last First M.I.

Student Number __922-43-1219__

Sex: Male [X] Female [ ] Class __Jr__

Mathematics:

- ___ 30011 Pre-Algebra
- ___ **30013 Applied Math**
- ___ 30015 Statistics
- ___ 30018 Algebra 1
- ___ 30030 Geometry
- ___ 30053 Trig.
- ___ 30272 Pre-Calculus
- ___ 30230 Calculus
- [X] 30250 Computer Sci.

Language Arts:

- ___ 91004 World Lit.
- ___ 91009 Am. Lit. (1)
- ___ 91010 Am. Lit. (2)
- ___ 91023 Communications
- ___ 91024 Adv. Comm.
- ___ 91026 Drama
- ___ 91029 Mass Media
- ___ 91031 Short Stories
- [X] 91035 Develop. Studies

Social Science:

- ___ 11007 Sociology
- ___ 11017 Psychology 1
- ___ 11018 Psychology 2
- [X] 11021 Economics
- ___ 11083 World History
- ___ 11206 Family Studies
- ___ 11207 Social Research

Science:

- ___ 02001 Biology
- ___ 02101 Chemistry
- ___ 02102 Chem. Lab.
- ___ **02201 Physics**
- ___ 02213 Geology
- [X] 02401 Research

Electives:

__Business Management__   __Health__
Elective 1   Elective 2   Elective 3

For Office Use   For Office Use   For Office Use

GRANT JOHNSON STATE COLLEGE
REGISTRATION

Name __Puterbaugh__ __Dorane__ __N__
Last First M.I.

Student Number __948-91-9172__

Sex: Male [X] Female [ ] Class __Fr__

Mathematics:

- ___ 30011 Pre-Algebra
- ___ **30013 Applied Math**
- [X] 30015 Statistics
- ___ 30018 Algebra 1
- ___ 30030 Geometry
- ___ 30053 Trig.
- ___ 30272 Pre-Calculus
- ___ 30230 Calculus
- ___ 30250 Computer Sci.

Language Arts:

- [X] 91004 World Lit.
- ___ 91009 Am. Lit. (1)
- ___ 91010 Am. Lit. (2)
- ___ 91023 Communications
- ___ 91024 Adv. Comm.
- ___ 91026 Drama
- ___ 91029 Mass Media
- ___ 91031 Short Stories
- ___ 91035 Develop. Studies

Social Science:

- ___ 11007 Sociology
- [X] 11017 Psychology 1
- ___ 11018 Psychology 2
- ___ 11021 Economics
- ___ 11083 World History
- ___ 11206 Family Studies
- ___ 11207 Social Research

Science:

- ___ 02001 Biology
- [X] 02101 Chemistry
- ___ 02102 Chem. Lab.
- ___ **02201 Physics**
- ___ 02213 · Geology
- ___ 02401 Research

Electives:

__Small Engines__   __Business Management__   __Word Processing__
Elective 1   Elective 2   Elective 3

For Office Use   For Office Use   For Office Use

GRANT JOHNSON STATE COLLEGE
REGISTRATION

Student Number **948-12-5141**

Name: **Middleton** (Last)   **Allison** (First)   **C** (M.I.)

Sex: Male ☐   Female ☒   Class **So**

Language Arts:
- ___ 91004 World Lit.
- _X_ 91009 Am. Lit. (1)
- ___ 91010 Am. Lit. (2)
- ___ 91023 Communications
- ___ 91024 Adv. Comm.
- ___ 91026 Drama
- ___ 91029 Mass Media
- ___ 91031 Short Stories
- ___ 91035 Develop. Studies

Mathematics:
- ___ 30011 Pre-Algebra
- ___ 30013 Applied Math
- _X_ 30015 Statistics
- ___ 30018 Algebra 1
- ___ 30030 Geometry
- ___ 30053 Trig.
- ___ 30272 Pre-Calculus
- ___ 30230 Calculus
- ___ 30250 Computer Sci.

Science:
- ___ 02001 Biology
- ___ 02101 Chemistry
- _X_ 02102 Chem. Lab.
- ___ 02201 Physics
- ___ 02213 Geology
- ___ 02401 Research

Social Science:
- ___ 11007 Sociology
- ___ 11017 Psychology 1
- _X_ 11018 Psychology 2
- ___ 11021 Economics
- ___ 11083 World History
- ___ 11206 Family Studies
- ___ 11207 Social Research

Electives:
- **Health** — Elective 1 — For Office Use
- **Advanced Phys. Ed.** — Elective 2 — For Office Use
- **Small Engines** — Elective 3 — For Office Use

GRANT JOHNSON STATE COLLEGE
REGISTRATION

Student Number **938-64-2131**

Name: **Brockett** (Last)   **Bennett** (First)   **O** (M.I.)

Sex: Male ☒   Female ☐   Class **So**

Language Arts:
- ___ 91004 World Lit.
- _X_ 91009 Am. Lit. (1)
- ___ 91010 Am. Lit. (2)
- ___ 91023 Communications
- ___ 91024 Adv. Comm.
- ___ 91026 Drama
- _X_ 91029 Mass Media
- ___ 91031 Short Stories
- ___ 91035 Develop. Studies

Mathematics:
- ___ 30011 Pre-Algebra
- ___ 30013 Applied Math
- _X_ 30015 Statistics
- ___ 30018 Algebra 1
- ___ 30030 Geometry
- ___ 30053 Trig.
- ___ 30272 Pre-Calculus
- ___ 30230 Calculus
- ___ 30250 Computer Sci.

Science:
- _X_ 02001 Biology
- ___ 02101 Chemistry
- ___ 02102 Chem. Lab.
- ___ 02201 Physics
- ___ 02213 Geology
- ___ 02401 Research

Social Science:
- _X_ 11007 Sociology
- _X_ 11017 Psychology 1
- ___ 11018 Psychology 2
- ___ 11021 Economics
- ___ 11083 World History
- ___ 11206 Family Studies
- ___ 11207 Social Research

Electives:
- **Notetaking** — Elective 1 — For Office Use
- **Business Management** — Elective 2 — For Office Use
- **Keyboarding** — Elective 3 — For Office Use

GRANT JOHNSON STATE COLLEGE
REGISTRATION

Student Number **929-86-1270**

Name: **Farnham** (Last) **Corliss** (First) **S** (M.I.)

Sex: Male [ ] Female [X] Class **Sr**

Mathematics:
- ___ 30011 Pre-Algebra
- ___ **30013** Applied Math
- ___ 30015 Statistics
- ___ 30018 Algebra 1
- ___ 30030 Geometry
- ___ 30053 Trig.
- ___ 30272 Pre-Calculus
- ___ 30230 Calculus
- X 30250 Computer Sci.

Language Arts:
- ___ 91004 World Lit.
- ___ 91009 Am. Lit. (1)
- ___ 91010 Am. Lit. (2)
- ___ 91023 Communications
- X 91024 Adv. Comm.
- ___ 91026 Drama
- ___ 91029 Mass Media
- ___ 91031 Short Stories
- ___ 91035 Develop. Studies

Social Science:
- ___ 11007 Sociology
- ___ 11017 Psychology 1
- ___ 11018 Psychology 2
- X 11021 Economics
- ___ 11083 World History
- ___ 11206 Family Studies
- ___ 11207 Social Research

Science:
- ___ 02001 Biology
- ___ 02101 Chemistry
- ___ 02102 Chem. Lab.
- ___ **02201 Physics**
- ___ 02213 Geology
- X 02401 Research

Electives:

Small Engines — Elective 1
For Office Use

Keyboarding — Elective 2
For Office Use

Intermed. Phys. Ed. — Elective 3
For Office Use

GRANT JOHNSON STATE COLLEGE
REGISTRATION

Student Number **955-46-4264**

Name: **Collamore** (Last) **Marilyn** (First) **A** (M.I.)

Sex: Male [ ] Female [X] Class **Fr**

Mathematics:
- ___ 30011 Pre-Algebra
- ___ **30013** Applied Math
- ___ 30015 Statistics
- ___ 30018 Algebra 1
- X 30030 Geometry
- ___ 30053 Trig.
- ___ 30272 Pre-Calculus
- ___ 30230 Calculus
- ___ 30250 Computer Sci.

Language Arts:
- X 91004 World Lit.
- ___ 91009 Am. Lit. (1)
- ___ 91010 Am. Lit. (2)
- ___ 91023 Communications
- ___ 91024 Adv. Comm.
- ___ 91026 Drama
- ___ 91029 Mass Media
- ___ 91031 Short Stories
- ___ 91035 Develop. Studies

Social Science:
- ___ 11007 Sociology
- ___ 11017 Psychology 1
- ___ 11018 Psychology 2
- ___ 11021 Economics
- ___ 11083 World History
- ___ 11206 Family Studies
- X 11207 Social Research

Science:
- X 02001 Biology
- ___ 02101 Chemistry
- ___ 02102 Chem. Lab.
- ___ **02201 Physics**
- ___ 02213 Geology
- ___ 02401 Research

Electives:

Construction — Elective 1
For Office Use

Keyboarding — Elective 2
For Office Use

Drawing — Elective 3
For Office Use

GRANT JOHNSON STATE COLLEGE
REGISTRATION

Student Number __938-40-8137__

Name __Lindsey__ / __Susan__ / __E__
Last / First / M.I.

Sex: Male ☐ Female ☒ Class __Jr__

Language Arts:
- ___ 91004 World Lit.
- ___ 91009 Am. Lit. (1)
- ___ 91010 Am. Lit. (2)
- ___ 91023 Communications
- _X_ 91024 Adv. Comm.
- ___ 91026 Drama
- ___ 91029 Mass Media
- ___ 91031 Short Stories
- ___ 91035 Develop. Studies

Mathematics:
- ___ 30011 Pre-Algebra
- ___ 30113 Applied Math
- ___ 30015 Statistics
- ___ 30018 Algebra 1
- ___ 30030 Geometry
- _X_ 30053 Trig.
- ___ 30272 Pre-Calculus
- ___ 30230 Calculus
- ___ 30250 Computer Sci.

Science:
- ___ 02001 Biology
- ___ 02101 Chemistry
- ___ 02102 Chem. Lab.
- _X_ 02201 Physics
- ___ 02213 Geology
- ___ 02401 Research

Social Science:
- ___ 11007 Sociology
- ___ 11017 Psychology 1
- ___ 11018 Psychology 2
- ___ 11021 Economics
- _X_ 11083 World History
- ___ 11206 Family Studies
- ___ 11207 Social Research

Electives:

__Graphics__
Elective 1

__Interior Design__
Elective 2

__Keyboarding__
Elective 3

For Office Use

GRANT JOHNSON STATE COLLEGE
REGISTRATION

Student Number __948-10-1163__

Name __Morton__ / __Julie__ / __K__
Last / First / M.I.

Sex: Male ☐ Female ☒ Class __So__

Language Arts:
- ___ 91004 World Lit.
- _X_ 91009 Am. Lit. (1)
- ___ 91010 Am. Lit. (2)
- ___ 91023 Communications
- ___ 91024 Adv. Comm.
- ___ 91026 Drama
- ___ 91029 Mass Media
- ___ 91031 Short Stories
- ___ 91035 Develop. Studies

Mathematics:
- _X_ 30011 Pre-Algebra
- ___ 30013 Applied Math
- ___ 30013 Statistics
- ___ 30018 Algebra 1
- ___ 30030 Geometry
- ___ 30053 Trig.
- ___ 30272 Pre-Calculus
- ___ 30230 Calculus
- ___ 30250 Computer Sci.

Science:
- ___ 02001 Biology
- ___ 02101 Chemistry
- ___ 02102 Chem. Lab.
- _X_ 02201 Physics
- ___ 02213 Geology
- ___ 02401 Research

Social Science:
- ___ 11007 Sociology
- _X_ 11017 Psychology 1
- ___ 11018 Psychology 2
- ___ 11021 Economics
- ___ 11083 World History
- ___ 11206 Family Studies
- ___ 11207 Social Research

Electives:

__Drafting__
Elective 1

__Child Develop.__
Elective 2

__Keyboarding__
Elective 3

For Office Use

GRANT JOHNSON STATE COLLEGE
REGISTRATION

Student Number **923-43-8165**

Name **Detweiler** (Last) **John** (First) **C** (M.I.)

Class **Sr**

Sex: Male **X** Female

Mathematics:
____	30011	Pre-Algebra
____	**30013**	Applied Math
____	30015	Statistics
____	30018	Algebra 1
____	30030	Geometry
____	30053	Trig.
X	30272	Pre-Calculus
____	30230	Calculus
____	30250	Computer Sci.

Language Arts:
____	91004	World Lit.
____	91009	Am. Lit. (1)
____	91010	Am. Lit. (2)
____	91023	Communications
____	91024	Adv. Comm.
____	91026	Drama
X	91029	Mass Media
____	91031	Short Stories
____	91035	Develop. Studies

Social Science:
____	11007	Sociology
____	11017	Psychology 1
____	11018	Psychology 2
X	11021	Economics
____	11083	World History
____	11206	Family Studies
____	11207	Social Research

Science:
____	02001	Biology
____	02101	Chemistry
____	02102	Chem. Lab.
____	02201	Physics
____	02213	Geology
X	02401	Research

Electives:

Interior Design — Elective 1 — For Office Use

Notetaking — Elective 2 — For Office Use

Auto Repair — Elective 3 — For Office Use

GRANT JOHNSON STATE COLLEGE
REGISTRATION

Student Number **951-67-1280**

Name **Wilcoxon** (Last) **Wilson** (First) **D** (M.I.)

Class **Fr**

Sex: Male **X** Female

Mathematics:
____	30011	Pre-Algebra
____	**30013**	Applied Math
____	30015	Statistics
____	30018	Algebra 1
X	30030	Geometry
____	30053	Trig.
____	30272	Pre-Calculus
____	30230	Calculus
____	30250	Computer Sci.

Language Arts:
X	91004	World Lit.
____	91009	Am. Lit. (1)
____	91010	Am. Lit. (2)
____	91023	Communications
____	91024	Adv. Comm.
____	91026	Drama
____	91029	Mass Media
____	91031	Short Stories
____	91035	Develop. Studies

Social Science:
____	11007	Sociology
____	11017	Psychology 1
____	11018	Psychology 2
____	11021	Economics
____	11083	World History
____	11206	Family Studies
X	11207	Social Research

Science:
X	02001	Biology
____	02101	Chemistry
____	02102	Chem. Lab.
____	02201	Physics
____	02213	Geology
____	02401	Research

Electives:

Word Processing — Elective 1 — For Office Use

Gen. Business — Elective 2 — For Office Use

Bus. Management — Elective 3 — For Office Use

Form 1

GRANT JOHNSON STATE COLLEGE
REGISTRATION

Student Number **927-89-5186**

Name: **Ostormeckian** (Last) **Amie** (First) **D** (M.I.)

Sex: Male ☐ Female ☒ Class **Sr**

Language Arts:
___	91004	World Lit.
___	91009	Am. Lit. (1)
___	91010	Am. Lit. (2)
X	91023	Communications
___	91024	Adv. Comm.
___	91026	Drama
___	91029	Mass Media
___	91031	Short Stories
___	91035	Develop. Studies

Mathematics:
___	30011	Pre-Algebra
___	30013	Applied Math
___	30015	Statistics
___	30018	Algebra 1
___	30030	Geometry
___	30053	Trig.
X	30272	Pre-Calculus
___	30230	Calculus
___	30250	Computer Sci.

Science:
___	02001	Biology
___	02101	Chemistry
___	02102	Chem. Lab.
X	02201	Physics
___	02213	Geology
___	02401	Research

Social Science:
___	11007	Sociology
___	11017	Psychology 1
___	11018	Psychology 2
X	11021	Economics
___	11083	World History
___	11206	Family Studies
___	11207	Social Research

Electives:

Drafting _____ Elective 1

For Office Use

Adv. Physical Ed. _____ Elective 2

For Office Use

_____ Elective 3

For Office Use

Form 2

GRANT JOHNSON STATE COLLEGE
REGISTRATION

Student Number **947-26-8255**

Name: **Chaidez** (Last) **Timothy** (First) **N** (M.I.)

Sex: Male ☒ Female ☐ Class **So**

Language Arts:
X	91004	World Lit.
___	91009	Am. Lit. (1)
___	91010	Am. Lit. (2)
___	91023	Communications
___	91024	Adv. Comm.
___	91026	Drama
___	91029	Mass Media
___	91031	Short Stories
___	91035	Develop. Studies

Mathematics:
___	30011	Pre-Algebra
___	30013	Applied Math
___	30015	Statistics
___	30018	Algebra 1
___	30030	Geometry
X	30053	Trig.
___	30272	Pre-Calculus
___	30230	Calculus
___	30250	Computer Sci.

Science:
___	02001	Biology
X	02101	Chemistry
___	02102	Chem. Lab.
___	02201	Physics
___	02213	Geology
___	02401	Research

Social Science:
___	11007	Sociology
X	11017	Psychology 1
___	11018	Psychology 2
___	11021	Economics
___	11083	World History
___	11206	Family Studies
___	11207	Social Research

Electives:

Auto Repair _____ Elective 1

For Office Use

Foods _____ Elective 2

For Office Use

Drafting _____ Elective 3

For Office Use

GRANT JOHNSON STATE COLLEGE
REGISTRATION

Student Number __926-88-9180__

Name __Ormsby__ / __Marguerite__ / __M__
Last / First / M.I.

Class __Sr__

Sex: Male ☐ Female ☒

Language Arts:
- ____ 91004 World Lit.
- ____ 91009 Am. Lit. (1)
- ____ 91010 Am. Lit. (2)
- ____ 91023 Communications
- ____ 91024 Adv. Comm.
- ____ 91026 Drama
- ____ 91029 Mass Media
- __X__ 91031 Short Stories
- ____ 91035 Develop. Studies

Mathematics:
- ____ 30011 Pre-Algebra
- ____ **30013** Applied Math
- ____ 30015 Statistics
- ____ 30018 Algebra 1
- ____ 30030 Geometry
- ____ 30053 Trig.
- ____ 30272 Pre-Calculus
- __X__ 30230 Calculus
- ____ 30250 Computer Sci.

Social Science:
- ____ 11007 Sociology
- ____ 11017 Psychology 1
- ____ 11018 Psychology 2
- ____ 11021 Economics
- __X__ 11083 World History
- ____ 11206 Family Studies
- ____ 11207 Social Research

Science:
- ____ 02001 Biology
- ____ 02101 Chemistry
- ____ 02102 Chem. Lab.
- __X__ 02201 **Physics**
- ____ 02213 Geology
- ____ 02401 Research

Electives:

Small Engines	Health	Bus. Machines
Elective 1	Elective 2	Elective 3
For Office Use	For Office Use	For Office Use

GRANT JOHNSON STATE COLLEGE
REGISTRATION

Student Number __959-98-3106__

Name __Maplewood__ / __Bruce__ / __P__
Last / First / M.I.

Class __Fr__

Sex: Male ☒ Female ☐

Language Arts:
- __X__ 91004 World Lit.
- ____ 91009 Am. Lit. (1)
- ____ 91010 Am. Lit. (2)
- ____ 91023 Communications
- ____ 91024 Adv. Comm.
- ____ 91026 Drama
- ____ 91029 Mass Media
- ____ 91031 Short Stories
- ____ 91035 Develop. Studies

Mathematics:
- ____ 30011 Pre-Algebra
- ____ **30013** Applied Math
- ____ 30015 Statistics
- ____ 30018 Algebra 1
- __X__ 30030 Geometry
- ____ 30053 Trig.
- ____ 30272 Pre-Calculus
- ____ 30230 Calculus
- ____ 30250 Computer Sci.

Social Science:
- __X__ 11007 Sociology
- ____ 11017 Psychology 1
- ____ 11018 Psychology 2
- ____ 11021 Economics
- ____ 11083 World History
- ____ 11206 Family Studies
- ____ 11207 Social Research

Science:
- __X__ 02001 Biology
- ____ 02101 Chemistry
- ____ 02102 Chem. Lab.
- ____ 02201 **Physics**
- ____ 02213 Geology
- ____ 02401 Research

Electives:

Word Processing	Graphics	Gen. Business
Elective 1	Elective 2	Elective 3
For Office Use	For Office Use	For Office Use

GRANT JOHNSON STATE COLLEGE
REGISTRATION

Name __Chen__ __Tracy__ __H__
  Last First M.I.

Student Number __938-37-9196__   Class __Jr__

Sex: Male [X] Female [ ]

Language Arts:
- ___ 91004 World Lit.
- ___ 91009 Am. Lit. (1)
- ___ 91010 Am. Lit. (2)
- ___ 91023 Communications
- ___ 91024 Adv. Comm.
- ___ 91026 Drama
- _X_ 91029 Mass Media
- ___ 91031 Short Stories
- ___ 91035 Develop. Studies

Mathematics:
- ___ 30011 Pre-Algebra
- ___ **30013 Applied Math**
- ___ 30015 Statistics
- ___ 30018 Algebra 1
- ___ 30030 Geometry
- ___ 30053 Trig.
- ___ 30272 Pre-Calculus
- _X_ 30230 Calculus
- ___ 30250 Computer Sci.

Science:
- ___ 02001 Biology
- ___ 02101 Chemistry
- ___ 02102 Chem. Lab.
- ___ **02201 Physics**
- _X_ 02213 Geology
- ___ 02401 Research

Social Science:
- ___ 11007 Sociology
- ___ 11017 Psychology 1
- ___ 11018 Psychology 2
- ___ 11021 Economics
- _X_ 11083 World History
- ___ 11206 Family Studies
- ___ 11207 Social Research

Electives:

Accounting
Elective 1
_____
For Office Use

Drafting
Elective 2
_____
For Office Use

Elective 3
_____
For Office Use

GRANT JOHNSON STATE COLLEGE
REGISTRATION

Name __Anderson__ __Virgil__ __E__
  Last First M.I.

Student Number __927-81-9415__   Class __Sr__

Sex: Male [X] Female [ ]

Language Arts:
- ___ 91004 World Lit.
- ___ 91009 Am. Lit. (1)
- ___ 91010 Am. Lit. (2)
- ___ 91023 Communications
- ___ 91024 Adv. Comm.
- _X_ 91026 Drama
- ___ 91029 Mass Media
- ___ 91031 Short Stories
- ___ 91035 Develop. Studies

Mathematics:
- ___ 30011 Pre-Algebra
- ___ **30013 Applied Math**
- ___ 30015 Statistics
- ___ 30018 Algebra 1
- ___ 30030 Geometry
- ___ 30053 Trig.
- ___ 30272 Pre-Calculus
- _X_ 30230 Calculus
- ___ 30250 Computer Sci.

Science:
- ___ 02001 Biology
- ___ 02101 Chemistry
- ___ 02102 Chem. Lab.
- ___ **02201 Physics**
- _X_ 02213 Geology
- ___ 02401 Research

Social Science:
- ___ 11007 Sociology
- ___ 11017 Psychology 1
- ___ 11018 Psychology 2
- _X_ 11021 Economics
- ___ 11083 World History
- ___ 11206 Family Studies
- ___ 11207 Social Research

Electives:

Keyboarding
Elective 1
_____
For Office Use

Gen. Business
Elective 2
_____
For Office Use

Graphics
Elective 3
_____
For Office Use

GRANT JOHNSON STATE COLLEGE
REGISTRATION

Student Number **958-33-9347**

Name: **Colkitt** (Last) **Martha** (First) **R** (M.I.)

Sex: Male ☐ Female ☒ Class **Fr**

Language Arts:
- ☒ 91004 World Lit.
- ___ 91009 Am. Lit. (1)
- ___ 91010 Am. Lit. (2)
- ___ 91023 Communications
- ___ 91024 Adv. Comm.
- ___ 91026 Drama
- ___ 91029 Mass Media
- ___ 91031 Short Stories
- ___ 91035 Develop. Studies

Mathematics:
- ___ 30011 Pre-Algebra
- ___ **30013 Applied Math**
- ___ 30015 Statistics
- ☒ 30018 Algebra 1
- ___ 30030 Geometry
- ___ 30053 Trig.
- ___ 30272 Pre-Calculus
- ___ 30230 Calculus
- ___ 30250 Computer Sci.

Social Science:
- ☒ 11007 Sociology
- ___ 11017 Psychology 1
- ___ 11018 Psychology 2
- ___ 11021 Economics
- ___ 11083 World History
- ___ 11206 Family Studies
- ☒ 11207 Social Research

Science:
- ☒ 02001 Biology
- ___ 02101 Chemistry
- ___ 02102 Chem. Lab.
- ___ **02201 Physics**
- ___ 02213 Geology
- ___ 02401 Research

Electives:

Woodworking
Elective 1 _____
For Office Use _____

Drafting
Elective 2 _____
For Office Use _____

Word Processing
Elective 3 _____
For Office Use _____

GRANT JOHNSON STATE COLLEGE
REGISTRATION

Student Number **935-90-4182**

Name: **Robichaud** (Last) **Harry** (First) **C** (M.I.)

Sex: Male ☒ Female ☐ Class **So**

Language Arts:
- ___ 91004 World Lit.
- ___ 91009 Am. Lit. (1)
- ___ 91010 Am. Lit. (2)
- ___ 91023 Communications
- ___ 91024 Adv. Comm.
- ___ 91026 Drama
- ☒ 91029 Mass Media
- ___ 91031 Short Stories
- ___ 91035 Develop. Studies

Mathematics:
- ___ 30011 Pre-Algebra
- ___ **30013 Applied Math**
- ☒ 30015 Statistics
- ___ 30018 Algebra 1
- ___ 30030 Geometry
- ___ 30053 Trig.
- ___ 30272 Pre-Calculus
- ___ 30230 Calculus
- ___ 30250 Computer Sci.

Social Science:
- ___ 11007 Sociology
- ___ 11017 Psychology 1
- ___ 11018 Psychology 2
- ___ 11021 Economics
- ☒ 11083 World History
- ___ 11206 Family Studies
- ___ 11207 Social Research

Science:
- ___ 02001 Biology
- ___ 02101 Chemistry
- ___ 02102 Chem. Lab.
- ___ 02201 Physics
- ☒ 02213 Geology
- ___ 02401 Research

Electives:

Drafting
Elective 1 _____
For Office Use _____

Bus. Machines
Elective 2 _____
For Office Use _____

Woodworking
Elective 3 _____
For Office Use _____

Activity 12

RADIO STATION SURVEY

→ **1** Define programming and listener survey.

2 Explain two resons why listener surveys are important to a radio station.

3 List the type of information advertisers want to know about a radio station's listeners.

4 Describe the general activities involved in gathering and tallying data about radio listeners.

5 Key-enter data for radio station listener surveys.

DATA ENTRY APPLICATION AND JOB DESCRIPTION

*A*ll of us have listened to a radio. Many of us have a favorite station. It may be our favorite because it plays the type of music we like or because it doesn't play much music at all. It may be an all-talk station that offers advice to its listeners or invites well-known authorities to discuss current issues.

How does a radio station decide if it will play music or not? If the station decides to play music, how does it determine if it will concentrate on jazz, classical, country western, rock, top forty, or adult contemporary? The answers to these questions influence a station's **programming** decisions. A station's programming depends on the type of listener the station is trying to attract. In order to determine which type of listener a station should try to attract, that station must conduct a **listener survey** in the broadcast area. Even after a station decides the type of programming it wants to provide, it must continue to survey the people in the listening area to make sure that the station is still serving a need and still has a satisfied audience.

Listener surveys are also conducted to help sell advertising. Most radio stations must sell air time to companies for advertising their products or services. Advertising is the major form of income for most non-public radio stations. To convince companies to buy air time on their stations, station managers must be able to prove that they have a large audience of listeners. However, it is not enough to provide these potential advertisers with just the number of listeners. Advertisers may also want to know at what time of the day most people listen to the station, where people listen to the station, where the most listeners live, the age or income level of the average listener, and so forth. To get the answers to these questions, the radio station must again survey the people in its listening area. The station must continue to conduct listener surveys to keep up to date on the type of audience it serves.

HOW LISTENER SURVEYS ARE TAKEN AND RESULTS TALLIED

Different methods are available to conduct listener surveys. Some radio stations hire research companies to complete these surveys for them. Other stations prefer to conduct the surveys themselves, usually by telephone. Phone numbers are randomly selected and called. If the person called agrees to participate in the survey, the surveyors ask questions and usually records the answers on a preprinted survey form. The survey itself can vary from two or three questions to a survey with numerous questions covering many areas of the listening audience. An example listener survey is shown in Figure 12.1. At a later time, all of the responses will be entered into a computer to have the results tallied. In some cases, the answers are entered into a computer as the survey is taken.

FIGURE 12.1 Listener Survey

HOW DATA IS ANALYZED

In most cases, the data collected during the survey is analyzed with the use of a computer. By using a computer, this analysis can be done more quickly than it was before computers were available. In addition, the computerized data can be used in many ways to develop various reports and statistics. From these reports, the radio station can determine the answers to its programming questions and the answers to questions raised by potential advertisers.

● ●

INPUT FIELDS

*I*n this activity you will key-enter data from listener surveys. Information from listener surveys is key-entered into input fields on the data entry screen. The input fields for this activity are provided below.

No. This field identifies the survey number. It is a three-digit numerical field.

Age. This field identifies the age of the listener. This data is used to determine the average listener's age and the number of listeners in various age categories.

Sex. This field contains the appropriate abbreviation for the sex of an individual, either F for a female, or M for a male.

ZIP code. This field contains the listener's nine-character ZIP code.

Type Of Music. This field contains the code letter identifying the type of music the listener prefers. This code appears directly on the source document.

Radio Station. This field identifies the listener's preferred radio station. In order to input the data in this field accurately, you will key-enter the first four letters, the hyphen, and the last two letters (AM or FM).

Time Of Day. This field contains the time of day the person most often listens to the radio. In this activity you will be using military time, where the p.m. hours are numbered 13-24. You will key-enter the hour as the first two digits. For example, 3 a.m. would be key-entered as "03" and 3 p.m. would be key-entered as "15." The colon separating the hour from the minutes will be inserted by the computer.

Where Do You Listen. This field identifies where people are when they listen to the radio. You will need to key-enter the data as it appears on the survey, except that "School" will be key-entered as "Schl".

Number Of Radios In Home. The field contains the number of radios the listener has in the home.

(OBJECTIVE 5)

GET READY

Follow the start-up procedures for your computer.

COMPLETE ALPHA-NUMERIC DEXTERITY DRILL

```
08953 WXEL-FM 00372 21800 4247 3627M 171
12302 0865860 CAR2 B1226 SCHL5 213053341
WKIK-FM 1130245 173158 038066 18WORK 35M
4356 OTHER 1900 429M086 0487 SHOP 190035
62581829 SCHLF FABB3835 1630 11068 FORTY
```

STEP 1   From the *Activities* menu, select *Activity 12 Radio Listener Survey*.

STEP 2   Select *Alpha-Numeric Dexterity Drill*.

STEP 3   Enter the data for each line. Press *enter* or *return* at the end of each line.

STEP 4   Select *OK* when you are finished key-entering. Review your score.

STEP 5   Select *Review* to review any errors that were made. After you have reviewed your performance, select *OK*.

Repeat the Alpha-Numeric Dexterity Drill as many times as instructed by your teacher.

COMPLETE KEYPAD DEXTERITY DRILL

```
03715 72049 86759 76347 91806 76209 0794
91745 21134 16020 96256 02525 70446 9172
05433 48899 53673 41897 28835 08712 4203
84426 50251 39436 24945 83824 50016 8532
08946 21691 43234 64827 30977 12318 0231
```

STEP 1   From the *Activities* menu, select *Activity 12 Radio Listener Survey.*

STEP 2   Select *Keypad Dexterity Drill.*

STEP 3   Enter the data for each line. Press *enter* or *return* at the end of each line.

STEP 4   Select *OK* when you are finished key-entering. Review your score.

STEP 5   Select *Review* to review any errors that were made. After you have reviewed your performance, select *OK.*

Repeat the Keypad Dexterity Drill as many times as instructed by your teacher.

COMPLETE RADIO LISTENER SURVEY FORMS

STEP 1   Remove the Radio Listener Survey forms that are located at the end of this activity.

STEP 2   From the *Activities* menu, select *Activity 12: Radio Listener Survey.*

STEP 3   Select *Survey Form.* Your screen will be similar to that shown in Figure 12.2.

FIGURE 12.2

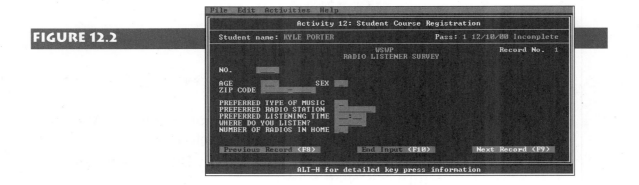

STEP 4   Key-enter the No., Age, Sex, ZIP Code, Preferred Type of Music, Preferred Radio Station, Preferred Listening Time, Where Do You Listen?, Number of Radios In Home, in the appropriate fields for your first record.

STEP 5   Select *Next Record.*

STEP 6   Key-enter the remaining records.

✎ **Note: If you are interrupted before key-entering all of the records, follow the necessary procedures to end input.**

STEP 7 After key-entering all of the Radio Listener Survey forms, select *End Input*. If you notice errors after you have selected End Input, select *Edit* and then move to the appropriate fields to key-enter the corrections.

STEP 8 Print the radio listener survey forms if instructed by your teacher.

STEP 9 Select *Analyze*. Review the information presented.

STEP 10 Select *Review*. Any errors will be highlighted.

STEP 11 Select *Done*.

STEP 12 You may generate a report of your performance.

✎ **Note: In a real work situation, you would strive for completely accurate records. Therefore, it is suggested that once you have completed all the steps listed here, you should go back into the records and correct all errors. To do this:**

From the *Activities* menu, select *Activity 12 Radio Listener Survey*.

- Select *Survey Form*.

- Use the appropriate keys to locate the proper record and field and then key-enter the correction.

- Select *End Input*.

- Select *Analyze*.

- Select *Review*.

- Select *Done*.

- Print the radio listener survey forms if instructed by your teacher.

VOCABULARY

listener survey
programming

Activity 12 Study Guide

RADIO STATION SURVEY

PART 1

OBJECTIVES 1, 2, 3, AND 4 (2 POINTS EACH)

● **Match the vocabulary terms with the best definitions. Write the letter of the term in the space to the left of the definition.**

A. **advertisers**　　　C. **over half billion**　　　E. **random**
B. **listener survey**　　D. **programming decisions**

_____　**1.** A station's answer to the type of music a listener wishes to hear.

_____　**2.** The station wants to check to see that the music it is providing is listened to by the people.

_____　**3.** These are companies who sell merchandise over the radio.

_____　**4.** The number of radios in the United States.

_____　**5.** Method most often used in selecting household to participate in a radio survey.

PART 2

OBJECTIVES 1 AND 3 (1 POINT EACH)

● **Each of the following statements is either true or false. Indicate your choice by circling T for a true statement or F for a false statement.**

T　　F　**1.** Radio stations may want to know the time of day most listeners are listening to the radio.

T　　F　**2.** A typical question in a listener survey could relate to the number of radios a listener has in the home.

T　　F　**3.** A radio station takes a survey to determine the type of music it plays.

T　　F　**4.** "Programming decisions" refer to the type of computer the radio station uses to tally its surveys.

T　　F　**5.** Advertising is the major form of income of most radio stations.

T F   **6.** It is up to the radio station to decide if it is going to be purely a talk station.

T F   **7.** Listener surveys are important to radio stations only if advertisers want to know what kind of people listen to each station.

T F   **8.** The radio station does not have to keep up with listeners' surveys once they have taken them.

T F   **9.** Age is not important to include when designing a listener survey.

T F   **10.** A radio station may hire an outside company to conduct its listener survey.

PART 3

OBJECTIVES 1, 3 AND 4 (3 POINTS EACH)

Briefly answer each of the following items. Write your answers on the lines provided.

1. Name some ways station managers would convince companies to buy air time.

_____

_____

_____

2. Explain why advertisers want to know what type of person listens to a radio station.

_____

_____

_____

3. How does a listener survey influence a radio station's programming decisions?

_____

_____

_____

4. Explain what general activities are involved in gathering and tallying data about radio listeners.

_____

_____

5. List five pieces of data that would be collected in a listener survey.

_____

_____

_____

_____

_____

☛ **Remove the Activity 12 Study Guide from your text-workbook and hand it to your instructor for correcting.**

Total Points Possible	35
(Minus) Incorrect Points	_____
Total Points Earned	_____
Percent Correct	_____
Grade	_____

WSWP RADIO LISTENER SURVEY — No. 001

Age: **23**   Sex: M [X]   F [ ]
Zip Code **07438-4247**

Preferred Type of Music:
- _____ A **Adult Contemporary**
- _____ O Oldies
- _____ K Classical
- _____ C Contemporary Hit Radio
- _____ E Easy Listening
- _____ G Gospel
- _____ J Jazz
- _____ W Modern Country Western
- **X** R Rhythm and Blues
- _____ F Top Forty
- _____ T Traditional Country Western

Preferred Radio Station **WCLA-FM**
Preferred Listen Time **18:00**

Where do you listen?
[ ] Home [X] Work [ ] Car
[ ] School [ ] Gym [ ] Other

Number of Radios in Home? **4**

WSWP RADIO LISTENER SURVEY — No. 002

Age: **40**   Sex: M [X]   F [ ]
Zip Code **07604-3627**

Preferred Type of Music:
- _____ A **Adult Contemporary**
- _____ O Oldies
- _____ K Classical
- **X** C Contemporary Hit Radio
- _____ E Easy Listening
- _____ G Gospel
- _____ J Jazz
- _____ W Modern Country Western
- _____ R Rhythm and Blues
- _____ F Top Forty
- _____ T Traditional Country Western

Preferred Radio Station **WKIK-AM**
Preferred Listen Time **20:00**

Where do you listen?
[X] Home [ ] Work [ ] Car
[ ] School [ ] Gym [ ] Other

Number of Radios in Home? **4**

WSWP RADIO LISTENER SURVEY — No. 003

Age: **72**   Sex: M [X]   F [ ]
Zip Code **08953-0795**

Preferred Type of Music:
- _____ A **Adult Contemporary**
- _____ O Oldies
- **X** K Classical
- _____ C Contemporary Hit Radio
- _____ E Easy Listening
- _____ G Gospel
- _____ J Jazz
- _____ W Modern Country Western
- _____ R Rhythm and Blues
- _____ F Top Forty
- _____ T Traditional Country Western

Preferred Radio Station **WXEL-FM**
Preferred Listen Time **08:00**

Where do you listen?
[X] Home [ ] Work [ ] Car
[ ] School [ ] Gym [ ] Other

Number of Radios in Home? **2**

WSWP RADIO LISTENER SURVEY — No. 004

Age: **46**   Sex: M [ ]   F [X]
Zip Code **08658-6097**

Preferred Type of Music:
- _____ A **Adult Contemporary**
- _____ O Oldies
- _____ K Classical
- _____ C Contemporary Hit Radio
- _____ E Easy Listening
- _____ G Gospel
- _____ J Jazz
- _____ W Modern Country Western
- **X** R Rhythm and Blues
- _____ F Top Forty
- _____ T Traditional Country Western

Preferred Radio Station **WSWP-AM**
Preferred Listen Time **12:30**

Where do you listen?
[ ] Home [x] Work [ ] Car
[ ] School [ ] Gym [ ] Other

Number of Radios in Home? **2**

WSWP RADIO LISTENER SURVEY — No. 005

Age: **23**   Sex: M [X]   F [ ]

Zip Code: **08091-9240**

Preferred Type of Music:

- _____ A **Adult Contemporary**
- _____ O Oldies
- _____ K Classical
- _____ C Contemporary Hit Radio
- _____ E Easy Listening
- _____ G Gospel
- _____ J Jazz
- _____ W Modern Country Western
- __X____ R Rhythm and Blues
- _____ F Top Forty
- _____ T Traditional Country Western

Preferred Radio Station: **WSWP-AM**

Preferred Listen Time: **08:00**

Where do you listen?

- [ ] Home   [X] Work   [ ] Car
- [ ] School   [ ] Gym   [ ] Other

Number of Radios in Home? **2**

WSWP RADIO LISTENER SURVEY — No. 006

Age: **15**   Sex: M [X]   F [ ]

Zip Code: **07240-7125**

Preferred Type of Music:

- _____ A **Adult Contemporary**
- _____ O Oldies
- _____ K Classical
- _____ C Contemporary Hit Radio
- _____ E Easy Listening
- _____ G Gospel
- _____ J Jazz
- _____ W Modern Country Western
- _____ R Rhythm and Blues
- __X____ F Top Forty
- _____ T Traditional Country Western

Preferred Radio Station: **WTRO-AM**

Preferred Listen Time: **18:00**

Where do you listen?

- [ ] Home   [ ] Work   [ ] Car
- [X] School   [ ] Gym   [ ] Other

Number of Radios in Home? **2**

WSWP RADIO LISTENER SURVEY — No. 007

Age: **18**   Sex: M [X]   F [ ]

Zip Code: **07589-9820**

Preferred Type of Music:

- _____ A **Adult Contemporary**
- _____ O Oldies
- _____ K Classical
- _____ C Contemporary Hit Radio
- _____ E Easy Listening
- _____ G Gospel
- _____ J Jazz
- _____ W Modern Country Western
- __X____ R Rhythm and Blues
- _____ F Top Forty
- _____ T Traditional Country Western

Preferred Radio Station: **WSWP-AM**

Preferred Listen Time: **18:00**

Where do you listen?

- [X] Home   [ ] Work   [ ] Car
- [ ] School   [ ] Gym   [ ] Other

Number of Radios in Home? **4**

WSWP RADIO LISTENER SURVEY — No. 008

Age: **19**   Sex: M [X]   F [ ]

Zip Code: **08399-9656**

Preferred Type of Music:

- _____ A **Adult Contemporary**
- _____ O Oldies
- _____ K Classical
- _____ C Contemporary Hit Radio
- _____ E Easy Listening
- _____ G Gospel
- _____ J Jazz
- _____ W Modern Country Western
- _____ R Rhythm and Blues
- __X____ F Top Forty
- _____ T Traditional Country Western

Preferred Radio Station: **WTRO-AM**

Preferred Listen Time: **16:00**

Where do you listen?

- [ ] Home   [X] Work   [ ] Car
- [ ] School   [ ] Gym   [ ] Other

Number of Radios in Home? **5**

WSWP RADIO LISTENER SURVEY No. 009

Age: __43__ Sex: M [X] F [ ]
Zip Code __08631-1226__
Preferred Type of Music:
_____ A **Adult Contemporary**
_____ O Oldies
_____ K Classical
__X_____ C Contemporary Hit Radio
_____ E Easy Listening
_____ G Gospel
_____ J Jazz
_____ W Modern Country Western
_____ R Rhythm and Blues
_____ F Top Forty
_____ T Traditional Country Western
Preferred Radio Station __WKIK-AM__
Preferred Listen Time __20:30__
Where do you listen?
[X] Home [ ] Work [ ] Car
[ ] School [ ] Gym [ ] Other
Number of Radios in Home? __3__

WSWP RADIO LISTENER SURVEY No. 010

Age: __51__ Sex: M [X] F [ ]
Zip Code __07778-1440__
Preferred Type of Music:
_____ A **Adult Contemporary**
_____ O Oldies
_____ K Classical
_____ C Contemporary Hit Radio
_____ E Easy Listening
_____ G Gospel
__X_____ J Jazz
_____ W Modern Country Western
_____ R Rhythm and Blues
_____ F Top Forty
_____ T Traditional Country Western
Preferred Radio Station __WJZZ-FM__
Preferred Listen Time __20:00__
Where do you listen?
[ ] Home [X] Work [ ] Car
[ ] School [ ] Gym [ ] Other
Number of Radios in Home? __4__

WSWP RADIO LISTENER SURVEY No. 011

Age: __47__ Sex: M [ ] F [X]
Zip Code __07067-3341__
Preferred Type of Music:
_____ A **Adult Contemporary**
_____ O Oldies
_____ K Classical
_____ C Contemporary Hit Radio
_____ E Easy Listening
_____ G Gospel
_____ J Jazz
_____ W Modern Country Western
_____ R Rhythm and Blues
_____ F Top Forty
__X_____ T Traditional Country Western
Preferred Radio Station __WSTR-FM__
Preferred Listen Time __13:00__
Where do you listen?
[X] Home [ ] Work [ ] Car
[ ] School [ ] Gym [ ] Other
Number of Radios in Home? __2__

WSWP RADIO LISTENER SURVEY No. 012

Age: __56__ Sex: M [X] F [ ]
Zip Code __08288-6955__
Preferred Type of Music:
_____ A **Adult Contemporary**
_____ O Oldies
_____ K Classical
_____ C Contemporary Hit Radio
_____ E Easy Listening
_____ G Gospel
_____ J Jazz
_____ W Modern Country Western
_____ R Rhythm and Blues
__X_____ F Top Forty
_____ T Traditional Country Western
Preferred Radio Station __WSWP-AM__
Preferred Listen Time __22:30__
Where do you listen?
[ ] Home [X] Work [ ] Car
[ ] School [ ] Gym [ ] Other
Number of Radios in Home? __5__

WSWP RADIO LISTENER SURVEY — No. 013

Age: 17 Sex: M ☐ F ☒
Zip Code 07989-6867
Preferred Type of Music:
_____ A **Adult Contemporary**
_____ O Oldies
_____ K Classical
_____ C Contemporary Hit Radio
_____ E Easy Listening
_____ G Gospel
_____ J Jazz
___X___ W Modern Country Western
_____ R Rhythm and Blues
_____ F Top Forty
_____ T Traditional Country Western
Preferred Radio Station WSTR-FM
Preferred Listen Time 17:30
Where do you listen?
☒ Home ☐ Work ☐ Car
☐ School ☐ Gym ☐ Other
Number of Radios in Home? 2

WSWP RADIO LISTENER SURVEY — No. 014

Age: 32 Sex: M ☒ F ☐
Zip Code 08834-8294
Preferred Type of Music:
_____ A **Adult Contemporary**
_____ O Oldies
___X___ K Classical
_____ C Contemporary Hit Radio
_____ E Easy Listening
_____ G Gospel
_____ J Jazz
_____ W Modern Country Western
_____ R Rhythm and Blues
_____ F Top Forty
_____ T Traditional Country Western
Preferred Radio Station WXEL-FM
Preferred Listen Time 17:30
Where do you listen?
☐ Home ☒ Work ☐ Car
☐ School ☐ Gym ☐ Other
Number of Radios in Home? 4

WSWP RADIO LISTENER SURVEY — No. 015

Age: 66 Sex: M ☐ F ☒
Zip Code 08158-0380
Preferred Type of Music:
_____ A **Adult Contemporary**
_____ O Oldies
_____ K Classical
_____ C Contemporary Hit Radio
___X___ E Easy Listening
_____ G Gospel
_____ J Jazz
_____ W Modern Country Western
_____ R Rhythm and Blues
_____ F Top Forty
_____ T Traditional Country Western
Preferred Radio Station WKIK-AM
Preferred Listen Time 18:00
Where do you listen?
☒ Home ☐ Work ☐ Car
☐ School ☐ Gym ☐ Other
Number of Radios in Home? 1

WSWP RADIO LISTENER SURVEY — No. 016

Age: 35 Sex: M ☒ F ☐
Zip Code 08655-1841
Preferred Type of Music:
_____ A **Adult Contemporary**
_____ O Oldies
_____ K Classical
_____ C Contemporary Hit Radio
_____ E Easy Listening
_____ G Gospel
_____ J Jazz
_____ W Modern Country Western
_____ R Rhythm and Blues
_____ F Top Forty
___X___ T Traditional Country Western
Preferred Radio Station WSTR-FM
Preferred Listen Time 19:00
Where do you listen?
☐ Home ☒ Work ☐ Car
☐ School ☐ Gym ☐ Other
Number of Radios in Home? 3

WSWP RADIO LISTENER SURVEY — No. 017

Age: 29   Sex: M [X] F [ ]
Zip Code: 08663-4358
Preferred Type of Music:
_____ A **Adult Contemporary**
_____ O Oldies
_____ K Classical
_____ C Contemporary Hit Radio
____X____ E Easy Listening
_____ G Gospel
_____ J Jazz
_____ W Modern Country Western
_____ R Rhythm and Blues
_____ F Top Forty
_____ T Traditional Country Western
Preferred Radio Station WKIK-AM
Preferred Listen Time 19:00
Where do you listen?
[ ] Home   [ ] Work   [X] Car
[ ] School [ ] Gym   [ ] Other
Number of Radios in Home? 4

WSWP RADIO LISTENER SURVEY — No. 018

Age: 35   Sex: M [X] F [ ]
Zip Code: 07607-5332
Preferred Type of Music:
_____ A **Adult Contemporary**
_____ O Oldies
_____ K Classical
_____ C Contemporary Hit Radio
____X____ E Easy Listening
_____ G Gospel
_____ J Jazz
_____ W Modern Country Western
_____ R Rhythm and Blues
_____ F Top Forty
_____ T Traditional Country Western
Preferred Radio Station WKIK-AM
Preferred Listen Time 18:00
Where do you listen?
[X] Home   [ ] Work   [ ] Car
[ ] School [ ] Gym   [ ] Other
Number of Radios in Home? 3

WSWP RADIO LISTENER SURVEY — No. 019

Age: 46   Sex: M [ ] F [X]
Zip Code: 07019-6443
Preferred Type of Music:
_____ A **Adult Contemporary**
_____ O Oldies
_____ K Classical
_____ C Contemporary Hit Radio
_____ E Easy Listening
_____ G Gospel
_____ J Jazz
_____ W Modern Country Western
____X____ R Rhythm and Blues
_____ F Top Forty
_____ T Traditional Country Western
Preferred Radio Station WIGT-AM
Preferred Listen Time 08:00
Where do you listen?
[X] Home   [ ] Work   [ ] Car
[ ] School [ ] Gym   [ ] Other
Number of Radios in Home? 3

WSWP RADIO LISTENER SURVEY — No. 020

Age: 47   Sex: M [X] F [ ]
Zip Code: 07636-0487
Preferred Type of Music:
_____ A **Adult Contemporary**
_____ O Oldies
_____ K Classical
_____ C Contemporary Hit Radio
_____ E Easy Listening
_____ G Gospel
_____ J Jazz
_____ W Modern Country Western
____X____ R Rhythm and Blues
_____ F Top Forty
_____ T Traditional Country Western
Preferred Radio Station WSWP-AM
Preferred Listen Time 09:00
Where do you listen?
[X] Home   [ ] Work   [ ] Car
[ ] School [ ] Gym   [ ] Other
Number of Radios in Home? 4

WSWP RADIO LISTENER SURVEY — No. 021

Age: **62**   Sex: M [X]   F [ ]
Zip Code **08063-5957**

Preferred Type of Music:
- **X** A **Adult Contemporary**
- _____ O Oldies
- _____ K Classical
- _____ C Contemporary Hit Radio
- _____ E Easy Listening
- _____ G Gospel
- _____ J Jazz
- _____ W Modern Country Western
- _____ R Rhythm and Blues
- _____ F Top Forty
- _____ T Traditional Country Western

Preferred Radio Station **WXEL-FM**
Preferred Listen Time **18:00**
Where do you listen?
[ ] Home [ ] Work [X] Car
[ ] School [ ] Gym [ ] Other
Number of Radios in Home? **4**

WSWP RADIO LISTENER SURVEY — No. 022

Age: **58**   Sex: M [ ]   F [X]
Zip Code **08634-1149**

Preferred Type of Music:
- _____ A **Adult Contemporary**
- _____ O Oldies
- _____ K Classical
- _____ C Contemporary Hit Radio
- _____ E Easy Listening
- _____ G Gospel
- _____ J Jazz
- _____ W Modern Country Western
- **X** R Rhythm and Blues
- _____ F Top Forty
- _____ T Traditional Country Western

Preferred Radio Station **WKIK-AM**
Preferred Listen Time **16:30**
Where do you listen?
[X] Home [ ] Work [ ] Car
[ ] School [ ] Gym [ ] Other
Number of Radios in Home? **3**

WSWP RADIO LISTENER SURVEY — No. 023

Age: **18**   Sex: M [ ]   F [X]
Zip Code **08611-7316**

Preferred Type of Music:
- _____ A **Adult Contemporary**
- _____ O Oldies
- _____ K Classical
- _____ C Contemporary Hit Radio
- _____ E Easy Listening
- _____ G Gospel
- _____ J Jazz
- _____ W Modern Country Western
- _____ R Rhythm and Blues
- **X** F Top Forty
- _____ T Traditional Country Western

Preferred Radio Station **WYLR-AM**
Preferred Listen Time **16:30**
Where do you listen?
[ ] Home [ ] Work [ ] Car
[X] School [ ] Gym [ ] Other
Number of Radios in Home? **1**

WSWP RADIO LISTENER SURVEY — No. 024

Age: **29**   Sex: M [ ]   F [X]
Zip Code **08976-5283**

Preferred Type of Music:
- _____ A **Adult Contemporary**
- _____ O Oldies
- _____ K Classical
- _____ C Contemporary Hit Radio
- _____ E Easy Listening
- _____ G Gospel
- _____ J Jazz
- _____ W Modern Country Western
- **X** R Rhythm and Blues
- _____ F Top Forty
- _____ T Traditional Country Western

Preferred Radio Station **WSWP-AM**
Preferred Listen Time **17:30**
Where do you listen?
[ ] Home [ ] Work [ ] Car
[ ] School [ ] Gym [X] Other
Number of Radios in Home? **2**

WSWP RADIO LISTENER SURVEY — No. 025

Age: **25**   Sex: M ☐   F **X**
Zip Code **07740-3384**

Preferred Type of Music:

_____	A	**Adult Contemporary**
_____	O	Oldies
_____	K	Classical
_____	C	Contemporary Hit Radio
X	E	Easy Listening
_____	G	Gospel
_____	J	Jazz
_____	W	Modern Country Western
_____	R	Rhythm and Blues
_____	F	Top Forty
_____	T	Traditional Country Western

Preferred Radio Station **WTRO-AM**
Preferred Listen Time **18:00**
Where do you listen?
☐ Home   **X** Work   ☐ Car
☐ School   ☐ Gym   ☐ Other
Number of Radios in Home? **3**

WSWP RADIO LISTENER SURVEY — No. 026

Age: **18**   Sex: M ☐   F **X**
Zip Code **08324-7778**

Preferred Type of Music:

_____	A	**Adult Contemporary**
_____	O	Oldies
_____	K	Classical
_____	C	Contemporary Hit Radio
_____	E	Easy Listening
_____	G	Gospel
_____	J	Jazz
X	W	Modern Country Western
_____	R	Rhythm and Blues
_____	F	Top Forty
_____	T	Traditional Country Western

Preferred Radio Station **WSTR-FM**
Preferred Listen Time **20:00**
Where do you listen?
☐ Home   ☐ Work   ☐ Car
X School   ☐ Gym   ☐ Other
Number of Radios in Home? **2**

WSWP RADIO LISTENER SURVEY — No. 027

Age: **33**   Sex: M **X**   F ☐
Zip Code **08680-3627**

Preferred Type of Music:

_____	A	**Adult Contemporary**
_____	O	Oldies
_____	K	Classical
_____	C	Contemporary Hit Radio
_____	E	Easy Listening
_____	G	Gospel
_____	J	Jazz
_____	W	Modern Country Western
X	R	Rhythm and Blues
_____	F	Top Forty
_____	T	Traditional Country Western

Preferred Radio Station **WSWP-AM**
Preferred Listen Time **08:00**
Where do you listen?
☐ Home   ☐ Work   **X** Car
☐ School   ☐ Gym   ☐ Other
Number of Radios in Home? **3**

WSWP RADIO LISTENER SURVEY — No. 028

Age: **32**   Sex: M ☐   F **X**
Zip Code **07227-2053**

Preferred Type of Music:

_____	A	**Adult Contemporary**
_____	O	Oldies
_____	K	Classical
_____	C	Contemporary Hit Radio
_____	E	Easy Listening
_____	G	Gospel
_____	J	Jazz
_____	W	Modern Country Western
X	R	Rhythm and Blues
_____	F	Top Forty
_____	T	Traditional Country Western

Preferred Radio Station **WCLA-FM**
Preferred Listen Time **20:00**
Where do you listen?
X Home   ☐ Work   ☐ Car
☐ School   ☐ Gym   ☐ Other
Number of Radios in Home? **2**

WSWP RADIO LISTENER SURVEY — No. 029

Age: **17**   Sex: M [X]   F [ ]

Zip Code **07797-9586**

Preferred Type of Music:

_____	A	**Adult Contemporary**
_____	O	Oldies
_____	K	Classical
_____	C	Contemporary Hit Radio
_____	E	Easy Listening
X	G	Gospel
_____	J	Jazz
_____	W	Modern Country Western
_____	R	Rhythm and Blues
_____	F	Top Forty
_____	T	Traditional Country Western

Preferred Radio Station **WIGT-AM**

Preferred Listen Time **08:00**

Where do you listen?

[ ] Home   [X] Work   [ ] Car
[ ] School   [ ] Gym   [ ] Other

Number of Radios in Home? **4**

WSWP RADIO LISTENER SURVEY — No. 030

Age: **33**   Sex: M [ ]   F [X]

Zip Code **08271-5860**

Preferred Type of Music:

X	A	**Adult Contemporary**
_____	O	Oldies
_____	K	Classical
_____	C	Contemporary Hit Radio
_____	E	Easy Listening
_____	G	Gospel
_____	J	Jazz
_____	W	Modern Country Western
_____	R	Rhythm and Blues
_____	F	Top Forty
_____	T	Traditional Country Western

Preferred Radio Station **WWUX-AM**

Preferred Listen Time **08:00**

Where do you listen?

[ ] Home   [X] Work   [ ] Car
[ ] School   [ ] Gym   [ ] Other

Number of Radios in Home? **2**

WSWP RADIO LISTENER SURVEY — No. 031

Age: **59**   Sex: M [ ]   F [X]

Zip Code **07079-8919**

Preferred Type of Music:

_____	A	**Adult Contemporary**
_____	O	Oldies
_____	K	Classical
_____	C	Contemporary Hit Radio
_____	E	Easy Listening
X	G	Gospel
_____	J	Jazz
_____	W	Modern Country Western
_____	R	Rhythm and Blues
_____	F	Top Forty
_____	T	Traditional Country Western

Preferred Radio Station **WXEL-FM**

Preferred Listen Time **17:00**

Where do you listen?

[ ] Home   [X] Work   [ ] Car
[ ] School   [ ] Gym   [ ] Other

Number of Radios in Home? **4**

WSWP RADIO LISTENER SURVEY — No. 032

Age: **37**   Sex: M [ ]   F [X]

Zip Code **08824-0954**

Preferred Type of Music:

_____	A	**Adult Contemporary**
_____	O	Oldies
_____	K	Classical
X	C	Contemporary Hit Radio
_____	E	Easy Listening
_____	G	Gospel
_____	J	Jazz
_____	W	Modern Country Western
_____	R	Rhythm and Blues
_____	F	Top Forty
_____	T	Traditional Country Western

Preferred Radio Station **WWUX-AM**

Preferred Listen Time **19:00**

Where do you listen?

[X] Home   [ ] Work   [ ] Car
[ ] School   [ ] Gym   [ ] Other

Number of Radios in Home? **3**

WSWP RADIO LISTENER SURVEY — No. 033

Age: 28   Sex: M ☐   F [X]
Zip Code: 08604-0712

Preferred Type of Music:
- _____ A **Adult Contemporary**
- _____ O Oldies
- _____ K Classical
- _____ C Contemporary Hit Radio
- _____ E Easy Listening
- _____ G Gospel
- _____ J Jazz
- _____ W Modern Country Western
- _____ R Rhythm and Blues
- __X__ F Top Forty
- _____ T Traditional Country Western

Preferred Radio Station: WSWP-AM
Preferred Listen Time: 19:00

Where do you listen?
☐ Home   ☐ Work   [X] Car
☐ School ☐ Gym   ☐ Other
Number of Radios in Home? 3

WSWP RADIO LISTENER SURVEY — No. 034

Age: 22   Sex: M ☐   F [X]
Zip Code: 07253-8878

Preferred Type of Music:
- _____ A **Adult Contemporary**
- _____ O Oldies
- _____ K Classical
- _____ C Contemporary Hit Radio
- _____ E Easy Listening
- _____ G Gospel
- _____ J Jazz
- _____ W Modern Country Western
- _____ R Rhythm and Blues
- __X__ F Top Forty
- _____ T Traditional Country Western

Preferred Radio Station: WTRO-AM
Preferred Listen Time: 18:00

Where do you listen?
☐ Home   [X] Work   ☐ Car
☐ School ☐ Gym   ☐ Other
Number of Radios in Home? 5

WSWP RADIO LISTENER SURVEY — No. 035

Age: 39   Sex: M ☐   F [X]
Zip Code: 07599-8203

Preferred Type of Music:
- _____ A **Adult Contemporary**
- _____ O Oldies
- _____ K Classical
- _____ C Contemporary Hit Radio
- __X__ E Easy Listening
- _____ G Gospel
- _____ J Jazz
- _____ W Modern Country Western
- _____ R Rhythm and Blues
- _____ F Top Forty
- _____ T Traditional Country Western

Preferred Radio Station: WKIK-AM
Preferred Listen Time: 09:00

Where do you listen?
[X] Home   ☐ Work   ☐ Car
☐ School ☐ Gym   ☐ Other
Number of Radios in Home? 7

WSWP RADIO LISTENER SURVEY — No. 036

Age: 42   Sex: M [X]   F ☐
Zip Code: 08654-9656

Preferred Type of Music:
- _____ A **Adult Contemporary**
- _____ O Oldies
- __X__ K Classical
- _____ C Contemporary Hit Radio
- _____ E Easy Listening
- _____ G Gospel
- _____ J Jazz
- _____ W Modern Country Western
- _____ R Rhythm and Blues
- _____ F Top Forty
- _____ T Traditional Country Western

Preferred Radio Station: WXEL-FM
Preferred Listen Time: 06:30

Where do you listen?
☐ Home   [X] Work   ☐ Car
☐ School ☐ Gym   ☐ Other
Number of Radios in Home? 6

WSWP RADIO LISTENER SURVEY — No. 037

Age: **45**   Sex: M ☐   F **X**
Zip Code: **07458-3880**

Preferred Type of Music:
- _____ A **Adult Contemporary**
- _____ O Oldies
- _____ K Classical
- _____ C Contemporary Hit Radio
- **X** E Easy Listening
- _____ G Gospel
- _____ J Jazz
- _____ W Modern Country Western
- _____ R Rhythm and Blues
- _____ F Top Forty
- _____ T Traditional Country Western

Preferred Radio Station **WKIK-AM**
Preferred Listen Time **07:30**

Where do you listen?
☐ Home   ☐ Work   **X** Car
☐ School   ☐ Gym   ☐ Other

Number of Radios in Home? **2**

WSWP RADIO LISTENER SURVEY — No. 038

Age: **83**   Sex: M ☐   F **X**
Zip Code: **08155-1841**

Preferred Type of Music:
- _____ A **Adult Contemporary**
- _____ O Oldies
- _____ K Classical
- _____ C Contemporary Hit Radio
- _____ E Easy Listening
- **X** G Gospel
- _____ J Jazz
- _____ W Modern Country Western
- _____ R Rhythm and Blues
- _____ F Top Forty
- _____ T Traditional Country Western

Preferred Radio Station **WCLA-FM**
Preferred Listen Time **08:30**

Where do you listen?
X Home   ☐ Work   ☐ Car
☐ School   ☐ Gym   ☐ Other

Number of Radios in Home? **6**

WSWP RADIO LISTENER SURVEY — No. 039

Age: **32**   Sex: M ☐   F **X**
Zip Code: **07969-4358**

Preferred Type of Music:
- _____ A **Adult Contemporary**
- _____ O Oldies
- _____ K Classical
- _____ C Contemporary Hit Radio
- **X** E Easy Listening
- _____ G Gospel
- _____ J Jazz
- _____ W Modern Country Western
- _____ R Rhythm and Blues
- _____ F Top Forty
- _____ T Traditional Country Western

Preferred Radio Station **WXEL-FM**
Preferred Listen Time **17:00**

Where do you listen?
☐ Home   ☐ Work   **X** Car
☐ School   ☐ Gym   ☐ Other

Number of Radios in Home? **1**

WSWP RADIO LISTENER SURVEY — No. 040

Age: **23**   Sex: M ☐   F **X**
Zip Code: **08607-5332**

Preferred Type of Music:
- _____ A **Adult Contemporary**
- _____ O Oldies
- _____ K Classical
- _____ C Contemporary Hit Radio
- **X** E Easy Listening
- _____ G Gospel
- _____ J Jazz
- _____ W Modern Country Western
- _____ R Rhythm and Blues
- _____ F Top Forty
- _____ T Traditional Country Western

Preferred Radio Station **WKIK-AM**
Preferred Listen Time **11:00**

Where do you listen?
☐ Home   **X** Work   ☐ Car
☐ School   ☐ Gym   ☐ Other

Number of Radios in Home? **7**

Quiz 4

PART 1

(2 POINTS EACH)

☛ **Match the vocabulary terms with the best definitions. Write the letter of the term in the space to the left of the definition.**

A. **advertisers**
B. **automobile registration**
C. **canceled**
D. **certificate of title**

E. **closed class**
F. **elective courses**
G. **lien holder**
H. **listener survey**
I. **mandatory insurance**

J. **master schedule**
K. **programming decisions**
L. **sticker tab**

_____ 1. The most common method used by each state to monitor automobile ownership.

_____ 2. True ownership of an automobile is verifiable by this document.

_____ 3. Courses that give a student a chance to explore different areas.

_____ 4. A radio station wants to check to see that the music it is providing is listened to by the people.

_____ 5. A method that a state uses to tell police that a vehicle is registered for the current year.

_____ 6. A matrix that connects curricular offerings to available staff and student enrollment.

_____ 7. A maximum number of students have enrolled or registered in a class.

_____ 8. A minimum amount of insurance coverage for all vehicles is required in some states.

_____ 9. A radio station's answer to the type of music a listener wishes to hear.

_____ 10. What may happen to a course that does not attract enough student interest.

_____ 11. The person from whom the money has been borrowed to purchase an automobile.

_____ 12. These are companies who sell merchandise over the radio.

PART 2

➥ **Each of the following statements is either true or false. Indicate your choice by circling T for a true statement or F for a false statement.**

T   F   **1.** A vehicle does not have an identifying serial number.

T   F   **2.** Every administration does much planning to determine an effective class registration.

T   F   **3.** Radio stations may want to know the time of day most listeners are listening to the radio.

T   F   **4.** Most colleges use three methods to determine their course offerings.

T   F   **5.** The certificate of registration must be in the vehicle any time it is in use.

T   F   **6.** A typical question in a listener survey could be regarding the number of radios the listener has in his/her home.

T   F   **7.** A radio station takes a survey to determine the type of music it plays.

T   F   **8.** Vehicle registration data is considered public information in many states.

T   F   **9.** The number of teachers need not be taken into consideration when scheduling.

T   F   **10.** Registration usually requires no limit (minimum or maximum) to the size of a class.

T   F   **11.** A closed class is one for which students may still register.

T   F   **12.** This bureau will create a new title for a vehicle.

T   F   **13.** Advertising is the major form of income for most radio stations.

T   F   **14.** Age is not an important category to include when designing a listener's survey.

T   F   **15.** A radio station may hire outside companies to conduct surveys.

T   F   **16.** Students make their class choices on registration forms.

T   F   **17.** The course number is a random number assigned to each student.

PART 3

(3 POINTS EACH)

👉 **Briefly answer each of the following items. Write your answers on the lines provided.**

1. Explain the difference, if any, between the speedometer and the odometer.

_____

_____

2. Explain the two major methods of course scheduling.

_____

_____

3. Give several reasons why states require automobile registration.

_____

_____

👉 **Remove Quiz 4 from your text-workbook and hand it to your instructor for correcting.**

Total Points Possible	50
(Minus) Incorrect Points	_____
Total Points Earned	_____
Percent Correct	_____
Grade	_____

Final Quiz

PART 1

(2 POINTS EACH)

➥ Match the vocabulary terms with the best definitions. Write the letter of the term in the space to the left of the definition.

A. **accounts receivable ledger**
B. **accounts payable ledger**
C. **census**
D. **certificate of title**
E. **comprehensive insurance**
F. **required courses**
G. **data**

H. **deductible**
I. **Department of Commerce**
J. **discount**
K. **elective courses**
L. **endorsement**
M. **gross pay**
N. **net pay**
O. **periodic inventory**
P. **perpetual inventory**

Q. **policy**
R. **premium**
S. **purchase order**
T. **restrictions**
U. **salary**
V. **sale on account**
W. **sales invoice**
X. **statement**

_____ 1. Raw facts that are processed by the microcomputer.

_____ 2. A written agreement between a buyer of insurance and an insurance company.

_____ 3. Each time a charge customer purchases merchandise, the seller completes this form.

_____ 4. The total amount of pay due to an individual employee before any deductions are subtracted.

_____ 5. A form that shows all items purchased, the amount of all payments, and the total amount owed.

_____ 6. Courses such as English and Science.

_____ 7. A record of all customers and the amount they owe, arranged alphabetically.

_____ 8. The total amount a company owes all of its vendors for purchases on account is recorded in this account.

_____ 9. Conditions that must be met in order for a driver's license to be valid.

_____ 10. This term identifies a decrease in the premium amount due to good grades, low miles driven daily, or a good driving record of the policyholder.

349

_____ **11.** This document is prepared by the buyer and lists the description, quantity, and price of the goods to be purchased.

_____ **12.** This pay type is a fixed amount paid to an employee each pay period.

_____ **13.** The Bureau of Census is an agency of the federal government under this government body.

_____ **14.** The amount deducted by an insurance company before they pay for a repair.

_____ **15.** Continually monitoring inventory levels by recording the quantities of merchandise bought and sold after each transaction.

_____ **16.** The process whereby an actual count is taken of items on hand at least once a year.

_____ **17.** A population survey of the United States that must be taken every ten years.

_____ **18.** Policyholders pay this amount to be covered for insurance protection.

_____ **19.** This type of sale occurs when the customer buys the merchandise now but pays for it later.

_____ **20.** The amount paid to the employee after deductions are subtracted from gross pay.

_____ **21.** The true ownership of an automobile is verifiable by this document.

_____ **22.** Courses that give students a chance to explore different areas.

_____ **23.** Coverage that protects you when your automobile is damaged from something other than a collision.

_____ **24.** An additional right to drive specialized vehicles.

PART 2

(1 POINT EACH)

➥ **Each of the following statements is either true or false. Indicate your choice by circling T for a true statement or F for a false statement.**

T   F   **1.** Data is recorded on tracks on a disk.

T   F   **2.** When the "in-use" light of the disk drive is on, the disk should be removed from the drive.

T   F   **3.** Perpetual inventory allows a business to monitor its inventory only once a year.

T   F   **4.** A discrepancy report can be used to notify management if more or less merchandise is on hand than the inventory record shows.

T   F   **5.** Credit card sales are treated the same as cash sales.

T   F   **6.** Point-of-sale terminals do not reduce errors in the checkout process.

T   F   **7.** A purchase order is completed by a supplier of goods.

T   F   **8.** A vendor uses information contained on an invoice to prepare a purchase order.

T   F   **9.** Advertising is the main source of income for most radio stations.

T   F   **10.** A complete U. S. census is taken every seven years.

T   F   **11.** To update the census data, the government usually conducts sample surveys.

T   F   **12.** An insurance company will pay for the loss up to the level of protection purchased.

T   F   **13.** Auto insurance is required in all states.

T   F   **14.** A driver may hold a driver's license in two or more states at one time.

T   F   **15.** It is against the law to lend your driver's license to anyone else.

T   F   **16.** A certificate of registration identifies both an automobile and an owner.

PART 3

(3 POINTS EACH)

➥ **Briefly answer each of the following items. Write your answers on the lines provided.**

1. Define accounts payable.

_____

_____

_____

2. What is the purpose of an insurance agent?

_____

_____

_____

3. Define collision insurance.

_____

_____

4. What is a commission?

_____

_____

_____

5. Define electronic spreadsheet.

_____

_____

6. What is an actuarial table?

_____

_____

_____

7. Define information.

_____

_____

8. Define inventory.

_____

_____

9. What do the initials UPC stand for?

_____

_____

10. What is a lien holder?

_____

_____

_____

11. Explain overtime rate.

_____

_____

_____

12. What are vendors?

_____

_____

_____

☞ **Remove the Final Quiz from your text-workbook and hand it to your instructor for correcting.**

Total Points Possible	100
(Minus) Incorrect Points	_____
Total Points Earned	_____
Percent Correct	_____
Grade	_____

Activity 13

SUMMARY PROJECT

LEARNING OBJECTIVES

Upon completion of this activity, you will be able to:

→ 1 Explain the payroll activities of a sporting goods store.

2 Explain the accounts payable activities of a sporting goods store.

3 Explain the importance of inventory control in a sporting goods store.

4 Key-enter data for payroll, accounts payable, and inventory systems.

DATA ENTRY APPLICATION AND JOB DESCRIPTION

*I*n this activity you will key-enter data for The Sports Closet, a locally owned sporting goods store. The Sports Closet sells all types of sports equipment, athletic clothing, and sports accessories. This store is the most popular sporting goods store in the city. In addition to selling to many retail customers, the store sells uniforms and equipment to many local athletic teams. Some of the most popular items carried by The Sports Closet are sporting goods labeled with the names of professional sports teams.

This final activity will focus on three different record-keeping areas—payroll, accounts payable, and inventory control.

PAYROLL

The payroll department of a sporting goods store is similar to the payroll department of most other companies. The employees are usually paid according to one of three pay methods: hourly, salary, or salary plus commission. Hourly employees are paid per hour worked. Therefore, if an employee misses a day of work, he/she does not get paid for that day. If the employee works longer than the normal work period (40 hours), he/she receives extra compensation for the overtime hours. Overtime pay is usually one and one-half times the normal pay.

Salaried employees are paid the same amount every week, even if they work more or less than an average work week. Supervisors and office workers are common examples of salaried positions. If employees are in a salaried position, they do not receive overtime pay, even if they work longer than the average work week.

Salary plus commission personnel are typically paid a small salary plus a percentage of the total amount of the sales they make. For example, a salesperson may receive a salary of $150 plus 1% of sales each week. Let us assume that a salesperson has sales of $40,000 for one week. That person would receive the salary ($150) plus the commission on sales (.01 × 40,000 = $400), which totals $550. The purpose of this pay method is to encourage sales personnel to sell as much as possible in order to increase the salesperson's pay and, thereby, increase store's total clothing sales.

All payroll data can be controlled by using a computer. Data entry operators are needed to keep the records up to date and to enter the weekly payroll accounts.

ACCOUNTS PAYABLE

Just like every other company, a sporting goods store must keep accurate accounts payable records. When a store purchases sporting goods, it usually does not pay cash. Instead, the supplier will send an invoice to the store. When the invoice is received, the information must be entered into the computer system. The computer may be able to update the inventory (add the newly purchased sporting goods to the current inventory), as well as check to see that the store was charged the correct price for the items purchased. The computer can also be programmed to keep track of the date when each invoice must be paid and print the check. Data entry operators are employed to enter all of this data into the computer system.

SPORTING GOODS INVENTORY

Accurate inventory control is essential for a sporting goods store. Management must always know the amount of merchandise available for sale to customers. In a fully integrated computer system, the inventory is automatically updated when accounts payable data and sales data are entered. For example, as the data entry operator enters accounts payable data for the purchase of merchandise, the inventory automatically increases. As the data entry operator enters sales information, the inventory automatically decreases. However, with many computer systems, the data entry operator must enter the inventory data and the accounts payable data separately.

INPUT FIELDS

In this comprehensive activity you will enter the payroll, accounts payable, and inventory data for The Sports Closet. Specifically, you will enter payroll records for ten employees and enter five updates to the payroll data. You will enter data for ten sales invoices received by The Sports Closet. Finally, you will enter the beginning inventory data for ten products, sales information from twelve sales tickets, and five inventory updates.

The fields used in this activity are similar to the fields used in Activity 6 (Payroll Records), Activity 5 (Accounts Payable), and Activity 2 (Merchandise Inventory). If necessary, refer to those activities for a further explanation of each field.

(OBJECTIVE 4)

GET READY

Follow the start-up procedures for your computer.

COMPLETE ALPHA-NUMERIC DEXTERITY DRILL

```
28223  CHARLOTTE  17032  1305  684  53416  402
7963  S  1750  2354  BELMONT  23M  46131  31649
5315  34072  PINEVILLE  4736  28211  20S  4951
62825  SWEATSHIRT  45019  1150  FAIRVIEW  256
FOOTBALL  JERSEY  44925  395080  MESH  SHIRTS
```

STEP 1   From the *Activities* menu, select *Activity 13 Summary Project.*

STEP 2   Select *Alpha-Numeric Dexterity Drill.* Complete the drill.

STEP 3   Repeat the Alpha-Numeric Dexterity Drill as many times as instructed by your teacher.

COMPLETE KEYPAD DEXTERITY DRILL

```
08566  93228  84910  56363  50725  06206  0950
60905  83621  93186  07008  18126  16935  6138
52866  22155  46295  47774  01334  02186  5206
47834  10188  09140  54078  54279  31663  2534
73445  16919  57531  99245  24256  60193  5041
```

STEP 1   From the *Activities* menu, select *Activity 13 Summary Project.*

STEP 2   Select *Keypad Dexterity Drill.* Complete the drill.

STEP 3   Repeat the Keypad Dexterity Drill as many times as instructed by your teacher.

COMPLETE FINAL PROJECT

STEP 1   Remove all of the payroll setup forms for The Sports Closet that are located at the end of this activity. The payroll setup forms may be key-entered in any order.

STEP 2   Key-enter the data for all records. Follow the procedures for editing and correcting records.

STEP 3   Print the payroll setup form if instructed by your teacher.

> **Note: You may generate a report of your performance for each project in this activity.**

> **Note: In a real work situation, you would strive for completely accurate records. Therefore, it is suggested that after you have completed each project in Activity 13, you should go back into the records and correct any remaining errors.**

STEP 4   Remove the payroll update form for The Sports Closet that is located at the end of this activity.

STEP 5   Key-enter the corrected data. Follow all procedures for editing and correcting records.

STEP 6   Print the payroll update form if instructed by your teacher.

STEP 7   Remove all of the sales invoices that are located at the end of this activity.

STEP 8   Key-enter the data for all records. Follow the procedures for editing and correcting records.

STEP 9   Print each sales invoice if instructed by your teacher.

STEP 10   Remove all of the inventory tickets for The Sports Closet that are located at the end of this activity.

STEP 11   Key-enter the data for all records. The stock taker and date will not be key-entered. They are kept on the original forms for reference only. Follow all procedures for editing and correcting records.

STEP 12   Print each inventory ticket if instructed by your teacher.

STEP 13   Remove the inventory setup form for The Sports Closet that is located at the end of the activity.

STEP 14   Key-enter the data for all records. Follow the procedures for editing and correcting records.

STEP 15   Print the inventory setup form if instructed by your teacher.

STEP 16   Remove all of the sales tickets for The Sports Closet that are located at the end of this activity.

STEP 17   Key-enter the data for all records. Follow the procedures for editing and correcting records.

STEP 18   Print each sales ticket if instructed by your teacher.

STEP 19   Remove the inventory update form for The Sports Closet that is located at the end of this activity.

STEP 20   Key-enter the data for all records. Follow the procedures for editing and correcting records.

STEP 21   Print the inventory update form if instructed by your teacher.

Payroll Setup Form

EMPLOYEE NUMBER: 92477

NAME (LAST, FIRST): Polk   Barbara

STREET ADDRESS: 1790 Park Rd.

CITY: Charlotte   STATE: NC   ZIP: 28203-1370

SSN: 129-19-0700   MARITAL STATUS: S   DEPENDENTS: 1

PAY TYPE: 2   HOURLY RATE: $ _____   SALARY: $ 468.00   COMMISSION: _____

HEALTH INSURANCE: $ 23.54   PENSION: $ 37.44

PAY TYPE CODE: HOURLY = 1	SALARY = 2	COMMISSION + SALARY = 3

Payroll Setup Form

EMPLOYEE NUMBER: 17032

NAME (LAST, FIRST): Easley   Ellen

STREET ADDRESS: 1305 Craig Ave.

CITY: Charlotte   STATE: NC   ZIP: 28211-2011

SSN: 961-29-9505   MARITAL STATUS: M   DEPENDENTS: 2

PAY TYPE: 1   HOURLY RATE: $ 6.84   SALARY: $ _____   COMMISSION: _____

HEALTH INSURANCE: $ 47.36   PENSION: $ 21.89

PAY TYPE CODE: HOURLY = 1	SALARY = 2	COMMISSION + SALARY = 3

Payroll Setup Form

EMPLOYEE NUMBER: 53416

NAME (LAST, FIRST): Walker   Paul

STREET ADDRESS: 402 Wilcrest Dr.

CITY: Matthews   STATE: NC   ZIP: 20105-1501

SSN: 334-85-8629   MARITAL STATUS: M   DEPENDENTS: 2

PAY TYPE: 3   HOURLY RATE: $ _____   SALARY: $ 390.00   COMMISSION: 6

HEALTH INSURANCE: $ 47.36   PENSION: $ 31.20

PAY TYPE CODE: HOURLY = 1	SALARY = 2	COMMISSION + SALARY = 3

Payroll Setup Form

The **SPORTS CLOSET** 9

EMPLOYEE NUMBER: _82948_

NAME (LAST, FIRST): _Seifert_   _Charles_

STREET ADDRESS: _760 Laurel Dr._

CITY: _Charlotte_   STATE: _NC_   ZIP: _28212-1947_

SSN: _775-81-6379_   MARITAL STATUS: _S_ DEPENDENTS: _0_

PAY TYPE: _1_   HOURLY RATE: $ _7.50_   SALARY: $ _____ COMMISSION: _____

HEALTH INSURANCE: $ _23.54_   PENSION: $ _24.00_

PAY TYPE CODE: HOURLY = 1	**SALARY = 2**	**COMMISSION + SALARY = 3**

Payroll Setup Form

The **SPORTS CLOSET** 9

EMPLOYEE NUMBER: _25774_

NAME (LAST, FIRST): _Brockman_   _Richard_

STREET ADDRESS: _301 Park St._

CITY: _Belmont_   STATE: _NC_   ZIP: _28012-1980_

SSN: _126-35-4613_   MARITAL STATUS: _M_ DEPENDENTS: _3_

PAY TYPE: _2_   HOURLY RATE: $ _____   SALARY: $ _420.00_ COMMISSION: _____

HEALTH INSURANCE: $ _47.36_   PENSION: $. _33.60_

PAY TYPE CODE: HOURLY = 1	**SALARY = 2**	**COMMISSION + SALARY = 3**

Payroll Setup Form

The **SPORTS CLOSET** 9

EMPLOYEE NUMBER: _38857_

NAME (LAST, FIRST): _Adamson_   _Douglas_

STREET ADDRESS: _1761 Earle St._

CITY: _Charlotte_   STATE: _NC_   ZIP: _28206-1914_

SSN: _439-44-2880_   MARITAL STATUS: _S_ DEPENDENTS: _1_

PAY TYPE: _1_   HOURLY RATE: $ _6.70_   SALARY: $ _____ COMMISSION: _____

HEALTH INSURANCE: $ _23.54_   PENSION: $ _21.44_

PAY TYPE CODE: HOURLY = 1	**SALARY = 2**	**COMMISSION + SALARY = 3**

Payroll Setup Form

EMPLOYEE NUMBER: 24413

NAME (LAST, FIRST): Mueller   Tammy

STREET ADDRESS: 1513 Scarlet Cir.

CITY: Charlotte   STATE: NC   ZIP: 28201-3401

SSN: 063-41-2952   MARITAL STATUS: S   DEPENDENTS: 2

PAY TYPE: 1   HOURLY RATE: $ 7.50   SALARY: $ _____   COMMISSION: _____

HEALTH INSURANCE: $ 47.36   PENSION: $ 23.80

PAY TYPE CODE: HOURLY = 1   SALARY = 2   COMMISSION + SALARY = 3

Payroll Setup Form

EMPLOYEE NUMBER: 34072

NAME (LAST, FIRST): Wong   Marsha

STREET ADDRESS: 1206 Main St.

CITY: Pineville   STATE: NC   ZIP: 28134-7610

SSN: 250-83-2307   MARITAL STATUS: M   DEPENDENTS: 1

PAY TYPE: 1   HOURLY RATE: $ 8.10   SALARY: $ _____   COMMISSION: _____

HEALTH INSURANCE: $ 23.54   PENSION: $ 19.52

PAY TYPE CODE: HOURLY = 1   SALARY = 2   COMMISSION + SALARY = 3

Payroll Setup Form

EMPLOYEE NUMBER: 04542

NAME (LAST, FIRST): Hernandez   Maria

STREET ADDRESS: 413 Briarwood Dr.

CITY: Charlotte   STATE: NC   ZIP: 28215-2115

SSN: 558-55-6941   MARITAL STATUS: S   DEPENDENTS: 0

PAY TYPE: 2   HOURLY RATE: $ _____   SALARY: $ 495.00   COMMISSION: _____

HEALTH INSURANCE: $ 23.54   PENSION: $ 39.60

PAY TYPE CODE: HOURLY = 1   SALARY = 2   COMMISSION + SALARY = 3

→

Payroll Setup Form

EMPLOYEE NUMBER: 21999

NAME (LAST, FIRST): Mulligan   Neil

STREET ADDRESS: 3134 Walker Rd.

CITY: Charlotte   STATE: NC   ZIP: 28211-6586

SSN: 859-36-4952   MARITAL STATUS: M DEPENDENTS: 2

PAY TYPE: 1   HOURLY RATE: $ 8.10   SALARY: $ _____ COMMISSION: _____

HEALTH INSURANCE: $ 47.36   PENSION: $ 25.92

PAY TYPE CODE: HOURLY = 1   SALARY = 2   COMMISSION + SALARY = 3

Payroll Setup Form

EMPLOYEE NUMBER: _____

NAME (LAST, FIRST): _____   _____

STREET ADDRESS: _____

CITY: _____   STATE: _____ ZIP: _____

SSN: _____   MARITAL STATUS: ____ DEPENDENTS: _____

PAY TYPE: _____ HOURLY RATE: $ _____   SALARY: $ _____ COMMISSION: _____

HEALTH INSURANCE: $ _____   PENSION: $ _____

PAY TYPE CODE: HOURLY = 1   SALARY = 2   COMMISSION + SALARY = 3

Payroll Setup Form

EMPLOYEE NUMBER: _____

NAME (LAST, FIRST): _____   _____

STREET ADDRESS: _____

CITY: _____   STATE: _____ ZIP: _____

SSN: _____   MARITAL STATUS: ____ DEPENDENTS: _____

PAY TYPE: _____ HOURLY RATE: $ _____   SALARY: $ _____ COMMISSION: _____

HEALTH INSURANCE: $ _____   PENSION: $ _____

PAY TYPE CODE: HOURLY = 1   SALARY = 2   COMMISSION + SALARY = 3

Payroll Update Form

EMP. NO.	LAST NAME	FIRST NAME	STREET ADDRESS	CITY	STATE	ZIP	SS #	MAR. STAT.	DEP.	PAY TYPE	HOUR RATE	SAL.	COMM.	HEALTH INSUR.	PENSION
17032			3506 Monroe Rd.			28205-1205									
53416								M	1			450.00	7		32.00
82948															
24413	Hollister		791 Kenilworth Ave.			28204-1400		M	3						
34072									2						

Shorts & Sweats, Inc.   3116 NORTH TYRON ST. / CHARLOTTE, NC 28279-7679

SALES INVOICE

VENDOR NUMBER:	62825
TERMS:	N/30
INVOICE NUMBER:	45019
DATE:	04/12

SOLD TO: The Sports Closet
650 Pressley Rd.
Charlotte, NC 28217-3183

QTY	UPC NO.	DESCRIPTION	PRICE	EXTENDED AMOUNT
50	27000 60801	Sweatshirt	23.00	1150.00
24	11205 02324	Baseball Cap	12.95	310.80
			GRAND TOTAL	1460.80

NTB International   6010 Fairview Road • Charlotte, NC 28298-8664

SALES INVOICE

Sold To: The Sports Closet
650 Pressley Rd.
Charlotte, NC 28217-3183

Vendor Number:	16815
Terms:	1/15, N/30
Invoice Number:	76152
Date:	04/15

QTY	UPC NO.	DESCRIPTION	PRICE	EXTENDED AMOUNT
20	85162 20949	Men's Swim. Trunks	29.50	590.00

GRAND TOTAL _____ 590.00

MASON MANUFACTURING

148 MOREHEAD ST. / CHARLOTTE, NC 28276-4576

SALES INVOICE

SOLD TO:	The Sports Closet 650 Pressley Rd. Charlotte, NC 28217-3183

VENDOR NUMBER:	64535
TERMS:	N/30
INVOICE NUMBER:	02775
DATE:	04/12

QTY	UPC NO.	DESCRIPTION	PRICE	EXTENDED AMOUNT
50	00050 84550	Tee-Shirt	14.95	747.50
15	74000 32180	Football Jersey	29.95	449.25
			GRAND TOTAL	1196.75

SALES INVOICE

 Donhill, Inc.

914 Baxter St. • Charlotte, NC 28276-9894

Sold To:	The Sports Closet 650 Pressley Rd. Charlotte, NC 28217-3183

Vendor Number:	12544
Terms:	2/10, N/30
Invoice Number:	64024
Date:	04/17

QTY	UPC NO.	DESCRIPTION	PRICE	EXTENDED AMOUNT
75	21000 04115	Hooded Pullover	48.00	3600.00
20	51000 17170	Mesh Shirt	17.99	359.80
			GRAND TOTAL	3959.80

2615 Scarlet Drive
Charlotte, NC 28248-7150

SALES INVOICE

VENDOR NUMBER:	86902
TERMS:	N/30
INVOICE NUMBER:	20453
DATE:	04/17

SOLD TO: The Sports Closet
650 Pressley Rd.
Charlotte, NC   28217-3183

QTY	UPC NO.	DESCRIPTION	PRICE	EXTENDED AMOUNT
40	35616 02240	Women's Jog. Shorts	23.00	920.00
30	21010 56511	Ski Gloves	20.00	600.00
			GRAND TOTAL	1520.00

DENNISON Manufacturing
170 East Trade St. ● Matthews, NC 28273-8181

SALES INVOICE

Vendor Number:	00697
Terms:	N/30
Invoice Number:	53944
Date::	04/16

Sold To: The Sports Closet
650 Pressley Rd.
Charlotte, NC   28217-3183

QTY	UPC NO.	DESCRIPTION	PRICE	EXTENDED AMOUNT
25	12587 18108	Gym Bag	22.29	557.25
			GRAND TOTAL	557.25

SALES INVOICE

Weaver & Sons
309 Eastway Drive   Charlotte, NC 28279-3463

SOLD TO: The Sports Closet
650 Pressley Rd.
Charlotte, NC 28217-3183

VENDOR NUMBER: **72312**
TERMS: **N/30**
INVOICE NUMBER: **36197**
DATE: **04/12**

QTY	UPC NO.	DESCRIPTION	PRICE	EXTENDED AMOUNT
60	00510 70090	Sweatsocks	3.50	210.00
30	31220 00211	Knit Ski Cap	12.00	360.00
		GRAND TOTAL		570.00

SALES INVOICE

Weaver & Sons
309 Eastway Drive   Charlotte, NC 28279-3463

SOLD TO: The Sports Closet
650 Pressley Rd.
Charlotte, NC 28217-3183

VENDOR NUMBER: **67167**
TERMS: **N/30**
INVOICE NUMBER: **13918**
DATE: **04/13**

QTY	UPC NO.	DESCRIPTION	PRICE	EXTENDED AMOUNT
50	37000 11228	Sweatpants	38.00	1900.00
		GRAND TOTAL		1900.00

SALES INVOICE

SPORTS CLOTHING INC.
120 MOREHEAD ST. CHARLOTTE, NC 28276-8463

Sold To: The Sports Closet
650 Pressley Rd.
Charlotte, NC 28217-3183

Vendor Number: 25549
Terms: 2/10, N/30
Invoice Number: 13916
Date: 04/17

QTY	UPC NO.	DESCRIPTION	PRICE	EXTENDED AMOUNT
35	75600 12151	Athletic Jacket	79.50	2782.50
			GRAND TOTAL	2782.50

Sportswear, Ltd.
123 IVERSON WAY / CHARLOTTE, NC 28279-4080

SALES INVOICE

SOLD TO: The Sports Closet
650 Pressley Rd.
Charlotte, NC 28217-3183

VENDOR NUMBER: 21916
TERMS: N/30
INVOICE NUMBER: 12351
DATE: 04/13

QTY	UPC NO.	DESCRIPTION	PRICE	EXTENDED AMOUNT
30	00170 50466	Warm-up Suit	98.00	2940.00
24	40004 17611	Tank Top	12.99	311.76
			GRAND TOTAL	3251.76

The SPORTS CLOSET

Inventory Ticket

UPC Number	Bin No.	Quantity
85162 20949	90822	37

Stock Taker	Date

The SPORTS CLOSET

Inventory Ticket

UPC Number	Bin No.	Quantity
35616 02240	47075	41

Stock Taker	Date

The SPORTS CLOSET

Inventory Ticket

UPC Number	Bin No.	Quantity
00170 50466	91690	53

Stock Taker	Date

The SPORTS CLOSET

Inventory Ticket

UPC Number	Bin No.	Quantity
21000 04115	97662	164

Stock Taker	Date

The SPORTS CLOSET

Inventory Ticket

UPC Number	Bin No.	Quantity
75600 12151	55565	66

Stock Taker	Date

The SPORTS CLOSET

Inventory Ticket

UPC Number	Bin No.	Quantity
12587 18108	50605	19

Stock Taker	Date

Inventory Ticket — The SPORTS CLOSET 9

UPC Number	Bin No.	Quantity
00050 84550	09552	117

Stock Taker	Date

Inventory Ticket — The SPORTS CLOSET 9

UPC Number	Bin No.	Quantity
37000 11228	22716	133

Stock Taker	Date

Inventory Ticket — The SPORTS CLOSET 9

UPC Number	Bin No.	Quantity
00510 70090	43997	59

Stock Taker	Date

Inventory Ticket — The SPORTS CLOSET 9

UPC Number	Bin No.	Quantity
27000 60801	37680	102

Stock Taker	Date

Inventory Ticket — The SPORTS CLOSET 9

UPC Number	Bin No.	Quantity

Stock Taker	Date

Inventory Ticket — The SPORTS CLOSET 9

UPC Number	Bin No.	Quantity

Stock Taker	Date

Inventory Setup Form
November 1

UPC NO.	DESCRIPTION	BIN NO.	UNIT	UNIT PRICE	VENDOR #1	VENDOR #2	QTY. ON HAND	REORDER POINT	REORDER QUANTITY
21000 04115	Hooded Pullover	97662	Each	48.00	12544	88824	164	150	75
37000 11228	Sweatpants	22716	Each	38.00	67167	94372	133	125	50
84162 20949	Men's Swim. Trunks	90822	Each	29.50	16815	24369	37	30	20
12587 18108	Gym Bag	50605	Each	22.29	00697	64758	19	15	25
27000 60801	Sweatshirt	37680	Each	23.00	62825	82572	102	75	50
00170 50466	Warm-up Suit	91690	Each	98.00	21916	12234	53	30	30
00050 84550	Tee-Shirt	09552	Each	14.95	64535	74240	117	100	50
35616 02240	Women's Jog. Shorts	47075	Each	23.00	15035	86902	41	20	40
00510 70090	Sweatsocks	43997	Pair	3.50	72312	35126	59	40	60
75600 12151	Athletic Jacket	55565	Each	79.50	25549	64482	66	65	35

The SPORTS CLOSET
650 Pressley Rd.
Charlotte, NC 28217-3183

Date _____ 02/08

Sales Ticket

UPC No.	Quantity
21000 04115	48

The SPORTS CLOSET
650 Pressley Rd.
Charlotte, NC 28217-3183

Date _____ 01/24

Sales Ticket

UPC No.	Quantity
27000 60801	65

The SPORTS CLOSET
650 Pressley Rd.
Charlotte, NC 28217-3183

Date _____ 01/02

Sales Ticket

UPC No.	Quantity
00170 50466	24
00050 84550	75
35616 02240	30

The SPORTS CLOSET
650 Pressley Rd.
Charlotte, NC 28217-3183

Date _____ 01/23

Sales Ticket

UPC No.	Quantity
85162 20949	40
00510 70090	50

The SPORTS CLOSET
650 Pressley Rd.
Charlotte, NC 28217-3183

Date _____ 02/06

Sales Ticket

UPC No.	Quantity
37000 11228	60

The SPORTS CLOSET
650 Pressley Rd.
Charlotte, NC 28217-3183

Date _____ 01/17

Sales Ticket

UPC No.	Quantity
00050 84550	75
75600 12151	24

The SPORTS CLOSET

650 Pressley Rd.
Charlotte, NC 28217-3183

Date _01/19_

Sales Ticket

UPC No.	Quantity
85162 20949	48
12587 18108	18

The SPORTS CLOSET

650 Pressley Rd.
Charlotte, NC 28217-3183

Date _01/06_

Sales Ticket

UPC No.	Quantity
27000 60801	75

The SPORTS CLOSET

650 Pressley Rd.
Charlotte, NC 28217-3183

Date _01/03_

Sales Ticket

UPC No.	Quantity
00170 50446	24

The SPORTS CLOSET

650 Pressley Rd.
Charlotte, NC 28217-3183

Date _01/26_

Sales Ticket

UPC No.	Quantity
35616 02240	24
00510 70090	68
75600 12151	46

The SPORTS CLOSET

650 Pressley Rd.
Charlotte, NC 28217-3183

Date _01/22_

Sales Ticket

UPC No.	Quantity
21000 04115	50
37000 11228	50

The SPORTS CLOSET

650 Pressley Rd.
Charlotte, NC 28217-3183

Date _02/07_

Sales Ticket

UPC No.	Quantity
12587 18108	24

The Sports Closet

Inventory Update Form
November 15

UPC NO.	DESCRIPTION	BIN NO.	UNIT	UNIT PRICE	VENDOR #1	VENDOR #2	QTY. ON HAND	REORDER POINT	REORDER QUANTITY
37000 11228					03234				
84162 20949		07138							
27000 60801		01158			21982				
00050 84550									150
00510 70090						05187		125	

Appendix A

IBM PC, IBM PS/2 AND TANDY 1000

To run the Data Entry Activities software from a floppy disk:

STEP 1   Carefully insert a copy of the *Data Entry Activities for Microcomputers* software into the A: disk drive in your computer.

STEP 2   At the A:\> prompt, key-enter *data.* The program will boot up and you may begin the data entry exercises.

To install the Data Entry Activities software on a hard disk drive:

STEP 1   Carefully insert a copy of the *Data Entry Activities for Microcomputers* software into the A: disk drive in your computer.

STEP 2   At the A:\> prompt, key-enter *install.* Follow the directions that appear on your screen.

To run the Data Entry Activities software from the hard disk drive:

STEP 1   At the C:\> prompt, key-enter *data.* The program will boot up and you may begin the data entry exercises.

MACINTOSH COMPUTERS

To run the Data Entry Activities software from a floppy disk:

STEP 1 Carefully insert a copy of the *Data Entry Activities for Microcomputers* software into the disk drive in your computer.

STEP 2 Double-click on the disk icon that appears on your screen.

STEP 3 Double-click on the Data Entry Activities program icon. The program will boot up and you may begin the data entry exercises.

To install the Data Entry Activities software on a hard disk drive:

STEP 1 Carefully insert a copy of the *Data Entry Activities for Microcomputers* software into the disk drive in your computer.

STEP 2 Double-click on the disk icon that appears on your screen.

STEP 3 Drag the Data Entry Activities program icon onto your hard drive.

To run the Data Entry Activities software from the hard disk drive:

STEP 1 Find the Data Entry Activities program icon on your hard drive.

STEP 2 Double-click on the Data Entry Activities program icon. The program will boot up and you may begin the data entry exercises.

Appendix B

IBM PC, IBM PS/2, AND TANDY 1000

To format a disk from drive C:

STEP 1   At the C:\> prompt, key FORMAT A:.

STEP 2   Inset a disk into drive A. If you proceed, any data on this disk will be erased when formatting takes place.

STEP 3   Press the space bar. Disk drive A will spin for a few moments and the disk will be properly formatted. It is now ready for use as a student data disk with *Data Entry Activities for Microcomputers*.

To format a disk from drive A:

STEP 1   Carefully insert your DOS disk into drive A.

STEP 2   If your disk drive has a latch, close it.

STEP 3   Turn on the microcomputer. If the computer is already on, hold down the CTRL and ALT keys and press the DEL key. This will restart the computer.

STEP 4   You will see a prompt asking you to enter the date and time. Enter them in the format shown on the screen. Next, the prompt A:\> will be displayed.

STEP 5   If your microcomputer has one disk drive, do the following:

    A. Key-enter FORMAT A: (be sure to include the colon).

    B. Remove the DOS disk from disk drive A.

    C. Insert a disk into disk drive A. If you proceed, any data on this disk will be erased when formatting takes place.

    D. Press the space bar. Disk drive A will spin for a few moments and the disk will be properly formatted. It is now ready for use as a student data disk with *Data Entry Activities for Microcomputers*.

If your microcomputer has two disk drives, do the following:

A. Key-enter FORMAT B: (be sure to include the colon).

B. Insert a disk into disk drive B. If you proceed, any data on this disk will be erased when formatting takes place.

C. Press the space bar. Disk drive B will spin for a few moments and the disk will be properly formatted. It is now ready for use as a student data disk with *Data Entry Activities for Microcomputers*.

STEP 6   After the message FORMAT COMPLETE appears on the screen, a prompt asking if you wish to format another disk will appear.

STEP 7   If you want to format another disk, respond Y for yes and follow the screen prompts.

STEP 8   If you do not want to format another disk, respond N for no.

● ●

MACINTOSH

STEP 1   Turn on your Macintosh computer.

STEP 2   Carefully insert a disk into the disk drive, label-side facing up.

STEP 3   A disk icon will appear on the desktop. Make sure the disk icon is highlighted, by clicking on it once.

STEP 4   From the *Special* menu, choose *Erase Disk*.

STEP 5   A warning prompt will appear. If you are sure that you wish to format the selected disk, click on *OK*. If you proceed, any data on this disk will be erased when formatting takes place.

STEP 6   A dialog box may appear, asking if you wish to format the disk for 800K or 1.2 MB of storage. Select the appropriate size disk by clicking on the radio button in front of your choice. If you are unsure of which type of disk you have, you should stop here and determine the storage capacity of your disk.

STEP 7   When you are finished, you may leave the disk in or eject the disk by choosing *Eject Disk* from the *Special* menu. The disk is now ready for use as a student data disk with *Data Entry Activities for Microcomputers*.

Appendix C

Dexterity drills are designed to increase your speed and accuracy in key-entering data. There are two dexterity drills for each activity and at least one drill of each should be done each day. You may repeat drills as many times as directed by your instructor.

A dexterity drill is begun by selecting either *Alpha-Numeric* or *Keypad Drill* from an activity menu. The timing of the drill begins at the moment you type the first character. When you are finished, select *End Input*. The computer will display your words per minute, strokes per hour, and percentage of accuracy. You will have an option to print these scores.

ALPHA-NUMERIC DEXTERITY DRILLS

ACTIVITY 1

```
8125 4200229 TITANS 9500276 676CR 053665
1135520 06692 00815953 214663 HITS 52107
262119 008571 37182 RUNS 690016 6579 201
ERRORS 579442 311076 ME 631091 74259 567
36790 079524977 20010136 TEAM 638 575942
```

ACTIVITY 2

```
123 2748 9816 2503 52511 36003 21224 472
7525 8261 COTTON 2112 11946 58918 263523
CASE 2364 96518 50 2541 17507 304021 100
16824 28713 8 741 46273 12063 47 2290 48
RAZORS 3348 57443 8020 11759 MUSK 3336 2
```

ACTIVITY 3

2104 DESK SET 31 1 LC3035 2116 03021 217
KC3290 212250 TP8122 LEAD PENCIL 0201 24
0112 AS9878 10 DISKETTE TRAY 1128 0303 9
STIFF COVER BINDER BT0965 3529964 050 70
708020 1110 631798 SIDE ARM CHAIR CM6897

ACTIVITY 4

9193385 635852 117082 CORN 695750 825280
LASAGNA 390449 491978 42312 38285 762 78
69641 6822 4491 PEAS 1890 98006 4 ORANGE
72673 348501 STUFFED SHRIMP 1850 395 725
112577 HAM STEAKS 10045 8290 287228 1195

ACTIVITY 5

1321436 56109 TOOTHPASTE 788468 299 1966
47883 EYE DROPS 658-51 33400 16750 39748
539695 037802 BABY OIL 139 41143 02 3296
DEODORANT 77639 10500 16830 EMERY BOARDS
25669 123735 34 891126 MOUTHWASH 24 8670

ACTIVITY 6

43750 01136 80461 MO 968526 480063 33512
631211 CRESTON 320021 517942 05622 52506
304436 34634 16689 200058 ST CHARLES 375
531607 63033 4675250 PENSION 16631 69226
37397 SALARY L73438 462161 48969 7035442

ACTIVITY 7

80451 7287 DENVER 80204 3949 CO 58000 15
06001 834 061441 STANFORD CT 2281 687736
12 CONSTRUCTION 06783 14 09 61 38000 438
WILMINGTON 9 1628 061146 198050996 19958
050442 ATLANTA 30320 GA 14240 SAVANNAH 2

ACTIVITY 8

402 89063874 CARSON CITY 061341 10 00 53
HONDA GD222XJ 577160 04 0 08 53 RAYMONDX
25 10 24 48 RONALD 86 7554 DIPLOMAT 8950
8958101 NV 01 15 50 JK2TN5 68JB3228 1210
LEXINGTON 900S 0316 36 LIABILITY 8943140

ACTIVITY 9

223089726 511 160 NONE 022092 150170 602
FAIRFAX 26040442 29901 AUTOMATIC 0402924
20543992 STONEHEDGE 132 046 VA 510231025
MOPED 734402332 ABBES 155001 040421 2651
9600 L 510BL MOTORCYCLE 1180148 5753 022

ACTIVITY 1O

15623 63021 653890 CHEVROLET GU602337872
437453 2800 L986 3076525050261 CAPRICE E
13799 630318166 88 93 70995 J71134VU6519
HAZELWOOD GC438 83181788945 63042 439086
JT1126391 35 893076 CHEROKEE 101 0387731

ACTIVITY 11

818339344 02001 WOODWORKING 30018 910244
ANDERSON 01026 0221311 57791 9462 MARTHA
11021 302230 GENERAL BUSINESS 91026 0466
07211 91035 SMALL ENGINES 91009 BUSINESS
910123 02101 30053 DRAFTING 277268216 CA

ACTIVITY 12

08953 WXEL-FM 00372 21800 4247 3627M 171
12302 0865860 CAR2 B1226 SCHL5 213053341
WKIK-FM 1130245 173158 038066 18WORK 35M
4356 OTHER 1900 429M086 0487 SHOP 190035
62581829 SCHLF FABB3835 1630 11068 FORTY

ACTIVITY 13

28223 CHARLOTTE 17032 1305 684 53416 402
7963 S 1750 2354 BELMONT 23M 46131 31649
5315 34072 PINEVILLE 4736 28211 20S 4951
62825 SWEATSHIRT 45019 1150 FAIRVIEW 256
FOOTBALL JERSEY 44925 395080 MESH SHIRTS

KEYPAD DRILLS

ACTIVITY 1

47474 58585 69696 96969 85858 74747 4561
58585 69696 96969 85858 74747 4567 47474
69696 96969 85858 74747 4567 47474 58585
14725 36159 81972 58513 53619 75621 2378
15263 48597 45125 32838 97204 0314 58261

ACTIVITY 2

41414 52525 63636 41014 63636 52525 4142
52525 63636 41014 63636 52525 41414 5252
63636 36363 25252 14141 5252 41414 52525
55201 51594 11419 32945 46253 01255 0896
68203 57765 28839 21374 37009 09065 4324

ACTIVITY 3

10012 20023 30034 40045 50056 60067 7003
80089 90090 21212 31232 42345 53456 7456
56789 67890 78901 89012 90123 01234 0011
29057 28331 56123 50697 76852 34719 8476
28025 66782 86672 47104 58191 68954 5414

ACTIVITY 4

72875 65806 30543 48745 30458 37227 4034
81833 72285 49487 02825 97153 94439 4474
80780 25618 70948 40683 50309 55314 8166
52522 97783 11104 55898 08553 95523 2764
54271 12909 12266 00196 44104 14188 9051

ACTIVITY 5

```
51549  67365  35341  35353  08796  53657  9325
84575  29637  78333  42318  00231  16342  3526
08972  38079  28298  97705  82221  27444  7554
83375  46276  62315  97951  43925  71004  7496
50939  28257  30997  02215  30175  53353  5230
```

ACTIVITY 6

```
78924  97825  89565  27369  51531  47574  3506
20749  62358  45132  30075  50371  30157  7204
90387  22901  50417  18830  18609  78501  7183
45893  02754  32685  13245  00357  71530  7013
79689  34677  89053  28219  30997  90224  9329
```

ACTIVITY 7

```
63813  90114  30379  41137  77501  17549  2117
28382  69200  16498  01560  25250  04475  8266
92817  32736  98000  15432  00646  28962  1959
01777  49175  11512  60021  69256  54569  5661
94412  82238  96001  91648  20759  01838  2094
```

ACTIVITY 8

```
45748  62674  85682  38282  93606  70513  8258
99319  59347  39948  89375  21715  80626  6545
29651  29256  28529  48111  74431  75414  4428
15531  47575  86241  20067  97588  95063  9148
85403  20594  23568  53214  17003  37510  8213
```

ACTIVITY 9

```
56775  56199  74644  51332  50025  42625  3759
28033  11967  68319  56039  05967  94933  5456
48599  36375  18749  88532  88725  10872  2793
47051  83081  09167  69207  85017  31738  4883
54596  63851  11409  30739  13714  77107  5617
```

ACTIVITY 10

```
20155  94633  49542  38428  89889  27850  8210
56698  53488  69213  01255  34325  39176  2080
90736  24251  08352  12643  90370  89603  8513
52466  53455  25448  45863  25489  65723  2366
45465  45987  56354  37169  15080  60437  0589
```

ACTIVITY 11

```
87445  76246  98526  83822  06369  13750  1097
12157  97835  39984  93745  91939  25139  2919
57575  02651  29825  14811  17510  17514  5012
79020  77596  86518  24724  51323  00256  5078
88789  33280  69117  31698  23656  90563  2986
```

ACTIVITY 12

```
03715  72049  86759  76347  91806  76209  0794
91745  21134  16020  96256  02525  70446  9172
05433  48899  53673  41897  28835  08712  4203
84426  50251  39436  24945  83824  50016  8532
08946  21691  43234  64827  30977  12318  0231
```

ACTIVITY 13

```
08566  93228  84910  56363  50725  06206  0950
60905  83621  93186  07008  18126  16935  6138
52866  22155  46295  47774  01334  02186  5206
47834  10188  09140  54078  54279  31663  2534
73445  16919  57531  99245  24256  60193  5041
```

Appendix D

KEYBOARD NAVIGATION

Action	IBM keystroke	Macintosh keystroke
move cursor to the right	right arrow (→)	right arrow (→)
move cursor to the left	left arrow (←)	left arrow (←)
move cursor up one line or to nearest field above current field	up arrow ↑	up arrow ↑
move cursor down one line or to nearest field below current field	down arrow ↓	down arrow ↓
move cursor to next field	TAB	TAB
during data entry, move cursor to previous record	F8 key	⌘-J
during data entry, move cursor to next record	F9 key	⌘-K
end data input	F10 key	
edit data	F8 key	
analyze data entry results	F9 key	
move cursor to top of screen	HOME	HOME
move cursor to bottom of screen	END	END
delete character to left of cursor	DELETE	DELETE
causes all keyed characters to appear in upper case	CAPS LOCK	CAPS LOCK
causes computer to accept data	ENTER	RETURN
changes status of numeric keypad numbers and directional arrows	NUM LOCK	NUM LOCK

Photo Credits